School Reform from the Inside Out

Policy, Practice, and Performance

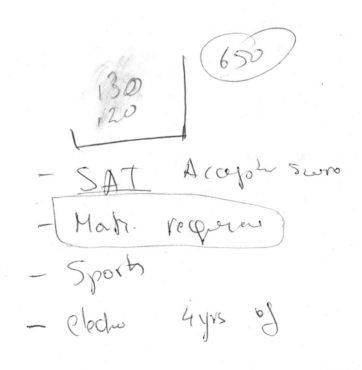

School Reform from the Inside Out

Policy, Practice, and Performance

RICHARD F. ELMORE

HARVARD EDUCATION PRESS

CAMBRIDGE, MASS.

Fifth Printing, 2008

Library of Congress Control Number 2004108773

Paperback ISBN 978-1-891792-24-3
Library Edition ISBN 978-1-891792-50-2

Published by Harvard Education Press,
an imprint of the Harvard Education Publishing Group

Harvard Education Press
8 Story Street
Cambridge, MA 02138

Cover Design: Alyssa Morris
Cover Photo: Corbis
Typography: Sheila Walsh

The typefaces used in this book are Castle and Afga Rotis Semisans
for display and ITC Veljovic for text.

Printed in Canada

Contents

Introduction

One test of decent research and analysis is whether it is topical at the time it is written and yet remains useful when times have changed. Readers of this volume will make their own judgments about how well the essays it includes, which span more than a decade of education reform, meet this standard. In collecting these pieces, I have been struck by the persistence of the problems they address over a period of sustained and dramatic transformation. *Plus ça change, plus c'est la même chose.* It is this theme of continuity and change in the landscape of educational reform, and in my own work on the subject, that I wish to address in this introduction.

More than twenty years ago, when states first began the current period of education reform, no one would have predicted that reform would be sustained and steadily developed over such an extended period. In the world of political analysis, the ebb and flow of policy issues —what political scientists call the issue attention cycle—typically proceeds in three- to five-year intervals. Rarely does a single policy issue command the attention of policymakers at the state or federal level for longer than this period; rarely do policymakers stay engaged in issues after the major bills have been passed and the implementation stage begins. Education reform seems to have defied this principle of political behavior, at least at the state and federal levels. Not only have the states sustained a high level of involvement in education reform over the entire period since the early 1980s, but they have also continued to extend the reach of state policy into schools and classrooms and to adjust state accountability systems to the strategic responses of schools and school systems. Even more surprising, this extended period of state policymaking hasn't deterred the federal government from extending its own institutional role in education reform. The Bush administration, with its centerpiece No Child Left Behind (NCLB) law, has presided over the largest single expansion of federal authority into state and local decisions in the history of the country. This level of activity shows no signs of abating.

The reform picture at the local level is murkier. Local reform initiatives are typically characterized by volatility—jumping nervously from one reform idea to the next over relatively short periods of time—and superficiality—choosing reforms that have little impact on instruction or student learning and implementing them in shallow ways. These patterns stem from political instability—superintendents' average tenure is between eighteen months and three years, and school board membership turns over regularly (Hess, 1999). Through the current reform period, local boards and administrators have continued to hold on to administrative control over what happens in schools and classrooms, although they have increasingly assumed a defensive and reactive posture toward reform measures at the state and federal level, rather than playing a central role in crafting policy. It is unclear whether sustained attention to reform at the state and federal level will have any impact on stability of focus at the local level; the anecdotal evidence at the moment cuts both ways.

The central theme of education reform policy since at least the early 1990s has been accountability for student performance. This represents a dramatic and sustained shift in the focus of federal, state, and local policy from the distribution of inputs (mainly money) to outputs (generally in the form of student test scores). All but one or two states have required some form of performance-based accountability for schools for at least five or six years; now, under NCLB, all states will be required to adhere to a relatively narrow set of design criteria for accountability systems—annual testing of all students between grades three and eight; disaggregation of student scores by demographic groups; progressive oversight and sanctions for poorly performing schools; and provision of parental choice for parents of students in chronically low-performing schools, among others. Regardless of how one feels about the specific provisions of NCLB—and there is considerable controversy at the moment—the idea of performance-based accountability as a theme for reform has proven to be extraordinarily robust over time.

Unfortunately, the root causes of the failure of education reform have also proven to be extraordinarily persistent and robust. Our capacity to initiate and sustain reform has exceeded, to a considerable degree, our capacity to solve the problems that undermine the effects of reforms. There is a cruel irony here. Performance-based accountability has stimulated an unprecedented demand for new knowledge of curriculum, pedagogy, and organizational improvement at the school and system levels. Research and development have focused to an unprecedented degree on improving instructional practice, especially in literacy and mathematics. But the fundamental problem of how to connect what we know about good practice to what schools actually do and replicate our successes on a large scale stubbornly persists. Variability in student performance in core content areas by school, by classroom, and by demographic group remains persistently, and unacceptably, large. High-performing classrooms and schools, especially in communities with high proportions of low-income minority children, are still the rare exception rather than the rule. Rigorous and engaging instruction remains all too rare across schools of all types. Indeed, the main stimulus for my work in the area of education reform has been the disconnect between what education policies prescribe and what seems to happen in schools and classrooms in response to those policies.

The essays in this book embody a particular analytic stance that has characterized my entire body of work as an academic. This stance is best expressed by the thesis that "the problems of the system are the problems of the smallest unit." This proposition operates in two directions: The effects of policies are determined in important ways by the conditions and constraints that operate every day in schools and classrooms. And the life of schools and classrooms has much to teach policymakers about the design and implementation of good policy. To succeed, school reform has to happen "from the inside out." This proposition has been a guiding principle of my research and writing, implicitly or explicitly, from the beginning.

My research began in the 1970s with a puzzle: Why do the actual consequences of policies bear only a vague resemblance to the ideas that shaped their design? Why, for example, in a federal program that was cleverly designed to test the relative effectiveness of alternative instructional approaches for educationally disadvantaged children, did it turn out that there was more variation in performance within instructional models than between instructional models (Elmore, 1975a, 1975b)? Why do policymakers persist in thinking about the effects of their actions in simplistic, mechanical ways when in fact they are operating in an environment characterized by multiple organizational, political, and human-relations dimensions (Elmore, 1978)? These initial questions gave rise to a concept that I labeled, with apologies to my public policy colleague Mark Moore, "backward mapping" (Elmore, 1979-1980). This term describes the process by which the effects of policies are determined: not by the way they are designed, which is often incomplete and provisional, but by the ways individuals and organizations respond to them. Teachers and principals, for example, operate in a crowded and complex organizational and political environment, of which formal accountability systems are only one component. The effects of accountability policies are determined by the interaction of those policies with the world in which educators work.

With my colleagues Penelope Peterson and Sarah McCarthey, I went on to examine the classroom- and school-level effects of a precursor to the present reform movement, the "school restructuring movement" (Elmore, 1996). The central idea of this reform was that teachers and principals were hampered by existing organizational structures from accomplishing what they knew to be their best instructional practices. *Ergo*, if we change school structures, we will change teaching practice. Our main finding, subsequently confirmed by others, was that changing structure did not change practice, it only relabeled existing practice with new names. The schools that succeed in changing practice are those that start with the practice and modify school structures to accommodate to it, often making more modest changes in structure than the advocates of school reform would recommend. Here, the intriguing problem was how to think concretely about school reform in the microcosm of the classroom and the school in ways that are useful in the macrocosm of reform policy. Policymakers like structures because they appear to be concrete and they can, at least in principle, be changed by mandate. What our research seemed to be saying was that it is pointless to work on structures until you know specifically what kind of practice you are trying to engender.

Following this work, I became engaged in exploratory research on the district role in school improvement as part of a larger agenda related to the problem of scale in educational reform. At a point where I had virtually given up on finding useful models of districtwide improvement of instructional practice, I stumbled onto a more or less fully developed model of districtwide improvement in Community District #2 in New York City. Here, my colleague Deanna Burney and I discovered, was a model of improvement that focused on particular teaching practices in literacy and mathematics and embodied structures and practices designed to enhance and develop those practices (Elmore, 1997). The focus on instructional content and pedagogy was central and stable, the organizational and managerial structures and practices were instrumental and variable. In short, the model embodied the principle of backward mapping: that system-level policymakers and administrators should base their decisions on a clear understanding of the results they want to achieve in the smallest unit—the classroom, the school—and let their organizational and policy decisions vary in response to the demands of the work at that level. Our work in District #2 also demonstrated how dependent we are as researchers on the work of practitioners who are willing to deliberately violate the conventional rules of management and organization in order to solve persistent problems and break the lock of traditional constraints. Anthony Alvarado, the longtime superintendent of District #2, embodied this attribute. Without his and his colleagues' leadership, we would have had nothing to study.

* * * * *

The articles in this book pick up around this period of my work. They embody the extension of the idea of backward mapping into the study of a number of areas: the problem of scale in school reform, school accountability, leadership, professional development, and school improvement in the context of the accountability movement. I have attempted, in the "Further Reading" notes for each article, to give some idea of the current work of other scholars on the same topic. I hope I have succeeded in acknowledging the full range of research, and I apologize to those whose work I may have omitted out of ignorance or inadvertence. My own thinking continues to develop, due increasingly to the work of gifted practitioners who have taken up the challenges I have tried to identify and who have pushed our knowledge far beyond where it was when I began this work.

I have focused on education as a field of study because I believe it is one way to do important work that contributes to the well-being of children and society. Studying educational policy and organization does not, however, engender optimism. It is often a Sisyphean enterprise— pushing the same rock up the hill time and again, only to see it roll back with the next generation of reform. Not the least effect of my work in District #2 was a subtle but marked shift in my own perspective on the possibilities of large-scale improvement of public schools. Seeing children and teachers working together in powerful ways in classrooms in District #2 brought me back to my original reasons for becoming an educator. The experience made me aware of how powerful our influence on the lives of children can be when we work with intensity and honesty and focus on the most basic issues of instructional practice. This inspiration continues to fuel my essential optimism in the work, although it may not always be evident in what I write.

1

Getting to Scale with Good Educational Practice

The issue of large-scale improvement has been at the center of contemporary school reform for a decade or more. In the mid-1990s, as I was preparing this essay, the federal government initiated a strategy designed to propagate and disseminate what it called comprehensive school reform models through a private, nonprofit agency called the New American Schools Development Corporation. The models were to be based on scientifically validated practices, and their sponsoring organizations received funding both to develop them and to implement them in multiple settings.

As with many prior attempts to influence educational practice "at scale," this one faded away, leaving behind some of the models and some of their connections to schools. This outcome confirms one of the central arguments presented in the essay that follows: that efforts to influence basic patterns of instructional practice in American schools on a large scale have never been sustained or deep enough to have an impact beyond the relatively small proportion of schools that are willing adopters of innovations.

One major contribution of this episode of educational reform has been the development of a substantial and interesting body of research on the problem of scale. The New American Schools project was the object of considerable research. Some of the sponsored programs in the project have done their own research, and a significant number of researchers have taken up the issue of scale. Taken together, their findings reinforce the conclusion put forth below:

that recent efforts to improve instructional practice at scale focus more on the number of adopters and the structural characteristics of reform than they do on fundamental changes in the instructional core—the relationships between teachers and students and the organizational practices that support those relationships. The difficulty of making changes at this level is the principal constraint on the large-scale adoption of promising new practices.

Why do good ideas about teaching and learning have so little impact on U.S. educational practice? This question, I argue, raises a central problem of U.S. education: A significant body of circumstantial evidence points to a deep, systemic incapacity of U.S. schools, and the practitioners who work in them, to develop, incorporate, and extend new ideas about teaching and learning in anything but a small fraction of schools and classrooms. This incapacity, I argue, is rooted primarily in the incentive structures in which teachers and administrators work. Therefore, solving the problem of scale means substantially changing these incentive structures.

CHANGING THE CORE: STUDENTS, TEACHERS, AND KNOWLEDGE

The problem of scale in educational innovation can be briefly stated as follows: Innovations that require large changes in the core of educational practice seldom penetrate more than a small fraction of U.S. schools and classrooms, and seldom last for very long when they do. By "the core of educational practice," I mean how teachers understand the nature of knowledge and the student's role in learning, and how these ideas about knowledge and learning are manifested in teaching and classwork. The "core" also includes structural arrangements of schools, such as the physical layout of classrooms, student grouping practices, teachers' responsibilities for groups of students, and relations among teachers in their work with students, as well as processes for assessing student learning and communicating it to students, teachers, parents, administrators, and other interested parties.

One can think of schools as generally representing a standard set of solutions to these problems of how to manage the core. Most teachers tend to think of knowledge as discrete bits of information about a particular subject and of student learning as the acquisition of this information through processes of repetition, memorization, and regular testing of recall (e.g., Cohen, 1988). The teacher, who is generally the center of attention in the classroom, initiates most of the talk and orchestrates most of the interaction in the classroom around brief factual questions, if there is any discussion at all.

Hence, the teacher is the main source of information, defined as discrete facts, and this information is what qualifies as knowledge. Often students are grouped by age, and again within age groups, according to their perceived capabilities to acquire information. The latter is generally accomplished either through within-class ability groups or, at higher grade levels, through "tracks," or clusters of courses for students whom teachers judge to have similar abilities. Individual teachers are typically responsible for one group of students for a fixed period of time. Seldom working in groups to decide what a given group of students should know or how that knowledge should be taught, teachers are typically solo practitioners operating in a structure that feeds them students and expectations about what students should be taught. Students' work is typically assessed by asking them to repeat information that has been conveyed by the teacher in the classroom, usually in the form of worksheets or tests that involve discrete, factual, right-or-wrong answers (Elmore, 1995).

At any given time, there are some schools and classrooms that deliberately violate these core patterns. For example, students may initiate a large share of the classroom talk, either in small groups or in teacher-led discussions, often in the context of some problem they are expected to solve. Teachers may ask broad, open-ended questions designed to elicit what students are thinking and how they are thinking, rather than to assess whether they have acquired discrete bits of information. Students' work might involve oral or written responses to complex, open-ended questions or problems for which they are expected to provide explanations that reflect not only their acquisition of information, but also their judgments about what kinds of information are most important or appropriate. Students may be grouped flexibly according to the teacher's judgment about the most appropriate array of strengths and weaknesses for a particular task or subject matter. Teachers may share responsibility for larger groups of students across different ages and ability levels and may work cooperatively to design classroom activities that challenge students working at different levels. In other words, students' learning may be assessed using a broad array of tasks, problems, mediums of expression, and formats.

In characterizing these divergences from traditional educational practice, I have deliberately avoided using the jargon of contemporary educational reform—"teaching for understanding," "whole language," "heterogeneous grouping," "team teaching," "cooperative learning," "authentic assessment," etc. I have done this because I do not want to confuse the problems associated with the implementation of particular innovations with the more general, systemic problem of what happens to practices, by whatever name, that violate or challenge the basic conventions of the core of schooling. The names of these practices change, and the intellectual traditions associated with particular versions of the practices ebb and flow. But, the fundamental problem remains: Attempts to change the stable patterns of the core of schooling, in the fundamental ways described above, are usually unsuccessful on anything more than a small scale. It is on this problem that I will focus.

Much of what passes for "change" in U.S. schooling is not really about changing the core, as defined above. Innovations often embody vague intentions of changing the core through modifications that are weakly related, or not related at all, to the core. U.S. secondary schools, for example, are constantly changing the way they arrange the schedule that students are expected to follow—lengthening or shortening class periods, distributing content in different ways across periods and days, increasing and decreasing class size for certain periods of the day, etc. These changes are often justified as a way to provide space in the day for teachers to do a kind of teaching they wouldn't otherwise be able to do, or to develop a different kind of relationship with students around knowledge.

However, the changes are often not explicitly connected to fundamental changes in the way knowledge is constructed, nor to the division of responsibility between teacher and student, the way students and teachers interact with each other around knowledge, or any of a variety of other stable conditions in the core. Hence, changes in scheduling seldom translate into changes in the fundamental conditions of teaching and learning for students and teachers. Schools, then, might be "changing" all the time—adopting this or that new structure or schedule or textbook series or tracking system—and never change in any fundamental way what teachers and students actually do when they are together in classrooms. I am not interested, except in passing, in changes that are unrelated to the core of schooling, as I have defined it above. My focus is on that narrower class of changes that directly challenge the fundamental relationships among student, teacher, and knowledge.

In some instances, such as the high-performance schools described by Linda Darling-Hammond (1996), a whole school will adopt a dramatically different form of organization, typically by starting from scratch rather than changing an existing school, and that form of organization will connect with teaching practices that are dramatically different from those traditionally associated with the core of schooling. At any given time there may be several such model schools, or exemplars of good practice, but as a proportion of the total number of schools, they are always a small fraction. In other words, it is possible to alter organization and practice in schools dramatically, but it has thus far never been possible to do it on a large scale.

The closer an innovation gets to the core of schooling, the less likely it is that it will influence teaching and learning on a large scale. The corollary of this proposition, of course, is that innovations that are distant from the core will be more readily adopted on a large scale. I will later develop some theoretical propositions about why this might be the case.

The problem of scale is a "nested" problem. That is, it exists in similar forms at different levels of the system. New practices may spring up in isolated classrooms or in clusters of classrooms within a given school, yet never move to most classrooms within that school. Likewise, whole schools may be created from scratch that embody very different forms of practice, but these schools remain a small proportion of all schools within a given district or state. And, finally, some local school systems may be more successful than others at spawning classrooms and schools that embody new practices, but these local systems remain a small fraction of the total number in a state.

The problem of scale is not a problem of the general resistance or failure of schools to change. Most schools are, in fact, constantly changing—adopting new curricula, tests, and grouping practices, changing schedules, creating new mechanisms for participation in decisionmaking, adding or subtracting teaching and administrative roles, and myriad other modifications. Within this vortex of change, however, basic conceptions of knowledge, of the teacher's and the student's roles in constructing knowledge, and of the role of classroom- and school-level structures in enabling student learning remain relatively static.

Nor is the problem of scale a failure of research or of systematic knowledge of what to do. At any given time, there is an abundance of ideas about how to change fundamental relationships in the core of schooling, some growing out of research and demonstration projects, some growing directly out of teaching practice. Many of these ideas are empirically tested and many are based on relatively coherent theories of student learning. We might wish that these ideas were closer to the language and thought processes of practitioners, and that they were packaged and delivered better, but there are more ideas circulating about how to change the core processes of schooling than there are schools and classrooms willing to engage them. There are always arguments among researchers and practitioners about which are the most promising ideas and conflicting evidence about their effects, but the supply of ideas is there. The problem, then, lies not in the supply of new ideas but in the demand for them. That is, the primary problem of scale is understanding the conditions under which people working in schools seek new knowledge and actively use it to change the fundamental processes of schooling.

WHY IS THE PROBLEM OF SCALE IMPORTANT TO EDUCATIONAL REFORM?

Two central ideas of the present period of U.S. educational reform raise fundamental, recurring problems of U.S. education. One idea is that teaching and learning in U.S. schools and classrooms is, in its most common form, emotionally flat and intellectually undemanding and unengaging; this idea is captured by that famous, controversial line from *A Nation at Risk:* "a rising tide of mediocrity" (National Commission on Excellence in Education, 1983). This is a perennial critique of U.S. education, dating back to the first systematic surveys of educational practice in the early twentieth century and confirmed by contemporary evidence.[1] One recent survey characterized typical classroom practice this way:

> No matter what the observational perspective, the same picture emerges. The two activities involving the most students were being lectured to and working on written assignments. . . . Students were working alone most of the time, whether individually or in groups. That is, the student listened as one member of a class being lectured,

or the student worked individually on a seat assignment. . . . In effect, then, the modal classroom configurations which we observed looked like this: the teacher explaining or lecturing to the total class or a single student, occasionally asking questions requiring factual answers; the teacher, when not lecturing, observing or monitoring students working individually at their desks; students listening or appearing to listen to the teacher and occasionally responding to the teacher's questions; students working individually at their desks on reading or writing assignments; and all with little emotion, from interpersonal warmth to expressions of hostility. (Goodlad, 1984, p. 230)

Every school can point to its energetic, engaged, and effective teachers; many students can recall at least one teacher who inspired in them an engagement in learning and a love of knowledge. We regularly honor and deify these pedagogical geniuses. But these exceptions prove the rule. For the most part, we regard inspired and demanding teaching as an individual trait, much like hair color or shoe size, rather than as a professional norm. As long as we consider engaging teaching to be an individual trait, rather than a norm that might apply to any teacher, we feel no obligation to ask the broader systemic question of why more evidence of engaging teaching does not exist. The answer to this question is obvious for those who subscribe to the individual trait theory of effective teaching: few teachers are predisposed to teach in interesting ways. Alternatively, other explanations for the prevalence of dull, flat, unengaging teaching might be that we fail to select and reward teachers based on their capacity to teach in engaging ways, or that organizational conditions do not promote and sustain good teaching when it occurs.

The other central idea in the present period of reform is captured by the slogan, "All students can learn." What reformers seem to mean by this idea is that "all" students—or most students—are capable of mastering challenging academic content at high levels of understanding, and the fact that many do not is more a testimonial to how they are taught than to whether they are suited for serious academic work. In other words, the slogan is meant to be a charge to schools to make challenging learning available to a much broader segment of students than they have in the past. The touchstone for this critique is consistent evidence over the last two decades or so that U.S. students do reasonably well on lower-level tests of achievement and cognitive skill, but relatively poorly on tests that require complex reasoning, inference, judgment, and transfer of knowledge from one type of problem to another (National Center for Education Statistics, 1993).

It is hard to imagine a solution to this problem of the distribution of learning among students that does not entail a solution to the first problem of increasing the frequency of engaging teaching. Clearly, getting more students to learn at higher levels has to entail some change in both the way students are taught and in the proportion of teachers who are teaching in ways that cause students to master higher-level skills and knowledge. It is possible, of course, that some piece of the problem of the distribution of learning can be solved by simply getting more teachers to teach more demanding academic content, even in boring and unengaging ways, to a broader population of students. But at some level it seems implausible that the large proportions of students presently disengaged from learning academic content at high levels of understanding will suddenly become more engaged if traditional teaching practices in the modal U.S. classroom remain the norm. Some students overcome the deadening effect of unengaging teaching through extraordinary ability, motivation, or family pressure. Other students, however, require extraordinary teaching to achieve extraordinary results. The problem of scale, then, can be seen in the context of the current reform debate as a need to change the core of schooling in ways that result in most students receiving engaging instruction in challenging academic content.

This view of educational reform, which focuses on changing fundamental conditions affecting the relationship of student, teacher, and knowledge, might be criticized as being either too narrow or too broad. My point in focusing the analysis wholly on the core of schooling is not to suggest that teaching and learning can be changed in isolation from an understanding of the contextual factors that influence children's lives. Nor is it to suggest that the object of reform should be to substitute one kind of uniformity of teaching practice for another. Rather, my point is that most educational reforms never reach, much less influence, long-standing patterns of teaching practice, and are therefore largely pointless if their intention is to improve student learning. I am interested in what is required before teaching practice can plausibly be expected to shift from its modal patterns toward more engaging and ambitious practices. These practices might be quite diverse. They might involve creative adaptations and responses to the backgrounds, interests, and preferences of students and their families. And they might be wedded in interesting ways to solutions to the multitude of problems that children face outside of school. But the fundamental problem I am interested in is why, when schools seem to be constantly changing, teaching practice changes so little, and on so small a scale.

THE EVIDENCE

The central claims of my argument, then, are that the core of schooling—defined as the standard solutions to the problem of how knowledge is defined, how teachers relate to students around knowledge, how teachers relate to other teachers in the course of their daily work, how students are grouped for purposes of instruction, how content is allocated to time, and how students' work is assessed—changes very little, except in a small proportion of schools and classrooms where the changes do not persist for very long. The changes that do tend to "stick" in schools are those that are most distant from the core.

The Progressive Period

To evaluate these claims, one would want to look at examples where reformers had ideas that challenged the core of schooling and where these ideas had time to percolate through the system and influence practice. One such example is the progressive period, perhaps the longest and most intense period of educational reform and ferment in the history of the country, running from roughly the early teens into the 1940s. What is most interesting about the progressive period, as compared with other periods of educational reform, is that its aims included explicit attempts to change pedagogy, coupled with a relatively strong intellectual and practical base. Noted intellectuals—John Dewey, in particular—developed ideas about how schools might be different, and these ideas found their way into classrooms and schools. The progressive period had a wide agenda, but one priority was an explicit attempt to change the core of schooling from a teacher-centered, fact-centered, recitation-based pedagogy to a pedagogy based on an understanding of children's thought processes and their capacities to learn and use ideas in the context of real-life problems.

In a nutshell, the progressive period produced an enormous amount of innovation, much of it in the core conditions of schooling. This innovation occurred in two broad forms. One was the creation of single schools that exemplified progressive pedagogical practices. The other was an attempt to implement progressive pedagogical practices on a large scale in public school systems. In discussing these two trends, I draw upon Lawrence Cremin's *The Transformation of the American School* (1961), which provides a detailed review of progressive education.

The single schools spawned by the progressive movement represented an astonishing range of pedagogical ideas and institutional forms, spread over the better part of four decades. In their seminal review of pedagogical reform in 1915, *Schools of To-Morrow*, John and Evelyn Dewey documented schools ranging from the Francis Parker School in Chicago to Caroline Pratt's Play School in New York, both exemplars of a single founder's vision. While these schools varied enormously in the particulars of their curricula, activities, grade and grouping structures, and teaching practices, they shared a common aim of breaking the lock of teacher-centered instruction and generating high levels of student engagement through student-initiated inquiry and group activities. Furthermore, these schools drew on a common wellspring of social criticism and prescription, exemplified in John Dewey's lecture, *The School and Society* (1899). According to Cremin, *The School and Society* focused school reform on shifting the center of gravity in education "back to the child. His natural impulses to conversation, to inquiry, to construction, and to expression were . . . seen as natural resources . . . of the educative process" (1961, pp. 118–119). Also included in this vision was the notion that school would be "recalled from isolation to the center of the struggle for a better life" (p. 119).

This dialectic between intellect and practice continued into the 1920s and 1930s, through the publication of several books: William Heard Kilpatrick's *Foundations of Method* (1925), an elaboration of Dewey's thinking about the connection between school and society; Harold Rugg and Ann Schumaker's *The Child-Centered School* (1928), another interpretive survey of pedagogical practice, like Dewey's *Schools of To-Morrow*; and Kilpatrick's *The Educational Frontier* (1933), a restatement of progressive theory and philosophy written by a committee of the National Society of College Teachers of Education (Cremin, 1961, pp. 216–229). Individual reformers and major social educational institutions, such as Teachers College and the University of Chicago, designed and developed schools that exemplified the key tenets of progressive thinking.

One example illustrates the power of this connection between ideas and institutions. In 1915, Abraham Flexner, the father of modern medical education, announced his intention to develop a model school that would do for general education what the Johns Hopkins Medical School had done for medical education. He wrote an essay called "A Modern School" (1917), a blueprint for reform describing a school that embodied major changes in curriculum and teaching. It was designed to serve as a laboratory for the scientific study of educational problems. In 1917, Teachers College, in collaboration with Flexner and the General Board of Education, opened the Lincoln School, which became a model and a gathering place for progressive reformers, a major source of new curriculum materials, and the intellectual birthplace of many reformers over the next two decades. The school survived until 1948, when it was disbanded in a dispute between its parents' association and the Teachers College administration (Cremin, 1961, pp. 280–291).

The second form of innovation in the progressive period, large-scale reforms of public school systems, drew on the same intellectual base as the founding of individual schools. A notable early example was the Gary, Indiana, school district. The Gary superintendent in 1907 was William Wirt, a former student of John Dewey at the University of Chicago. Wirt initiated the "Gary Plan," which became the leading exemplar of progressive practice on a large scale in the early progressive period. The key elements of the Gary Plan were "vastly extended educational opportunity" in the form of playgrounds, libraries, laboratories, machine shops, and the like; a "platoon system" of grouping, whereby groups of children moved *en masse* between classrooms and common areas, allowing for economies in facilities; a "community" system of school organization in which skilled tradespeople from the community played a role in teaching students; and a heavily project-focused curriculum (Cremin, 1961, pp. 153–160).

In 1919, Winnetka, Illinois, hired Carleton Washburn of the San Francisco State Normal School as its superintendent. Washburn launched a reform agenda based on the idea of individually paced instruction, where the "common essentials" in the curriculum were divided into "parcels," through which each student advanced, with the guidance of teachers, at his or her own pace. As students mastered each parcel, they were examined and moved on to the next. This individualized work was combined with "self-expressive" work in which students were encouraged to develop ideas and projects on their own, as well as group projects in which students worked on issues related to the community life of the school. Over the next decade, the Winnetka plan was imitated by as many as 247 other school districts, but with a crucial modification. Most districts found the practice of tailoring the curriculum to individual students far too complex for their tastes, so they organized students into groups to which they applied the idea of differential progress. In this way, a progressive reform focused on individualized learning led to the development of what is now called tracking (Cremin, 1961, pp. 295–298).

A number of cities, including Denver and Washington, DC, undertook massive curriculum reform projects in the late 1920s and early 1930s. These efforts were extraordinarily sophisticated, even by today's relatively rarefied standards. Typically, teachers were enlisted to meet in curriculum revision committees during regular school hours, and outside experts were enlisted to work with teachers in reformulating the curriculum and in developing new teaching practices. In Denver, Superintendent Jesse Newlon convinced his school board to appropriate $35,500 for this process. Denver became a center for teacher-initiated and teacher-developed curriculum, resulting in the development of a monograph series of course syllabi that attained a wide national circulation. The resulting curriculum changes were sustained in Denver over roughly two decades, when they were abandoned in the face of growing opposition to progressive pedagogy (Cremin, 1961, pp. 299–302; Cuban, 1984, pp. 67–83). In Washington, DC, Superintendent Frank Ballou led a pared-down version of the Denver curriculum revision model: Teacher committees chaired by administrators met after school, without the support of outside specialists. Despite these constraints, the process reached large numbers of teachers in both black and white schools in the city's segregated system (Cuban, 1984, pp. 83–93).

Larry Cuban concluded in *How Teachers Taught: Constancy and Change in American Classrooms, 1890–1980*, his study of large-scale reforms of curriculum and pedagogy in the late progressive period, that progressive practices, defined as movement away from teacher-centered and toward student-centered pedagogy, "seldom appeared in more than one-fourth of the classrooms in any district that systematically tried to install these varied elements" (1984, p. 135). Even in settings where teachers made a conscious effort to incorporate progressive practices, the result was more often than not a hybrid of traditional and progressive, in which the major elements of the traditional core of instruction were largely undisturbed:

> The dominant pattern of instruction, allowing for substantial spread of these hybrid progressive practices, remained teacher centered. Elementary and secondary teachers persisted in teaching from the front of the room, deciding what was to be learned, in what manner, and under what conditions. The primary means of grouping for instruction was the entire class. The major daily classroom activities continued with a teacher telling, explaining, and questioning students while the students listened, answered, read, and wrote. Seatwork or supervised study was an extension of these activities. (p. 137)

The fate of the progressive movement has been well documented. As the language of progressivism began to permeate educational talk, if not practice, the movement began to lose its intellectual edge and to drift into a series of empty clichés, the most extreme of which was life adjustment education. Opposition to progressivism, which had been building through the 1920s, came to a crescendo in the 1940s. The movement was increasingly portrayed by a skeptical public and press in terms of its most extreme manifestations—watered-down content, a focus on children's psychological adjustment at the expense of learning, and a preoccupation with self-expression rather than learning. Abraham Flexner, looking back on his experiences as a moderate progressive, observed that "there is something queer about the genus 'educator'; the loftiest are not immune. I think the cause must lie in their isolation from the rough and tumble contacts with all manner of men. They lose their sense of reality" (Cremin, 1961, p. 160).

The particular structure that educational reform took in the progressive period, though, is deeply rooted in American institutions and persists to this day. First, contrary to much received wisdom, intellectuals found ways to express their ideas about how education could be different in the form of real schools with structures and practices that were radically different from existing schools. There was a direct and vital connection between ideas and practice, a connection that persists up to the present, though in a much diluted form. But this connection took the institutional form of single schools, each an isolated island of practice, connected by a loosely defined intellectual agenda that made few demands for conformity, and each a particular, precious, and exotic specimen of a larger genus. So the most vital and direct connections between ideas and practice were deliberately institutionalized as separate, independent entities, incapable of and uninterested in forming replicates of themselves or of pursuing a broader institutional reform agenda.[2] A few exceptions, like the Lincoln School, were deliberately designed to influence educational practice on a larger scale, but the exact means by which that was to happen were quite vague. For the most part, progressive reformers believed that good ideas would travel, of their own volition, into U.S. classrooms and schools.

Second, where public systems did attempt to change pedagogical practice on a large scale, often using techniques that would be considered sophisticated by today's standards, they succeeded in changing practice in only a small fraction of classrooms, and then not necessarily in a sustained way over time. Sometimes, as in the case of Washburn's strategy of individualizing instruction in Winnetka, as the reforms moved from one district to another they became sinister caricatures of the original. The district-level reforms produced impressive tangible products, mostly in the form of new curriculum materials that would circulate within and outside the originating districts. The connection to classroom practice, however, was weak. Larry Cuban likens this kind of reform to a hurricane at sea—"storm-tossed waves on the ocean surface, turbulent water a fathom down, and calm on the ocean floor" (1984, p. 237).

Third, the very successes of progressive reformers became their biggest liabilities as the inevitable political opposition formed. Rather than persist in Dewey's original agenda of influencing public discourse about the nature of education and its relation to society through open public discussion, debate, and inquiry, the more militant progressives became increasingly like true believers in a particular version of the faith and increasingly isolated from public scrutiny and discourse. In this way, the developers of progressive pedagogy became increasingly isolated from the public mainstream and increasingly vulnerable to attack from traditionalists.

The pattern that emerges from the progressive period, then, is one where the intellectual and practical energies of serious reformers tended to turn inward, toward the creation of exemplary settings—classrooms or schools—that embodied their best ideas of practice, producing an impressive and attractive array of isolated examples of what practice *could* look like. At the same time, those actors with an interest in what would now be called systemic change focused on developing the tangible, visible, and material products of reform—plans, processes, curricula, materials—and focused much less, if at all, on the less tangible problem of what might cause a teacher to teach in new ways, if the materials and support were available to do so. These two forces produced the central dilemma of educational reform: We can produce many examples of how educational practice could look different, but we can produce few, if any, examples of large numbers of teachers engaging in these practices in large-scale institutions designed to deliver education to most children.

Large-Scale Curriculum Development Projects

Another, more recent body of evidence on these points comes from large-scale curriculum reforms of the 1950s and 1960s in the United States, which were funded by the National Science Foundation (NSF). In their fundamental structure, these reforms were quite similar to the progressive reforms, although much more tightly focused on content. The central idea of these curriculum reforms was that learning in school should resemble, much more than it usually does, the actual processes by which human beings come to understand their environment, culture, and social settings. That is, if students are studying mathematics, science, or social science, they should actually engage in activities similar to those of serious practitioners of these disciplines and, in the process, discover not only the knowledge of the subject, but also the thought processes and methods of inquiry by which that knowledge is constructed. This view suggested that construction of new curriculum for schools should proceed by bringing the best researchers in the various subjects together with schoolteachers and using the expertise of both groups to devise new conceptions of content and new strategies for teaching it. The earliest of these projects was the Physical Sciences Study Committee's (PSSC) high school physics curriculum, begun in 1956. Another of these was the Biological Sciences Curriculum Study (BSCS), begun in 1958. A third was Man: A Course of Study (MACOS), an ambitious social science curriculum development project, which began in 1959, but only received its first substantial funding from the Ford Foundation in 1962 and NSF support for teacher training in 1969 (Dow, 1991; Elmore, 1993;

Grobman, 1969; Marsh, 1964). These were among the largest and most ambitious of the curriculum reform projects, but by no means the only ones.

From the beginning, these curriculum reformers were clear that they aimed to change the core of U.S. schooling, and their aspirations were not fundamentally different from the early progressives. They envisioned teachers becoming coaches and co-investigators with students into the basic phenomena of the physical, biological, and social sciences. Students' work was to focus heavily on experimentation, inquiry, and study of original sources. The notion of the textbook as the repository of conventional knowledge was to be discarded, and in its place teachers were to use carefully developed course materials and experimental apparatus that were keyed to the big ideas in the areas under study. The object of study was not the assimilation of facts, but learning the methods and concepts of scientific inquiry by doing science in the same way that practitioners of science would do it.

The curriculum development projects grew out of the initiatives of university professors operating from the belief that they could improve the quality of incoming university students by improving the secondary school curriculum. Hence, university professors tended to dominate the curriculum development process, often to the detriment of relations with the teachers and school administrators who were expected to adopt the curricula once they were developed and tested in sample sites. The projects succeeded to varying degrees in engaging actual teachers in the development process, as opposed to simply having teachers field test lessons that had already been developed.

Teachers were engaged in one way or another at the developmental stage in all projects, but were not always co-developers. In PSSC, a few teachers judged to be talented enough to engage the MIT professors involved in the project were part of the development process; the main involvement of teachers came at the field-testing stage, but their feedback proved to be too voluminous to accommodate systematically in the final product (Marsh, 1964). In MACOS, one school in the Boston area was a summer test site, and teachers were engaged in the curriculum project relatively early in the process of development. Later versions of the curriculum were extensively tested and marketed in schools throughout the country (Dow, 1991).

By far the most ambitious and systematic involvement of teachers as co-developers was in BSCS. BSCS was designed to produce three distinct versions of a secondary biology curriculum (biochemical, ecological, and cellular) so that schools and teachers could have a choice of which approach to use. The development process was organized into three distinct teams, each composed of equal numbers of university professors and high school biology teachers. Lessons or units were developed by a pair composed of one professor and one secondary teacher, and each of these units was reviewed and critiqued by another team composed of equal partners. After the curriculum was developed, the teachers who participated in development were drafted to run study groups of teachers using the curriculum units during the school year, and the results of these study groups were fed back into the development process. Interestingly, once the curriculum was developed, NSF abandoned funding for the teacher study groups. NSF's rationale was that the teachers had accomplished their development task, but this cutoff effectively eliminated the teacher study groups, potentially the most powerful device for changing teaching practice (Elmore, 1993; Grobman, 1969).

Evaluations of the NSF-sponsored curriculum development projects generally conclude that their effects were broad but shallow. Hundreds of thousands of teachers and curriculum directors were trained in summer institutes. Tens of thousands of curriculum units were disseminated. Millions of students were exposed to at least some product or by-product of the various projects. In a few schools and school systems, teachers and administrators made concerted efforts to transform curriculum and teaching in accord with the new ideas, but in most instances the results looked like what Cuban (1984) found in his study of progressive teaching practices: A weak, diluted, hybrid form emerged in some settings in which new curricula were shoe-horned into old practices, and in most secondary classrooms the curricula had no impact on teaching and learning at all. While the curriculum development projects produced valuable materials that are still a resource to many teachers and shaped peoples' conceptions of the possibilities of secondary science curriculum, their tangible impact on the core of U.S. schooling has been negligible (Elmore, 1993; Stake & Easely, 1978).

Most academic critics agree that the curriculum development projects embodied a naive, discredited, and badly conceived model of how to influence teaching practice. The model, if there was one, was that "good" curriculum and teaching practice were self-explanatory and self-implementing. Once teachers and school administrators recognized the clearly superior ideas embodied in the new curricula, they would simply switch from traditional textbooks to the new materials and change long-standing practices in order to improve their teaching and the chances of their students succeeding in school.

What this model overlooked, however, was the complex process by which local curricular decisions get made, the entrenched and institutionalized political and commercial relationships that support existing textbook-driven curricula, the weak incentives operating on teachers to change their practices in their daily work routines, and the extraordinary costs of making large-scale, long-standing changes of a fundamental kind in how knowledge is constructed in classrooms. In the few instances where the advocates for the curriculum development projects appeared to be on the verge of discovering a way to change practice on a large scale—as in the BSCS teacher study groups, for example—they failed to discern the significance of what they were doing because they saw themselves as developers of new ideas about teaching and not as institution-changing actors.

The structural pattern that emerges from the large-scale curriculum development projects is strikingly similar to that of the progressive period. First, the ideas were powerful and engaging, and they found their way into tangible materials and into practice in a few settings. In this sense, the projects were a remarkable achievement in the social organization of knowledge, pulling the country's most sophisticated thinkers into the orbit of public education and putting them to work on the problem of what students should know and be able to do. Second, the curriculum developers proved to be inept and naive in their grasp of the individual and institutional issues of change associated with their reforms. They assumed that a "good" product would travel into U.S. classrooms on the basis of its merit, without regard for the complex institutional and individual factors that might constrain its ability to do so. Third, their biggest successes were, in a sense, also their biggest failures. Those few teachers who became accomplished teachers of PSSC physics, BSCS biology, or MACOS approaches to social studies only served to confirm what most educators think about talent in the classroom. A few have it, but most do not. A few have the extraordinary energy, commitment, and native ability required to change their practice in some fundamental way; most others do not. The existence of exemplars, without some way of capitalizing on their talents, only reinforces the notion that ambitious teaching is an individual trait, not a professional expectation.

What Changes?

Critiques of this argument posit that U.S. schools have changed in fundamental ways over the last one hundred years, and that focusing on the fate of what I have characterized as "good" classroom practice gives a biased picture. To be sure, schools have changed massively over the last century. David Cohen argues, for example, that in the critical period of the early twentieth century, when the secondary school population increased four-fold in three decades, massive institutional changes were necessary to accommodate newly arrived students. Larger, more complex schools, a more differentiated curriculum, and grading and retention practices designed to hold adolescents out of the labor force were just a few of those changes (Powell, Farrar, & Cohen, 1985). Vocational education emerged in the post–World War I era as a mechanism to bind schools more closely to the economy and to provide a more differentiated curriculum for a diverse student body. Kindergartens emerged on a large scale in the 1940s and 1950s, extending the period of life children were in school and altering the relationship between the family and school in important ways. The equity-based reforms of the 1960s and 1970s revealed the limits of earlier approaches to equality of opportunity, and new programs addressed the needs of students from disadvantaged backgrounds, many with physical and learning problems, and who spoke native languages other than English. In brief, this critique states that we face a much different educational system now than we did in the early decades of the twentieth century, and that these changes have surely had a significant impact on how teachers teach and how students learn.

I am inclined to agree with those who take an institutional perspective on educational change. In a nutshell, this argument states that it is possible, indeed practically imperative, for institutions to learn to change massively in their surface structures while at the same time changing little at their core (Cuban, 1990; March & Olsen, 1989; Meyer & Rowan, 1978; Tyack & Cuban, 1995; Tyack & Tobin, 1994). Institutions use their structures to buffer and assimilate the changing demands of a political and social order that is constantly in flux—they add new programs, they develop highly visible initiatives that respond to prevailing opinions in the community, they open new units in the organization to accommodate new clients, they mobilize and organize public opinion by creating new governance structures. But the gap between these institutional structures and the core patterns of schooling is slippery and elusive: The core of schooling remains relatively stable in the face of often massive changes in the structure around it. Schools legitimize themselves with their various conflicting publics by constantly changing external structures and processes, but shield their workers from any fundamental impact of these changes by leaving the core intact. This accounts for the resilience of practice within the context of constant institutional change.

THE ROLE OF INCENTIVES

Nested within this broad framework of institutional and political issues is a more specific problem of incentives that reforms need to address in order to get at the problem of scale. Institutional structures influence the behavior of individuals in part through incentives. The institution and its political context help set the values and rewards that individuals respond to within their daily work life. But individual values are also important. As David Cohen (1995) cogently argues in his discussion of rewards for teacher performance, incentives mobilize individual values; that is, individual values determine to some degree what the institution can elicit with incentives. For example, if teachers or students do not value student academic performance, do not see the relationship between academic performance and personal objectives, or do not believe it is possible to change student performance, then it is hard to use incentives to motivate them to action that would improve performance.

Thus, individual acts like the practice of teaching in complex institutional settings emanate both from incentives that operate on the individual and the individual's willingness to recognize and respond to these incentives as legitimate. Individual actions are also a product of the knowledge and the competence that the individual possesses. As Michael Fullan has argued, schools routinely undertake reforms for which they have neither the institutional nor the individual competence, and they resolve this problem by trivializing the reforms, changing the language they use, and modifying superficial structures around the practice, but without changing the practice itself (Fullan, 1982; Fullan & Miles, 1992). Individuals are embedded in institutional structures that provide them with incentives to act in certain ways, and they respond to these incentives by testing them against their values and their competence.

One way of thinking about the aforementioned evidence is that it demonstrates a massive failure of schools to harness their institutional incentives to the improvement of practice. I think this failure is rooted not only in the design of the institutions, but also in a deep cultural norm about teaching that I referred to earlier: that successful teaching is an individual trait rather than a set of learned professional competencies acquired over the course of a career.

Both the progressive reformers and the curriculum reforms of the 1950s and 1960s focused on connecting powerful ideas to practice, developing exemplars of good practice, and attracting true believers. These efforts largely failed, often in very interesting and instructive ways, to translate their ideas into broad-scale changes in practice. A very large incentive problem is buried in this strategy: Reform strategies of this kind rely on the intrinsic motivation of individuals with particular values and competencies—and a particular orientation toward the outside world—to develop and implement reforms in schools.

These intrinsically motivated individuals are typically highly engaged in the world outside of their workplace, and hence come in contact with the opportunities presented by new practices. They are usually willing to invest large amounts of their own time in learning new ways to think about their practice and in the messy and time-consuming work of getting others to cooperate in changing their practice. And, perhaps most importantly, they see their own practice in a broader social context and see certain parts of that social context as having authority over how they practice. Progressive teachers and school-builders, for example, saw themselves as participants in a broad movement for social reform and were willing to evaluate their own work in terms of its consistency with the goals of that reform (Tyack & Hansot, 1982). Some teachers who were directly involved in the curriculum reform projects formed an identity as science or math teachers affiliated with professional organizations that had authority and influence over their practice.

The problem of incentives is that these individuals are typically a small proportion of the total population of teachers. The demands required by this kind of ambitious, challenging, and time-consuming work seem at best formidable, and at worst hopelessly demanding. Friedrich Engels once said that the problem with socialism is that it spoils too many good evenings at home, and one could say the same about the reform of educational practice.

Ambitious and challenging practice in classrooms thus occurs roughly in proportion to the number of teachers who are intrinsically motivated to question their practice on a fundamental level and look to outside models to improve teaching and learning. The circumstantial evidence suggests that, at the peak of reform periods, this proportion of teachers is roughly 25 percent of the total population, and that it can decrease to considerably less than that if the general climate for reform is weak (Cuban, 1990). Our most successful and ambitious strategies of reform, then, embody incentive structures that can mobilize, at most, roughly one-fourth of the total population of teachers.

Given this interpretation of the evidence, then, it is possible to see the enormous power of a cultural norm that describes successful teaching as an individual attribute rather than a body of deliberately acquired professional knowledge and skills. If what a teacher does is based wholly or largely on individual traits, then it is highly unlikely that the incentive structures of schools could alter the proportion of teachers willing to engage in ambitious practice, other than changing the composition of the teaching force.

It is also possible to see the perverse incentives buried in typical reform strategies. The first step serious reformers typically take involves gathering up the faithful and concentrating them in one place in order to form a cohesive community of like-minded practitioners. In the case of the progressives, reformers started schools that embodied their ideas; in the case of the curriculum projects, reformers identified early adopters of their new curricula as exemplars of success. This strategy immediately isolates the teachers who are most likely to change from those who are least likely to embrace reform. This dynamic creates a social barrier between the two, virtually guaranteeing that the former will not grow in number and the latter will continue to believe that exemplary teaching requires extraordinary resources in an exceptional environment.

One can see vestiges of this perverse incentive structure in the design of current school reform movements. These reforms typically begin with a few teachers in a building and nurture a distinctive identity among those teachers, or they construct a new school from scratch and recruit teachers who are highly motivated to join the faculty. Both strategies guarantee the isolation of the small fraction of teachers who are willing to engage in change from the majority who find it an intimidating and threatening prospect, and are likely to instigate a conflict between the two groups of teachers that renders the scaling up of this reform highly unlikely.

Without some fundamental change in the incentive structure under which schools and teachers operate, we will continue more or less indefinitely to repeat the experience of the progressives and the curriculum reformers. Like our predecessors, we will design reforms that appeal to the intrinsic values and competencies of a relatively small proportion of the teaching force. We will gather these teachers together in ways that cut them off from contact and connection with those who find ambitious teaching intimidating and unfeasible. We will demonstrate that powerful ideas can be harnessed to changes in practice in a small fraction of settings, but continue to fail in moving those practices beyond the group of teachers who are intrinsically motivated and competent to engage in them.

WORKING ON THE PROBLEM OF SCALE

What might be done to change this self-reinforcing incentive structure? Probably the first step is to acknowledge that social problems of this complexity are not amenable to quick, comprehensive, rational solutions. Fundamental changes in patterns of incentives occur not by engaging in ambitious, discontinuous reforms, but rather by pushing hard in a few strategic places in the system of relations surrounding the problem and then carefully observing the results. My recommendations will be of this sort.

Furthermore, it seems important to continue to do what has yielded success in the past and to continue to do it with increasing sophistication. I have argued that the most successful part of the progressive and curriculum reform strategies was the creation of powerful connections between big ideas with large social implications and the micro-world of teaching practice. The progressives succeeded in creating versions of educational reform that both exemplified progressive ideals and embodied concrete changes in the core of schooling. Likewise, the curriculum reformers succeeded in harnessing the talent of the scientific elite to the challenge of secondary school curriculum and teaching.

This connection between the big ideas and the fine grain of practice in the core of schooling is a fundamental precondition for any change in practice. Capacity to make these connections waxes and wanes, and probably depends too heavily on the idiosyncrasies of particular individuals with a particular scientific or ideological ax to grind. One could imagine doing a much better job of institutionalizing the connection between big ideas and teaching practice. Examples might include routine major national curriculum reviews composed of groups with equal numbers of schoolteachers and university researchers, or a national curriculum renewal agenda that targeted particular parts of teaching and curriculum for renewal on a regular cycle. The more basic point, however, is that preserving the connection between big ideas and teaching practice, embodied in earlier reform strategies, is an essential element in tackling the problem of scale.

With these ideas as context, I offer four main proposals for how to begin to tackle the problem of scale. Each grows out of an earlier line of analysis in this article, and each embodies an argument about how incentives should be realigned to tackle the problem of scale.

1. Develop strong external normative structures for practice.

The key flaw in earlier attempts at large-scale reform was to rely almost exclusively on the intrinsic commitment of talented and highly motivated teachers to carry the burden of reform. Coupled with strong cultural norms about good teaching being an individual trait, this strategy virtually guarantees that good practice will stay with those who learn and will not travel to those who are less predisposed to learn. One promising approach, then, is to create strong professional and social normative structures for good teaching practice that are external to individual teachers and their immediate working environment, and to provide a basis for evaluating how many teachers are approximating good practice at what level of competence.

I use the concept of external normative structures, rather than a term like *standards,* because I think these structures should be diverse and need to be constructed on different bases of authority in order to be useful in influencing teaching practice. The category of external structures could include formal statements of good practice, such as content and performance standards developed by professional bodies like the National Council of Teachers of Mathematics. External structures might also include alternative credentialing systems, such as the National Board for Professional Teaching Standards.

But strong external structures could also include less imposing and more informal ways of communicating norms of good practice. For example, curriculum units designed to demonstrate more advanced forms of practice could be accompanied by videotapes of teachers engaging in these practices and then disseminated through teacher organizations. These external normative structures can be hooked to internal systems of rewards for teachers—salary increments for staff development related to changes in practice, release time to work on curriculum or performance standards, time to develop curriculum units that embody particular approaches to teaching, or opportunities to engage in demonstration teaching. There is no particular requirement for unanimity, consistency, or "alignment" among these various external structures, only that they embody well-developed notions of what it means for teachers to teach and students to learn at high levels of competency in a given area. The important feature of these structures is not their unanimity or consistency, which is probably illusory anyway, but the fact that the structures are external to the world in which teachers work, they form teachers' ideas about practice, and they carry some form of professional authority.

Why is the existence of external norms important? Because it institutionalizes the idea that professionals are responsible for looking outward at challenging conceptions of practice, in addition to looking inward at their values and competencies. Good teaching becomes a matter for public debate and disagreement, for serious reflection and discourse, for positive and negative feedback about one's own practices. Over time, as this predisposition to look outward becomes more routinized and ingrained, trait theories of teaching competence should diminish. Teachers would begin increasingly to think of themselves as operating in a web of professional relations that influence their daily decisions, rather than as solo practitioners inventing practice out of their personalities, prior experiences, and assessments of their own strengths and weaknesses. Without external normative structures, teachers have no incentive to think of their practice as anything other than a bundle of traits. The existence of strong external norms also has the effect of legitimating the proportion of teachers in any system who draw their ideas about teaching from a professional community, and who compare themselves against a standard external to their school or community. External norms give visibility and status to those who exemplify them.

2. Develop organizational structures that intensify and focus,
rather than dissipate and scatter, intrinsic motivation to engage
in challenging practice.

The good news about existing reform strategies is that they tend to galvanize commitment among the already motivated by concentrating them in small groups of true believers who reinforce each other. The bad news is that these small groups of self-selected reformers apparently seldom influence their peers. This conclusion suggests that structures should, at a minimum, create diversity among the energetic, already committed reformers and the skeptical and timid. But it also suggests that the unit of work in an organization that wants to change its teaching practice should be small enough so that members can exercise real influence over each others' practice. Certain types of structures are more likely than others to intensify and focus norms of good practice: organizations in which face-to-face relationships dominate impersonal, bureaucratic ones; organizations in which people routinely interact around common problems of practice; and organizations that focus on the results of their work for students, rather than on the working conditions of professionals. These features can be incorporated into organizations, as well as into the composition of their memberships.

Heather Lewis, an accomplished practitioner of school change with the Center for Collaborative Education in New York City, has argued that we will solve the problem of scaling up by scaling down.[3] By this, I think she means that more ambitious teaching practice is more likely to occur in smaller schools, where adults are more likely to work collaboratively and take common responsibility for students. Teachers in schools with a tighter sense of mutual commitment, which arguably comes with smaller size, are more likely to exert influence on each other around norms of good practice than are teachers in anonymous organizations in which bureaucratic controls are the predominant mechanism of influence.

The problem is that there is so little structural variation in U.S. public education that we have little conception of what kinds of structures would have this intensifying and focusing effect. The first job of structural reform should be to create more variation in structure—more small schools, more schools organized into smaller subunits, more structures that create stronger group norms inside larger schools, more ways of connecting adventurous teachers with their less ambitious and reflective colleagues—but not structures that isolate the true believers from the skeptical and the timid. In the absence of such structures, there will be no connective tissue to bind teachers together in a relationship of mutual obligation and force them to sort out issues of practice. Organizational forms that intensify and focus group norms, without nesting them in some system of external norms of good practice, will simply perpetuate whatever the prevailing conventional wisdom about practice happens to be in a given school.

3. Create intentional processes for reproduction of successes.
One of the major lessons from past large-scale reforms is their astounding naiveté about how to get their successes to move from one setting to another. The progressives seemed to think that a few good exemplars and a few energetic superintendents pursuing systemwide strategies of reform would ignite a conflagration that would consume all of U.S. education. If any social movement had the possibility of doing that, it was the progressive movement, since it had, at least initially, a high degree of focus, a steady supply of serious intellectual capital, and an infrastructure of committed reformers. But it did not succeed at influencing more than a small fraction of schools and classrooms. The curriculum reformers thought that good curriculum models would create their own demand, an astoundingly naive idea in retrospect, given what we know about the limits within which teachers work, the complex webs of institutional and political relationships that surround curriculum decisions, and the weak incentives for teachers to pay attention to external ideas about teaching practice.

This is not so much a failure of a theory of how to reproduce success as the absence of a practical theory that takes account of the institutional complexities that operate on changes in practice. I am skeptical that such a theory will emerge without serious experimentation, since I know of no clear a priori basis on which to construct such a theory. I suggest five theories that might serve as the basis for experimentation with processes designed to get exemplary practices to scale.

Incremental Growth: The usual way of thinking about increases in scale in social systems is incremental growth. For example, according to the incremental growth theory, the proportion of teachers teaching in a particular way would increase by some modest constant each year, until the proportion approached 100 percent. This model implies a fixed capacity for training a given number of teachers per year in an organization.

The problems with this model are not difficult to identify. The idea that new practice "takes" after a teacher has been trained is highly suspect. The notion that a fixed number of teachers could be trained to teach in a given way by circulating them through a training experience seems implausible, although it is probably the way most training programs are designed. Teaching practice is unlikely to change as a result of exposure to training, unless that training also brings with it some kind of external normative structure and a network of social relationships that personalize that structure, and unless that training supports interaction around problems of practice. The incremental model, if it is to work, needs a different kind of specification, which I will call the cumulative model.

Cumulative Growth: The cumulative growth model suggests that "getting to scale" is a slower, less linear process than that described by the incremental model. It involves not only creating interventions that expose teachers to new practices, but also monitoring the effects of these interventions on teaching practice. When necessary, processes may be created to compensate for the weaknesses of initial effects. Cumulative growth not only adds an increment of practitioners who are exposed to a new practice each year, but also involves a backlog of practitioners from previous years who may or may not have responded to past training. This problem requires a more complex solution than simply continuing to provide exposure to new practice at a given rate. It might require, for example, the creation of professional networks to support the practice of teachers who are in the process of changing their practice, or connecting the more advanced with the less advanced through some sort of mentoring scheme.

Discontinuous Growth: Another possibility is a sharply increasing, or discontinuous, growth model. This could occur through a process like a chain letter, in which an initial group of teachers learned a new kind of practice, and each member of that group worked with another group, and so on. The rate of growth might go, for example, from x, to $10x$, to $100x$, to $1000x$, etc.

This discontinuous growth model shares the same problem with the incremental growth model, but on a larger scale. As the number of teachers exposed to new practices increases, so too does the backlog of teachers for whom the initial intervention was inadequate, eventually reaching the point at which this accumulation of teachers overwhelms the system. It also seems likely that the discontinuous growth model would create serious quality control problems. As growth accelerates, it becomes more and more difficult to distinguish between teachers who are accomplished practitioners of new ways of teaching and those who are accomplished at making it appear as though they have mastered new ways of teaching.

In all the examples of growth models so far, teachers operate in a system of relationships that provides training and support, but not as members of organizations called schools. In addition to these three models that construct training and support around teachers, two additional models treat teachers as practitioners working in schools.

Unbalanced Growth: One of these models is the unbalanced growth model. This extends and modifies the standard model of innovation in education: collecting true believers in a few settings. Whereas the standard model socially isolates true believers from everyone else, virtually guaranteeing that new practices do not spread, versions of the unbalanced growth model correct for these deficiencies. A version of unbalanced growth might involve concentrating a critical mass of high-performing teachers in a few schools, with an explicit charge to develop each other's capacities to teach in new ways. The growth of new practice would be "unbalanced" initially because some schools would be deliberately constructed to bring like-minded practitioners together to develop their skills. Such schools might be called "pioneer" schools or "leading edge" schools to communicate that they are designed to serve as places where new practices are developed, nurtured, and taught to an ever-increasing number of practitioners. Over time, these schools would be deliberately staffed with larger proportions of less accomplished practitioners and teachers not yet introduced to new models of practice. The competencies developed in the high-performing organizations would then socialize new teachers into the norms of good practice.

The main problem with this model is that it goes against the grain of existing personnel practices in most school systems. Teaching assignments are typically made through collectively bargained seniority and/ or principal entrepreneurship, rather than on the basis of a systematic interest in using schools as places to socialize teachers to new practice. Younger teachers are typically assigned to schools with the largest proportions of difficult-to-teach children and spend their careers working their way into more desirable assignments. Principals who understand and have mastered the assignment system often use it to gather teachers with whom they prefer to work. In order for the unbalanced growth model to work, a school system would have to devise some deliberate strategy for placing teachers in settings where they would be most likely to develop new skills. Teachers, likewise, would have to be willing to work in settings where they could learn to develop their practice as part of their professional responsibility.

Cell Division, or Reproduction: The other model of growth that treats teachers as practitioners working in schools is the cell division, or reproduction, model. This model works from the analogy of reproductive biology. Rather than trying to change teaching practice by influencing the flow of teachers through schools, as in the unbalanced growth model, the cell division model involves systematically increasing the number and proportion of schools characterized by distinctive pedagogical practices.

The cell division model works by first creating a number of settings in which exemplary practitioners are concentrated and allowed to develop new approaches to teaching practice. Then, on a more or less predictable schedule, a number of these practitioners are asked to form another school, using the "genetic material" of their own knowledge and understanding to recruit a new cadre of teachers whom they educate to a new set of expectations about practice. Over time, several such schools would surface with strong communities of teachers invested in particular approaches to teaching.[4]

The reproduction model elicits more systematic thinking about what constitutes evidence of the "spread" of good teaching practice. Given the slipperiness of attempts to "replicate" successful programs or practices from one setting to another, the idea of getting to scale should not be equated with the exact replication of practices that work in one setting in others. For example, when we reproduce as human beings, children are not identical replicates of parents; rather, each child is a new human being with a distinctive personality that may bear a family resemblance to the mother and father. Children from the same family differ quite dramatically from each other, even though they may share certain common traits. The reproduction model broadens notions of evidence by allowing for the dissemination of good teaching practices with "family resemblances" in different settings. It causes us to look at the fundamental process by which practices are chosen for reproduction, while others are bypassed or significantly modified. It also prompts us to reproduce "family resemblances" in such a way as to have a meaningful impact on practice rather than merely promoting assimilation of symbols that do not go to the core.

These alternative models of growth each embody an explicit practical theory of how to propagate or reproduce practice. They also have a transparent logic that can be understood and adapted by others for use in other settings. More such theories, and more documented examples of how they work in use, should help in understanding how to get to scale with good educational practice.

4. Create structures that promote learning of new practices and incentive systems that support them.

Reformers typically make very heroic and unrealistic assumptions about what ordinary human beings can do, and they generalize these assumptions to a wide population of teachers. Cremin made the following observation about progressive education:

> From the beginning progressivism cast the teacher in an almost impossible role: [she] was to be an artist of consummate skill, properly knowledgeable in [her] field, meticulously trained in the science of pedagogy, and thoroughly imbued with a burning zeal for social improvement. It need hardly be said that here as elsewhere . . . the gap between the real and the ideal was appalling. (1961, p. 168)

Likewise, the curriculum reformers appeared to assume that teachers, given the existence of clearly superior content, would simply use the new curricula and learn what was needed in order to teach differently. Missing from this view is an explicit model of how teachers engage in intentional learning about new ways to teach. According to

Fullan and Miles, "Change involves learning and . . . all change involves coming to understand and to be good at something new" (1992, p. 749). While knowledge is not deep on this subject, the following seem plausible: teachers are more likely to learn from direct observation of practice and trial and error in their own classrooms than they are from abstract descriptions of new teaching; changing teaching practice, even for committed teachers, takes a long time and several cycles of trial and error; teachers have to feel that there is some compelling reason for them to practice differently, with the best direct evidence being that students learn better; and teachers need feedback from sources they trust about whether students are actually learning what they are taught.

These conditions accompany the learning of any new, complicated practice. Yet, reform efforts seldom, if ever, incorporate these conditions. Teachers are often tossed headlong into discussion groups to work out the classroom logistics of implementing a new curriculum. They are encouraged to develop model lessons as a group activity and then sent back to their classrooms to implement them as solo practitioners. Teachers are seldom asked to judge if this new curriculum translates well into concrete actions in the classroom, nor are they often asked to participate as codesigners of the ideas in the first place. The feedback teachers receive on the effects of their practice usually comes in the form of generalized test scores that have no relationship to the specific objectives of the new practice. In other words, the conditions under which teachers are asked to engage in new practices bear no relationship whatsoever to the conditions required for learning how to implement complex and new practices with success. Why would anyone want to change their practice under such conditions?

A basic prerequisite for tackling the problem of scale, then, is to insist that reforms that purport to change practice embody an explicit theory about how human beings learn to do things differently. Presently, there are few, if any, well-developed theories that meet this requirement, although I have sketched out a few above. Furthermore, these theories have to make sense at the individual and at the organizational level. That is, if you ask teachers to change the way they deal with students and to relate to their colleagues differently, the incentives that operate at the organizational level have to reinforce and promote those behaviors. Encouragement and support, access to special knowledge, time to focus on the requirements of the new task, time to observe others doing it—all suggest ways in which the environment of incentives in the organization comes to reflect the requirements of learning.

These four basic principles constitute departures from previous strategies of broad-scale reform, and they address fundamental problems of previous strategies. It is unlikely that teachers or schools will respond to the emergence of new practices any differently than they have in the past if those practices are not legitimated by norms that are external to the environment in which they work every day. It is unlikely that teachers who are not intrinsically motivated to engage in hard, uncertain work will learn to do so in large, anonymous organizations that do not intensify personal commitments and responsibilities. It is unlikely that successful practices will spontaneously reproduce themselves just because they are successful, in the absence of structures and processes based on explicit theories about how reproduction occurs. And it is unlikely that teachers will be successful at learning new practices if the organizations in which they work do not embody some explicit learning theory in the way they design work and reward people.

Each of these principles presents a formidable agenda for research and practice. The magnitude of the task suggests that we should not expect to see immediate large-scale adoption of promising new practices. It also suggests that progress will come from an explicit acknowledgment that the problems of scale are deeply rooted in the incentives and cultural norms of the institutions, and cannot be fixed with simple policy shifts or exhortations from people with money. The issue of getting to scale with good educational practice requires nothing less than deliberately creating and reproducing alternatives to the existing flawed institutional arrangements and incentives structures.

2

Building a New Structure for School Leadership*

Americans love the idea of leadership, though we are often deeply skeptical of our leaders. We expect our leaders to guide us through difficulties and crises in public life; we invest them with a wisdom, foresight, and competence greater than our own. But real leaders all too frequently prove themselves just as susceptible to confusion and error as we are.

The failure of leadership has become a focal point of public discourse. Courses in leadership and books about leadership are a staple of professional education programs in business, public policy, and education. The assumption is that people can be taught to be leaders. But if leadership can be taught, why does there seem to be so little difference between leaders who are trained for their role and those who are not? Why are so many of the exemplars of leadership featured in case studies and textbooks people who have received no formal education in being leaders?

Americans tend to treat leadership as a collection of personal attributes that inhere in leaders—attributes that, by definition, are difficult to teach precisely because they are character traits. At best, one can learn the behaviors that indicate such traits. But much of the work of leadership, especially in schools, requires real knowledge and skill. The idea that leaders need to know

* This paper was prepared for, and supported by, the Albert Shanker Institute. I am indebted to Eugenia Kemble, executive director of the Institute, for her guidance in thinking about these issues.

real things about the fundamental work of their organizations has not been central to the discourse about leadership in America.

This conundrum of leadership presents major challenges in the current phase of educational reform. Demands for accountability for student performance have never been greater. Hence, the demands on leaders in public education have never been greater. But what kind of knowledge and skill do school leaders need to respond to these demands? This essay sets out to demystify the notion of leadership in the context of school reform by focusing on the knowledge and skills leaders need to develop in order to improve instructional practice. It presents "a deliberately deromanticized, focused, and instrumental" vision of leadership: School leaders, the argument goes, will succeed or fail depending on whether they master the practice of instructional improvement at scale in classrooms and schools.

Attendant to this rather unglamorous idea of anchoring school leadership in the work of instructional practice is the emergence of a new definition of school leadership. Rather than focusing on the character traits and actions of individual leaders—in the heroic American tradition of charismatic leadership—we will increasingly have to focus on the distribution of leadership, dispersing responsibilities for guidance and direction along the same contours as the distribution of competence and expertise in improving the quality of instructional practice and the level of student learning.

Public schools and school systems, as they are presently constituted, are simply not led in ways that enable them to respond to the increasing demands they face under standards-based reform. Further, if schools, school systems, and their leaders respond to standards-based reforms the way they have responded to other attempts at broad-scale reform of public education over the past century, they will fail massively and visibly, with an attendant loss of public confidence and serious consequences for public education. The way out of this problem is through the large-scale improvement of instruction, something public education has been unable to do to date, but which is possible with dramatic changes in the way public schools define and practice leadership.

Contrary to the myth of visionary leadership that pervades American culture, most leaders in all sectors of society are creatures of the organizations they lead. Nowhere is this more true than in public education, where principals and district superintendents are recruited almost exclusively from the ranks of practice. As in the military and the church, one does not get to lead in education without being well socialized to the norms, values, predispositions, and routines of the organization one is leading.

Consequently, current education leaders are no better equipped than the organizations they lead to meet the challenges posed by standards-based reform (Lortie, 1987). So relying on leaders to solve the problem of systemic reform in schools is, to put it bluntly, asking people to do something they don't know how to do and have had no occasion to learn in the course of their careers. There are, of course, a few gifted and visionary leaders who are busy inventing solutions to the problems of systemic reform, just as there are a few gifted and visionary leaders at any moment of history in American education. These exceptions prove the rule. Few visionary leaders have had any effect on the dominant institutional patterns of American education.

Here, then, is the seeming conundrum: Schools are being asked by elected officials—policy leaders, if you will—to do things they are largely unequipped to do. School leaders are being asked to assume responsibilities they are largely unequipped to assume, and the risks and consequences of failure are high for everyone, but especially high for children. This paper attempts to chart a way out of this conundrum through an understanding of large-scale instructional improvement.

This paper looks outward—focusing on the imperatives of public school leadership and the demands standards-based accountability place upon it—rather than inward. It does not, in other words, focus on understanding how people in existing leadership positions define and do their work. I take this perspective because I don't think there is much in current conceptions of leadership in public schools that extends comfortably to the new conceptions. The logic of large-scale instructional improvement leads to differences in kind, rather than differences in degree. If public schools survive, leaders will look very different from the way they presently look, both in who leads and in what these leaders do.

Standards-based reform has a deceptively simple logic: schools and school systems should be held accountable for their contributions to student learning. Society should communicate its expectations for what students should know and be able to do in the form of standards, both for what should be taught and for what students should be able to demonstrate about their learning. School administrators and policymakers at the state, district, and school levels should regularly evaluate whether teachers are teaching what they are expected to teach and whether students can demonstrate what they are expected to learn. The fundamental unit of accountability should be the school, because that is the organizational unit where teaching and learning actually occur. Evidence from evaluations of teaching and student performance should be used to improve teaching and learning and, ultimately, to allocate rewards and sanctions (see Chapter 4).

This logic of standards-based reform has become, over the past fifteen years, a fundamental part of the architecture of policy and governance in American education. Virtually all states have adopted some form of content and/or performance standards. Most states are moving, in at least a rudimentary way, toward accountability systems that evaluate schools based on student performance. While the design of these policies leaves a great deal to be desired, both in specificity and internal logic, the politics that surround these policies are very energetic and visible. We may get the version of standards-based reform that advocates envision, or we may get a corrupted and poorly thought-out evil twin. But we will almost surely get some version of standards-based reform in virtually every jurisdiction over the next decade.

When historians of education look back at the late twentieth century, they will almost certainly describe it as a critical period of changing policy perspectives on public education in the United States. What they will describe by way of practices is considerably less certain. Like it or not, standards-based reform represents a fundamental shift in the relationship between policy and institutional practice.

In terms of policy, it is a direct attack on the most fundamental premises by which public education has been governed since its current structure emerged in the late nineteenth century. It is possible that the practice of public schooling will respond to standards-based reform in the same way it has responded to virtually every other large-scale reform in the twentieth century. It may, in other words, try to bend the logic of the policy to the logic of how the existing institutions function, making the policy unrecognizable upon its arrival in the classroom. If this is the case, the consequences for public education will be severe; the institutions that emerge will look nothing like the present ones, and the idea of a strong basic education system for all children will be lost in all but a rhetorical sense. It is also possible that public schools will find a way to incorporate the logic of standards-based reform into their practice of schooling, in which case the institutions that emerge will probably be very different from what exists today but will perpetuate a strong basic education system for all children. If public schools can adapt to the demands of standards-based reform, they will have a better chance of survival.

HOW DID WE GET HERE? THE BANE OF "LOOSE-COUPLING"

Early in the development of public schooling, the United States, through local elites and national opinion leaders, opted for a form of organization based on locally centralized school bureaucracy, governed by elected boards, with relatively low-status (mostly female) teachers working in relative isolation from each other under the supervision of (mostly male) administrators, whose expertise was thought to lie mainly in their mastery of administrative rather than pedagogical skills (Tyack, 1974; Tyack & Hansot, 1982).

As the scale of the enterprise grew, the institutional structure grew more elaborate and rigid. School districts expanded to include more schools, schools grew in size and complexity, and the extension of compulsory attendance through the secondary grades resulted in larger, more highly differentiated schools to deal with the diverse populations of previously uneducated students (Powell, Farrar et al., 1985). All this was done, again by local elites and national opinion leaders, in the name of solid progressive principles: providing universal access to learning; providing local communities with direct control over their schools through elected boards; assuring that the overall administrative guidance of locally centralized systems was safely lodged in the hands of administrative experts; providing local economies with a supply of reasonably qualified labor; holding a large proportion of the youth population out of the labor force; and providing a credentialing system to allocate access to higher education.

The by-products of this institutional form have been, among other things: relatively weak professionalization among teachers, since teaching was thought not to require expertise on a level with other, "real" professions, and conditions of work were not conducive to the formation of strong professional associations among teachers; a relatively elaborate system of administrative overhead at the district and school level, thought to be necessary for adequate supervision of the relatively low-skill teacher force; and relatively large schools, thought to be a logical extension of principles of scientific management requiring economies of scale to produce efficiencies.

By the 1960s and early 1970s, analysts of this institutional structure had converged on a model that came to be called "loose-coupling" (Meyer & Rowan, 1992; Rowan, 1990; Weick, 1976). Derived from institutional sociology, this view, in brief, posits that the "technical core" of education—detailed decisions about what should be taught at any given time, how it should be taught, what students should be expected to learn at any given time, how they should be grouped within classrooms for purposes of instruction, what they should be required to do to demonstrate their knowledge, and, perhaps most importantly, how their learning should be evaluated—resides in individual classrooms, not in the organizations that surround them.

Furthermore, the model posited that knowledge at the technical core is weak and uncertain (Bidwell, 1965; Lortie, 1975). It cannot be clearly translated into reproducible behaviors, it requires a high degree of individual judgment, and it is not susceptible to reliable external evaluation. Therefore, the loose-coupling argument continues, the administrative superstructure of the organization—principals, board members, and administrators—exists to "buffer" the weak technical core of teaching from outside inspection, interference, or disruption.

Administration in education, then, has come to mean not the management of instruction but the management of the structures and processes around instruction. That which cannot be directly managed must, in this view, be protected from external scrutiny. Buffering consists of creating structures and procedures around the technical core of teaching that, at the same time, 1) protect teachers from outside intrusions in their highly uncertain and murky work, and 2) create the appearance of rational management of the technical core, so as to allay the uncertainties of the public about the actual quality or legitimacy of what is happening in the technical core. This buffering creates what institutional theorists call a "logic of confidence" between public schools and their constituents.

Local board members, system-level administrators, and school administrators perform the ritualistic tasks of organizing, budgeting, managing, and dealing with disruptions inside and outside the system, all in the name of creating and maintaining public confidence in the institutions of public education.

Teachers, working in isolated classrooms under highly uncertain conditions, manage the technical core. This division of labor has been amazingly constant over the past century. The institutional theory of loose-coupling explains a great deal about the strengths and pathologies of the existing structure of public education. It explains why, for example, most innovation in schools (and the most durable innovations) occur in the structures that surround teaching and learning, and only weakly and idiosyncratically in the actual processes of teaching and learning. Most innovation is about maintaining the logic of confidence between the public and the schools, not about changing the conditions of teaching and learning for actual teachers and students. The theory of loose-coupling explains why schools continue to promote structures and to engage in practices that research and experience suggest are manifestly not productive for the learning of certain students.

They include extraordinarily large high schools that create anonymous and disengaging environments for learning; rigid tracking systems that exclude large numbers of students from serious academic work; athletic programs that keep large numbers of students from participation in extracurricular activities; grouping practices in elementary school classrooms that provide less stimulation for struggling learners; special programs that remove students from regular instruction in the name of remediation; instructional aide programs that are sometimes little more than public employment programs for community members; and site-based governance structures that engage in decisionmaking about everything except the conditions of teaching and learning.

Loose-coupling also explains why manifestly successful instructional practices that grow out of research or exemplary practice never take root in more than a small proportion of classrooms and schools (Cuban, 1984, 1990; Elmore, 1996; Tyack & Cuban, 1995). Because the administrative structure of schools exists to buffer the instructional core from disruptions and improvements, and because teaching is isolated work, instructional improvements occur most frequently as a consequence of purely voluntary acts among consenting adults. The educational change literature is full of injunctions to respect the autonomy of teaching and the mystery of its fundamental practices—hence the inviolability of individual teachers' choices about what to teach and how. This normative environment is a direct result of an institutional structure that is deliberately and calculatedly incompetent at influencing its core functions. Volunteerism is the only way to improve practice in an organization in which administrators do not purport to manage the core. Volunteerism leads to 1) innovations that are highly correlated with the personal values and predispositions of individual teachers and hence tend to be adopted only by a small proportion of receptive teachers at any given time; and 2) innovations that are largely disconnected from any collective goal or purpose of the school or the school system. Schools are consequently almost always aboil with some kind of "change," but they are only rarely involved in any deliberate process of *improvement*, where progress is measured against a clearly specified instructional goal.

Loose-coupling explains the elusive and largely unsuccessful quest over the past century for school administrators who are "instructional leaders." Instructional leadership is the equivalent of the holy grail in educational administration. Most credentialing programs for superintendents and principals purport, at least in part, to be in the business of preparing the next generation of instructional leaders. Most professional development for educational leaders makes at least symbolic reference to the centrality of instructional leadership to the work. Insofar as there is any empirical evidence on the frequency of actual instructional leadership in the work of school administrators, it points to a consistent pattern: Direct involvement in instruction is among the least frequent activities performed by administrators of any kind at any level, and those who do engage in instructional leadership activities on a consistent basis are a relatively small proportion of the total administrative force (Cuban, 1988; Murphy, 1990). School leaders are hired and retained based largely on their capacity to buffer teachers from outside interference and their capacity to support the prevailing logic of confidence between a school system and its constituencies. Again, the ethic of volunteerism prevails.

Principals who develop the skills and knowledge required to actually do instructional leadership in a serious way do so because of their personal preferences and values, often at some personal cost to their own careers, not because they are expected to do so as a condition of their work. Overall, we get about the proportion of instructional leaders in the administrative ranks that corresponds to the proportion of people in the population who are inclined to do that sort of work. The institutional structure does not promote, or select for, knowledge and skill related to instructional leadership; at best, it tolerates some proportion of the population who indulge in it out of personal commitment and taste.

Loose-coupling explains the nervous, febrile, and unstable condition of politics and leadership around most school systems of any size. The governance structure is designed to support the logic of confidence in the institutional structure of public schools, not to provide stability, guidance, or direction for the long-term improvement of school performance. Local politics is usually driven by pluralist imperatives: Local factions mobilize by neighborhood, by racial or ethnic group, or by moral principle; they galvanize electoral support; and they reproduce, not surprisingly, the same political divisions on school boards as exist in the community at large. Since politics is not about the instructional core but about the logic of confidence between the schools and the community, all policy decisions are essentially about the symbolism of mobilizing and consolidating political constituencies.

A smart board member, in this world, is one who spends most of his or her time using issues to consolidate political support. A smart superintendent is one who can count the number of board members, divide by two, and, if necessary, add one. Superintendents come and go based on their capacity to maintain a working majority on a relatively unstable elected board, rather than on their capacity to focus the institution on its core functions and make steady improvements over time.

Finally, loose-coupling explains the attachment of educators and the public to what I will call "trait theories" of competence in instructional practice and leadership. Good teachers, good principals, and good superintendents are thought to be so, under trait theories, because they have the necessary personal qualities for the work, not because they have mastered some body of professional knowledge or because they work in an organizational environment in which they are expected to be competent at what they do as a condition of employment. Hence, many prescriptions for improving schools focus on recruiting and retaining "better" people, meaning people who are naturally predisposed to do whatever we want them to do.

An organization that purports to have little or no influence over its core functions is one that can be expected to subscribe to trait theories of competence. If the organization cannot influence what goes on in its core through how it is organized and managed, then it can only influence the core by selections based on the personal attributes of whom it recruits and retains. Hence, the success of the organization depends more on who gets in and who stays than on what happens to them while they are actually working in the organization.

The idea that people should acquire additional competencies over the course of their careers, that the organization should systematically invest in the improvement of these competencies, or, more controversially, that people should be expected to meet higher expectations for competence over the course of their careers—these expectations don't exist, or exist only weakly and idiosyncratically, in organizations that purport not to be able to manage their core functions.

ENTER STANDARDS-BASED REFORM

With this overview of loose-coupling as background, it is not hard to identify why standards-based reform creates certain fundamental problems for public schooling—problems that probably can't be solved by tinkering with the existing institutional structure—and why standards-based reform is often greeted with dismay and disbelief by experienced educators who are battle-worn veterans of past educational reform campaigns. The logic of standards-based reform is fundamentally at odds with the logic of loose-coupling, and this difference is not likely to be resolved in the usual way, by simply bending and assimilating the new policy into the existing institutional structure.

First and most surprisingly, standards-based reform violates the fundamental premise of loose coupling—buffering the technical core from interference by external forces. With standards-based reform, policy reaches, at least in theory, directly into the instructional core of schools, making what actually gets taught a matter of public policy and open political discourse. Content standards, even in their current somewhat clumsy and overspecified form, carry the explicit message that students should receive and absorb instruction in certain subject areas and on certain topics. Performance standards are even more threatening to the technical core because they assert that schools are accountable for what students learn, meaning that *someone* should manage the conditions of learning in schools so as to produce a given result.

Not surprisingly, teachers and administrators who have fully assimilated the norms and values of loose-coupling find these intrusions into the technical core to be both disconcerting and threatening. They often respond with well-known arguments that conjure up the mystery and inviolability of the unique relationship between each student and teacher and its need for distance from bureaucratic or policy controls. What's remarkable in the present political climate is how little weight these arguments now carry in policy discussions. The course of standards-based reform seems largely immune to these traditional arguments.

Second, standards-based reform hits at a critical weakness of the existing institutional structure, namely, its inability to account for why certain students master academic content and can demonstrate academic performance while others do not. When the core technology of schools is buried in the individual decisions of classroom teachers and buffered from external scrutiny, outcomes are the consequence of mysterious processes that no one understands at the collective, institutional level.

Therefore, school people and the public at large are free to assign causality to whatever their favorite theory suggests: weak family structures, poverty, discrimination, lack of aptitude, peer pressure, diet, television, etc. Standards-based reform explicitly localizes accountability for student learning with the school and the people who work in it, and it carries the increasingly explicit message that students learn largely as a consequence of what goes on inside schools. Hence, schools are being asked to account for what students are actually taught and what they learn as a consequence of that teaching. And, whatever one may think about this theory—that students generally learn what they are taught, if they are taught with skill and understanding—it has a strong political, economic, and social appeal.

Third, standards-based reform undermines a basic premise of local governance of education because it identifies schools, not school districts, as the primary unit of accountability in virtually all state accountability systems. Governors and state legislators are typically polite and indirect about this issue, carefully constructing ways of including local school boards and superintendents in any description of how school accountability works. But the stark reality is that little more than a decade ago most states did not have the capacity to collect, analyze, and report data on individual schools.

Now most do, thanks largely to the political imperatives elected offi-cials feel to account for state education expenditures and to the miracles of modern information technology. When states have the capacity to collect data on individual schools, the individual school becomes the unit of accountability, and the remedies and sanctions that apply to low performance apply to schools. Districts may find a productive role to play in this system of accountability if they try, but the institutional drift of the system will create increasingly direct relationships between states and schools. The pluralist politics of local boards and administrators will increasingly be played out under a large, dark umbrella of state perfor-mance accountability requirements. Over time, it will become increas-ingly difficult to defend dysfunctional local politics in the face of in-creasing public scrutiny of individual school performance. Putting schools at the center of the accountability problem, in other words, has the effect of calling into question the purpose of locally centralized governance and administration.

These conflicts between the logic of standards-based reform and the logic of the traditional institutional structure of public education chal-lenge both public schools and the people who work in them. The tradi-tional arguments that have been used to defend the existing loosely cou-pled institutional structure—the mystery and inviolability of teaching and learning, the sanctity of local preferences in the governance of schools, the generally positive support of local schools by their elites, etc.—will probably become weaker and less persuasive as evidence about the performance of schools accumulates over time. The usual pro-cess by which public schools deal with these external threats is to bend the new policy requirements to the logic of the existing institutional structure. In this case, the response would mean that policymakers and the public would, over time, accept educators' arguments that the core technology of education is highly uncertain and unspecifiable, and that most matters of instructional quality and performance in education are matters of personal preference and taste, for both educators and their clients. The idea that schools should meet certain specified standards of quality and performance would then recede into the mists of policy his-tory. The problem with this scenario, of course, is that the imperative for school accountability will not go away, even if standards-based re-form does, because policymakers are still left with the problem of how to account for the public expenditures they are making and what to do about the governance structure of public education.

TAKING IT TO THE NEXT LEVEL:
CHALLENGES FROM THE MARKET MODEL

The hallmark of standards-based reform is school-site accountability for common measures of student performance. The standard critique of this model is that it ignores the complexity and idiosyncrasy of teaching and learning and the necessary variability of local and school-site tastes and preferences.

Within the current educational reform debate, the governance structure that best fits the view that all matters of quality and performance in education are matters of personal taste, preference, and judgment is, in fact, a market model. The most efficient way to allocate resources around matters of personal taste is to give public money directly to consumers to purchase education based on their own preferences (vouchers), or, in a slightly more domesticated version, to give money directly to schools based on the number of students they attract (capitation grants), or, in an even more domesticated version, to allow educators and their clients to escape the gravitational pull of the existing institutional structure by forming publicly supported schools that operate under independent charters (charter schools). Under each of these systems, the existing superstructure of local administration and governance in education becomes increasingly weak, unstable, and irrelevant to many educators and their clients.[1] Active choosers in each of these systems—on both the supply side and the demand side—have very strong incentives to escape the gravitational pull of locally centralized governance and administration. Entrepreneurial schools have little incentive to operate under local governance systems if they can function successfully, by the standards of consumer demand, as free agents. Parents and students with strong tastes and preferences, and the wherewithal to act on them, have little incentive to affiliate with centrally administered schools when they can express their preferences more directly through individual schools. Increasingly, then, the domain of centrally administered and governed public schools, under vouchers, capitation grants, or charters, becomes the domain of the nonchoosers and the unchosen. I frequently tell my students that, if they want to see a possible future for the public schools, they should visit the public hospital system—a subsystem in a largely capitation-based health-care market that specializes in clients no one else wants to serve, a subsystem that is also chronically underfinanced, and one in which the costs of serving clients bear little or no relationship to the reimbursements the hospitals receive through the capitation grant system. Such systems exist to catch the overflow of the unchosen from market-based capitation systems that work pretty well for active choosers.

So if public educators insist on pressing the inviolability of the instructional core of schools and the durability of the institutional structure that supports that view, they are inviting policymakers simply to agree. They are also inviting them to then begin to shift the structure of public education by degrees into one based entirely on personal taste, preference, and judgment. The stakes for the existing institutional structure of public education, and for the public at large, if this shift occurs, are extremely high. The shift, in essence, will mean that public responsibility toward education will be discharged when the available money is fully allocated to individual families or schools; what happens after the money has been allocated is the responsibility of the individuals and schools, not of the state. Any residual collective responsibility for whether students are exposed to high-quality teaching and learning as a consequence of public expenditures, for whether the differentials in exposure to high-quality teaching and learning are a matter of public concern, for what students know as a consequence of the teaching they have received, and for whether certain students routinely have access to more powerful knowledge than others—all these concerns become matters of individual taste, preference, and judgment, rather than matters of public policy discourse and debate.

So there are some reasons why public educators should be measured in their criticisms of standards-based reforms. The only thing that could be worse than opening up the instructional core of public schooling to external scrutiny and debate might be not doing so, and watching the public purposes of public education drift away into matters of individual taste and preference.

Standards-based reform has a deceptively simple logic: schools and school systems should be held accountable for their contributions to student learning. The rationale for maintaining local governance and ad-

ministration of education in the United States lies principally in the possibility of using the institutional structure for large-scale improvement
of instructional practice and student performance based on standards.
In the language of economics, large-scale improvement will increasingly be the main comparative advantage of local school districts in the
competitive market for clients that will arise as schools and parents increasingly attempt to escape the gravitational pull of local school bureaucracy. Individual schools, operating largely as individual firms,
have difficulty generating surplus resources for use in improving the
skills and knowledge of their teachers and administrators. Individual
schools that are part of larger corporations also have incentives, in mar-
kets largely defined by taste and preference, to underinvest in skill and
knowledge, since they market their reputations for quality rather than
any specific service or result. Most public school systems still have access to resources—largely now spent on non-instructional administrative overhead—that they can capture and invest in improvements in the
skills and knowledge of principals and teachers. In the present structure, these issues of instructional practice and performance are typically
left to individuals to decide. Principals and teachers declare whether a
given change has worked based on whether they individually think they
have altered their practice in useful ways and whether they think
students know and can do things they haven't known or done before.
Not surprisingly, this situation produces lots of change and not much
improvement.

Now add the problem of scale, a key weakness of the existing institutional structure. Improvement implies not just that any given unit in a
system is improving (classroom, grade level, school, etc.) but that all
units are improving at some rate. In the language of statistics, the mean,
or average, of quality and performance in all units is increasing over
time, while the variation among units in quality and performance is decreasing.

Next add the problem of context. The problems of the educational
system are the problems of the smallest units in that system, and each
unit faces a different version of the overall problem of the system. If the
overall problem of the system is student performance on higher order
cognitive tasks (explaining, e.g., why a change in temperature of a few
degrees in an ecosystem could produce a large change in the plant or an-
imal life in that system; why 3/5 and 18/30 are equivalent fractions; or

why Richard Wright and James Baldwin disagreed on the nature of blackness), this problem will be present in very different forms in every classroom where it occurs. Different groups of students will have different prior knowledge of the basic concepts and different attitudes toward the importance of knowing them. Different groups of students will bring different cultural, linguistic, and cognitive understandings to bear on the problem. At the school level, differences at the classroom level aggregate into differences in the overall culture of expectations for learning, order, and engagement, into the structure of opportunities that determine whether students get access to the content and teaching at all, and into whether they get it in a form that engages them. So the problem of improvement at each location in a system has to be solved in a way that produces results that are roughly consistent across many highly varied contexts.

Next add the problem of feedback. Most of what happens in organizations engaged in large-scale improvement is collective problem-solving, structured by a common set of expectations about what constitutes a good result. A major source of learning in such situations is analysis and discussion of successes and failures, and feedback about this into the larger pool of knowledge and skill in the organization. Improvement seldom, if ever, occurs on a straight trajectory; it typically involves bumps and slides, as well as gratifying leaps. Learning about improvement occurs in the growth and development of common understandings about why things happen the way they do. Notice also that learning depends to a very large degree on the existence of some variation in the overall system. If everyone is doing exactly the same thing in exactly the same way (a highly unlikely event in a situation where contexts vary dramatically by school and classroom), then we have no internal evidence on which to base judgments about how it might be done better.

Finally, add the problem of benchmarks or standards. Someone usually knows how to do something better than you do, no matter how well you may think you know how to do it. Using variation in practice and performance for purposes of improvement means exploiting situations in which someone, inside or outside the organization, knows more than you do about what works. Often the knowledge gleaned from other contexts is woefully incomplete; it comes with blank spaces in critical places. So the task of learning from other people in other contexts is an active one of analyzing similarities and differences, adapting what makes sense, and leaving behind what doesn't. The essential problem here, though, is that the knowledge we need to solve problems often doesn't reside close at hand; it has to be found through active inquiry and analysis.

Improvement, then, is change with direction, sustained over time, that moves entire systems, raising the average level of quality and performance while at the same time decreasing the variation among units, and engaging people in analysis and understanding of why some actions seem to work and others don't.

DEROMANTICIZING LEADERSHIP

Leadership is the guidance and direction of instructional improvement. This is a deliberately deromanticized, focused, and instrumental definition. Leadership tends to be romanticized in American culture, especially in the culture of schooling, both because we subscribe heavily to trait theories of success—people succeed because of their personal characteristics more than because of effort, skill, and knowledge—and because we like our heroes to have qualities that we think we don't have. The problem with this romanticized theory of leadership is that the supply of character traits we associate with "good" leaders is, by definition, limited, or we wouldn't envy and admire them so much in other people. Also, character traits are much less amenable to influence by education, training, and practice than are knowledge and skill. Deromanticizing leadership would have a very positive effect on the quality of schools.

A definition of leadership in terms of instruction is also far more focused than most conceptions of leadership in education. Reading the literature on the principalship can be overwhelming, because it suggests that principals should embody all the traits and skills that remedy all the defects of the schools in which they work. They should be in close touch with their communities, inside and outside the school; they should, above all, be masters of human relations, attending to all the conflicts and disagreements that might arise among students, among teachers, and among anyone else who chooses to create conflict in the school; they should be both respectful of the authority of district administrators and crafty at deflecting administrative intrusions that disrupt the autonomy of teachers; they should keep an orderly school; and so on.

Somewhere on the list one usually finds a reference to instruction, couched in strategically vague language, so as to include both those who are genuinely knowledgeable about and interested in instruction and those who regard it as a distraction from the main work of administration. But why not focus leadership on instructional improvement, and define everything else as instrumental to it?

The skills and knowledge that matter in leadership, under this definition, are those that can be connected to, or lead directly to, the improvement of instruction and student performance. Standards-based reform forces this question. It makes leadership instrumental to improvement. The leadership envisioned here differs from that typically described in the literature on management—leaders, or higher level managers, who exercise "control" over certain functions in the organization. There are, to be sure, certain routine organizational functions that require control—bus schedules, payroll, accounting, etc. But the term "control" applied to school improvement is a dubious concept because one does not "control" improvement processes so much as one guides them and provides direction for them, since most of the knowledge required for improvement must inevitably reside in the people who deliver instruction, not in the people who manage them. Control implies that the controller knows exactly what the controllee (if you will) should do, whereas guidance and direction imply some degree of shared expertise and some degree of difference in the level and kind of expertise among individuals. It is this problem of the distribution of knowledge required for large-scale improvement that creates the imperative for the development of models of distributed leadership.

The basic idea of distributed leadership is not very complicated.[2] In any organized system, people typically specialize or develop particular competencies that are related to their predispositions, interests, aptitudes, prior knowledge, skills, and specialized roles. Furthermore, in any organized system, competency varies considerably among people in similar roles; some principals and teachers, for example, are simply better at doing some things than others, either as a function of their personal preferences, their experience, or their knowledge. Organizing these diverse competencies into a coherent whole requires understanding how individuals vary, how the particular knowledge and skill of one person can be made to complement that of another, and how the competencies of some can be shared with others. In addition, organizing diverse competencies requires understanding when the knowledge and skill possessed by the people within the organization is not equal to the problem they are trying to solve, searching outside the organization for new knowledge and skill, and bringing it into the organization.

In a knowledge-intensive enterprise like teaching and learning, there is no way to perform these complex tasks without widely distributing the responsibility for leadership (again, guidance and direction) among roles in the organization, and without working hard at creating a common culture, or set of values, symbols, and rituals. Distributed leadership, then, means multiple sources of guidance and direction, following the contours of expertise in an organization, made coherent through a common culture. It is the "glue" of a common task or goal—improvement of instruction—and a common frame of values for how to approach that task—culture—that keeps distributed leadership from becoming another version of loose coupling.

To be sure, performance-based accountability in schools and good management practice generally require that certain people be held responsible for the overall guidance and direction of the organization, and ultimately for its performance. Distributed leadership does not mean that no one is responsible for the overall performance of the organization. It means, rather, that the job of administrative leaders is primarily about enhancing the skills and knowledge of people in the organization, creating a common culture of expectations around the use of those skills and knowledge, holding the various pieces of the organization together in a productive relationship with each other, and holding individuals accountable for their contributions to the collective result.

Since this view of leadership draws on several strands of research on school improvement, it is worth pausing here to take a brief inventory of how the idea emerges from the existing base of knowledge. Some time ago, Susan Rosenholtz (1986) observed, based on an empirical study of variations in school effectiveness, that there were two distinctively different types of school cultures or climates. One kind of normative climate, characterized by an emphasis on collaboration and continuous improvement, develops in schools where teacher effort, through a variety of principal actions, is focused on skill acquisition to achieve specific goals. In such schools, experimentation and occasional failure are expected and acceptable in the process of teacher learning. Further, seeking or giving collegial advice is not a gauge of relative competence, but rather a professional action viewed as desirable, necessary, and legitimate in the acquisition of new skills.

In schools characterized by norms of autonomy, on the other hand, there are ambiguous goals and no attempt to develop a shared teaching technology. There is no agreement among teachers and principals about the outcomes they seek and the means for reaching them. In such settings, therefore, definitions of teaching success and the manner in which it is attained are highly individualistic. Without these commonly held definitions, Rosenholtz (1986) says, collegial and principal assistance serves no useful purpose. These two cultures, she continues, result in "profoundly different opportunities for teachers' skill acquisition" (p. 101).

Rosenholtz argues that collegial support and professional development in schools are unlikely to have any effect on improvement of practice and performance if they are not connected to a coherent set of goals that give direction and meaning to learning and collegiality. Effective schools, she argues further, have "tighter congruence between values, norms, and behaviors of principals and teachers, and the activities that occur at the managerial level are aligned closely with, and facilitative of, the activities that occur at the technical level. There is an organizational basis for directing behavior, for motivating behavior, for justifying behavior, and for evaluating behavior" (1985, p. 360). Significantly, she found that principals' collegiality with teachers had no direct effect on school performance, but it did have an indirect effect when mediated by school-level goal setting, as well as teacher recruitment, socialization, and evaluation. In other words, principal collegiality with teachers affects school performance only when it is connected to activities that focus the school's purposes and that translate those purposes into tangible activities related to teaching (Rosenholtz, 1986).

In addition, Rosenholtz draws a direct relationship between teachers' uncertainty about the technical core of their work and the normative environment in which they work. Schools with a strong normative environment focused on instructional goals promote a view of teaching as a body of skill and knowledge that can be learned and developed over time, rather than as an idiosyncratic and mysterious process that varies with each teacher.

The issues of uncertainty also extend to principals. Principals who attributed a high level of uncertainty to teaching practice tended to be "turf minded" and were unwilling to relinquish control in order that teacher colleagues may render mutual assistance. "By contrast," Rosenholtz observes, "more certain principals seem able to galvanize their faculties for specific, goal-directed endeavors, increasing teachers' clarity about what to pursue" (1989, p. 69).

Similarly, in a broad-scale study of a national sample of high schools, Newmann and colleagues (Newmann, Rutter et al., 1989) found that teachers' knowledge of each other's courses and a focus on improved practice were, in addition to orderly student behavior, the cultural variables in schools that had the strongest relationship to teachers' sense of efficacy. They also found that the responsiveness of administrators to problems of practice—with help, support, and recognition—was most strongly related to teachers' perceptions of community within a school. Interestingly, they found no independent effect of teachers' perceptions of principals' leadership, teachers' participation in professional development, or teachers' participation in organizational decisions on either teachers' sense of efficacy or community. This latter finding is interesting not so much because of what it says about principal leadership and professional development per se, because the schools in the sample represented the full array of practice in this regard. It is interesting because it suggests that principal leadership, professional development, and participation in decisionmaking by teachers have no effect on teachers' sense of efficacy and community *unless* they are deliberately connected to tangible and immediate problems of practice.

Rowan found in his review of research on school improvement that participation of teachers in extended roles—that is, roles that require them to acquire knowledge and solve problems in groups and networks as opposed to individually—"fosters higher levels of commitment and satisfaction" (Rowan, 1990, p. 373). He also observed, though, that studies of teacher collegiality under naturally occurring conditions suggest that teachers focus the bulk of their interactions on relatively narrow issues of materials, discipline, and the problems of individual students, rather than on the acquisition of new knowledge and skill: "Teachers reasoned that they talked less about these issues because they already knew much about these subjects and because teacher behavior is personal, private, idiosyncratic, and intuitive. Few thought that time and opportunity prevent exchanges of information about teaching behaviors" (Rowan, 1990, p. 375). In other words, participation in collaborative work increases commitment and satisfaction among teachers, but it is unlikely to result in changes in teachers' practice, skill, or knowledge in the absence of a clear organizational focus on those issues.

Recent international research from the Third International Mathematics and Science Study (TIMSS) corroborates the idea that a focus on concrete instructional practice results in increased student learning. Countries in TIMSS that scored well in mathematics and science tended to have less complex curricula, greater coherence of curriculum across age levels, and greater emphasis on narrowing the range of quality in the curriculum actually delivered in the classroom. Hence, when school organization and policy reinforce a focus on curriculum and embody clear expectations about the range of acceptable quality in the delivered curriculum, a broader range of students learn at higher levels (Schmidt, McKnight, & Raizen, 1997; Stigler & Heibert, 1999).

These studies dovetail well with the line of work I have been pursuing with my colleagues on school restructuring and accountability. In our study of schools involved in significant, self-initiated restructuring activities, we found that these activities, all of which involved high levels of collegial interaction among teachers, did not result in classroom practice that reflected the rhetoric of reform, except in a school where the principal and teachers explicitly created a normative environment around a specific approach to instruction (Elmore, Peterson et al., 1996). Similarly, we found in our work on how schools construct their ideas about accountability that schools that lacked a strong internal normative environment—characterized by clear and binding expectations among teachers, among students and teachers, and among principals and teachers—were inclined to defer all judgments about what students could and should learn, and all decisions about to whom the school is collectively accountable for what, to individual teachers operating in isolation from each other. For example, teachers in most schools in our study were unable to provide specific evidence about ways in which their daily decisions about instruction and their expectations for student learning were influenced by administrators in their schools or by their colleagues.

Hence, when asked to whom they were accountable, they would reply either to no one or to themselves. In a small proportion of schools in our study, teachers were able to cite specific examples of how their practice and their expectations for student learning were influenced by their colleagues, by administrators, or by external networks of colleagues outside their schools. These latter schools tended to have a clearer idea of their purposes, stated in terms of expectations for student learning, and to manifest these purposes in detailed decisions about classroom instruction.

Organizational coherence on basic aims and values, then, is a precondition for the exercise of any effective leadership around instructional improvement. Collaboration and collegiality among teachers, and among teachers and principals, is a necessary but not sufficient condition for improvement. Distributed leadership poses the challenge of how to distribute responsibility and authority for guidance and direction of instruction, and learning about instruction, so as to increase the likelihood that the decisions of individual teachers and principals about what to do, and what to learn how to do, aggregate into collective benefits for student learning. I will discuss the practical implications of this challenge in a moment.

Before I advance, I would like to take a brief detour into the problem of learning and policy. David Cohen and Carol Barnes (1993) have suggested that we think about the pedagogical functions of policy in addition to the institutional and political functions. They argue that, while policy—say, in the form of content and performance standards—is usually intended to convey information and intentions to teachers and administrators, the policies themselves seldom pay much attention to what teachers and administrators would actually have to learn and what their activities should be to behave consistently with the policy. They conclude a review of reform policies with the observation that:

> The pedagogy of educational policy has been didactic and inconsistent. Policymakers have told teachers to do many different, hugely important things in a short time. And in each case policymakers have acted as though their assignment was to dispense answers, not to provoke thought, ask questions, or generate discussion. The pedagogy of policy has been teacher-centered. As policymakers taught, they created few opportunities to listen as teachers and other educators tried to make sense of new demands. Nor have policymakers cast policy as something that might be revised in light of what they learned from teachers' experience. (Cohen & Barnes, 1993, p. 226)

In other words, the same argument about distributed leadership that applies within schools and school systems applies between policy-makers and the organizations they attempt to influence. Policy itself, in its design and implementation, is unlikely to augment or stimulate improvement in practice and performance if it doesn't explicitly acknowledge the problems of expertise and learning embedded in its goals. Furthermore, policy is unlikely to result in improvement if it doesn't focus and deliver a coherent message about purposes and the practices that exemplify them, in the same sense that organizational coherence on purpose and practice is an important precondition for the success of school improvement.

There is, of course, strong evidence that asking policymakers to bring coherence and stability to education policy at the state and local level is akin to trying to change the laws of gravity. Instability and incoherence, in the form of pluralist politics, are the rule; coherence and stability, the exception. Pluralism—organized factions mobilizing and using political institutions as a means for legitimizing their particular interests in public policy—is hardwired into the culture and institutional structure of American politics. James Madison, in Federalist #10, puts the matter succinctly: institutions of government exist to play the interests of competing factions against each other, so as to prevent the tyranny of one faction over all others.

In his exhaustive survey of midsize urban school districts in the United States, Frederick Hess (1999) paints a deeply pessimistic picture for those, like myself, who see the future of urban school systems as lying in large-scale improvement of the instructional core. Hess found that local school boards and superintendents consistently engage in a kind of hyperactive policy dance—a phenomenon he calls "policy churn"—in which relatively unstable political factions advance new "reforms" as ways of satisfying their electoral constituencies, pausing only long enough to take credit for having acted and quickly moving on to new reforms, with no attention to the institutionalization or implementation of previous reforms. The political rewards in the pluralist structure, Hess argues, are in the symbolism of initiation and enactment of reform, not in its implementation. Among the pathologies the incentive structure creates is high turnover of leadership, both political and administrative. The average tenure of superintendents in Hess's sample was about two and one-half years. Factions are fickle, political opportunists abound. Board majorities hold onto school superintendents just long enough for them to advance their reform proposals (skillfully tailored to attaining their next job; after all, they are rational actors too) and, at the first sign of opposition, move on to the next superintendent.

Susan Fuhrman, while somewhat more sanguine about the prospects of coherent and stable reforms, identifies clear tendencies working against coherence in the recent drift of American politics toward term limitations for legislative and gubernatorial offices. This, coupled with a tendency for elected officials not to specialize in substantive policy areas long enough to develop understanding and expertise, leads to strong incentives for superficiality and instability (Fuhrman, 1993, 1994; Fuhrman & Elmore, 1994).

Notice the compatibility of this pattern of politics with the institutional theory of loose-coupling outlined in the first section of this paper. While the pace and intensity of policy churn may have picked up in recent years, owing, in large part, to the growth of new electoral factions in urban areas and the introduction of electoral reforms designed to increase turnover in political office, the phenomenon of policy churn has a deep history in American educational policy. The metaphor that Larry Cuban uses to describe the relationship between reform policy and teaching practice from the late nineteenth century through the final decades of the twentieth is the ocean in a severe storm: "The surface is agitated and turbulent, while the ocean floor is calm and serene (if a bit murky). Policy churns dramatically, creating the appearance of major changes, calculated to reinforce the symbolic rewards of action for policymakers and to cement the logic of confidence in the institutions, while deep below the surface, life goes on largely uninterrupted" (1984).

So whatever problems of leadership might lie in the administration of schools and school systems, these problems are reflected and amplified in policy leadership. Administrative and policy leaders are joined in a codependent, largely dysfunctional relationship, and as in most such relationships, the bond is strengthened by its pathology. We transform dysfunctional relationships into functional ones, not by continuing to do what we already know how to do more intensively and with greater enthusiasm, but by learning how to do new things and, perhaps more importantly, learning how to attach positive value to the learning and the doing of new things. Therein lies the challenge of harnessing leadership to the problem of large-scale improvement.

Creating a new model of distributed leadership consists of two main tasks: 1) describing the ground rules that leaders of various kinds would have to follow in order to engage in large-scale improvement; and 2) describing how leaders of various kinds in various roles and positions would share responsibility in a system of large-scale improvement. It should go without saying that this model is necessarily provisional and tentative, since it is a considerable departure from the status quo and its basic premise is that improvement involves both learning the ground rules and sharing responsibility for implementing them over time. It is impossible to say at the outset exactly what will be required at later stages.

Here, then, are five principles that lay the foundation for a model of distributed leadership focused on large-scale improvement:

1. The purpose of leadership is the improvement of instructional practice and performance, regardless of role.

Institutional theories of leadership, in the loose-coupling mode, stress the role of leaders as buffers of outside interference and as brokers between the institutions of public schooling and their clients. Political theories of group leadership stress the role of leaders as coalition-builders and brokers among diverse interests. Managerial theories of leadership stress the role of leaders as custodians of the institutions they lead—paterfamilias—and sources of managerial control. Cultural theories of leadership stress the role of leaders as manipulators of symbols around which individuals with diverse needs can rally. None of these theories captures the imperative for large-scale improvement, since none of them posits a direct relationship between the work that leaders should be doing and the core functions of the organization. One can be adept at any of these types of leadership and never touch the instructional core of schooling. If we put improvement of practice and performance at the center of our theory of leadership, then these other theories of leadership role must shift to theories about the possible skills and knowledge that leaders would have to possess to operate as agents of large-scale instructional improvement. If the purpose of leadership is the improvement of teaching practice and performance, then the skills and knowledge that matter are those that bear on the creation of settings for learning focused on clear expectations for instruction. All other skills are instrumental.

2. Instructional improvement requires continuous learning.

Learning is both an individual and a social activity. Therefore, collective learning demands an environment that guides and directs the acquisition of new knowledge about instruction. The existing institutional structure of public education does one thing very well: It creates a normative environment that values idiosyncratic, isolated, and individualistic learning at the expense of collective learning. This phenomenon holds at all levels: Individual teachers invent their own practice in isolated classrooms, small knots of like-minded practitioners operate in isolation from their colleagues within a given school, or schools operate as exclusive enclaves of practice in isolation from other schools. In none of these instances is there any expectation that individuals or groups are obliged to pursue knowledge as both an individual and a collective good. Unfortunately, the existing system doesn't value continuous learning as a collective good and does not make this learning the individual and social responsibility of every member of the system. Leadership must create conditions that value learning as both an individual and collective good. Leaders must create environments in which individuals expect to have their personal ideas and practices subjected to the scrutiny of their colleagues, and in which groups expect to have their shared conceptions of practice subjected to the scrutiny of individuals. Privacy of practice produces isolation; isolation is the enemy of improvement.

3. Learning requires modeling.

Leaders must lead by modeling the values and behavior that represent collective goods. Role-based theories of leadership wrongly envision leaders who are empowered to ask or require others to do things they may not be willing or able to do. But if learning, individual and collective, is the central responsibility of leaders, then they must be able to model the learning they expect of others. Leaders should be doing, and should be seen to be doing, that which they expect or require others to do. Likewise, leaders should expect to have their own practice subjected to the same scrutiny as they exercise toward others.

4. The roles and activities of leadership flow from the expertise required for learning and improvement, not from the formal dictates of the institution.

As we shall see shortly, large-scale improvement requires a relatively complex kind of cooperation among people in diverse roles performing diverse functions. This kind of cooperation requires understanding that learning grows out of differences in expertise rather than differences in formal authority. If collective learning is the goal, my authority to command you to do something doesn't mean much if it is not complemented by some level of knowledge and skill that, when joined with yours, makes us both more effective. Similarly, if we have the same roles, I have little incentive to cooperate with you unless we can jointly produce something that we could not produce individually. In both instances, the value of direction, guidance, and cooperation stems from acknowledging and making use of differences in expertise.

5. The exercise of authority requires reciprocity of accountability and capacity.

If the formal authority of my role requires that I hold you accountable for some action or outcome, then I have an equal and complementary responsibility to assure that you have the capacity to do what I am asking you to do (Elmore, 1997). All accountability relationships are necessarily reciprocal—unfortunately, often only implicitly. Policy usually states the side of accountability in which a person with formal authority requires another to do something he or she might not otherwise do except in the presence of such a requirement. Many educational professionals perceive standards in this way—as a set of requirements carrying formal legal authority—without attending to the circumstances that make doing the work possible. Furthermore, policymakers typically fail to acknowledge their own learning curve and to model it for others. This creates expectations that everyone should know what they don't know and without any preparation. The chief policy leaders—elected officials—are finally accountable to the public for providing the resources and authority necessary for improvement. The chief administrative leaders—superintendents and principals—are accountable for using these resources and authority to guide improvement. Both types of leaders are responsible for explicitly modeling in their own behavior the learning they expect of others. And leaders of practice—teachers and professional developers—are accountable for developing the new knowledge and skill required for the demands of broad-scale improvement. Distributed leadership makes the reciprocal nature of these accountability relationships explicit. My authority to require you to do something you might not otherwise do depends on my capacity to create the opportunity for you to learn how to do it, and to educate me on the process of learning how to do it, so that I become better at enabling you to do it the next time.

The practical side of a theory of distributed leadership describes how leadership roles would be defined if these principles were to work. Table 1 (p. 71) describes one possible way of defining leadership roles. The table makes little sense, however, without first describing some underlying assumptions about the nature of the work involved in large-scale improvement and how it translates into leadership roles. The first assumption has to do with distribution of expertise around the problem of improvement. There is a principle of comparative advantage, embedded in the table, that essentially says that people should engage in activities that are consistent with the comparative expertise of their roles and avoid activities that are beyond their expertise.

Policymakers (state and local board members and state legislators, for example) should, as elected officials, have a comparative advantage in adjudicating conflicts among competing interests, winnowing these interests down into goals and standards on what should be taught, setting the legal mandate within which rewards and sanctions are administered, and translating the feedback from various quarters into new guidance. Policymakers do *not* have a comparative advantage on issues relating to the specific content of standards or of practices that lead to student performance of a certain kind, no matter how well they do their jobs, no matter what their expertise has been in the past, no matter how much effort they invest in learning about standards and practice. They don't have a comparative advantage in these domains because *the nature of their work does not permit them to develop it;* in fact, the better they are at their work, the more they should recognize the limits of their expertise. The content of standards and instructional practice lies in the domain of professional knowledge, broadly defined as the intersection between instructional practice in classrooms and schools and systematic inquiry and evaluation of practice. To the extent that professional knowledge exists, it cuts across the specific community contexts in which it has to be used. Hence, the "professional community" might say that a particular kind of standard represents the best current conception of what should be taught, and the standard could be effectively enacted using a variety of instructional practices, but specific decisions about what a standard looks like when it is enacted in a given classroom, school, or school system would require expertise in both the practice and the context. This leads to a dependency across the professional community and leaders at the system, school, and classroom levels. So the functions described in Table 1 reflect the comparative advantages of different leadership roles in different positions, as well as their dependencies on each other.

I have used the language of "comparative advantage" here because I want to emphasize the degree to which large-scale improvement requires deference to and respect for expertise, coupled with reciprocity of accountability. I have self-consciously avoided using terms like *division of labor* or *division of responsibility* because I think it connotes a kind of balkanization that is more typical of loose-coupling than of distributed leadership. Spillane, in his important piece on distributed leadership, borrows from the language of distributed cognition and speaks of expertise and responsibilities as being "stretched over" people in different roles rather than neatly divided among them (Spillane, Halverson et al., 2002). The language fails us here, because the terminology that comes most readily to the surface in discussions of policy and management is the language of control rather than the language of reciprocity and mutual dependency.

Another aspect of Table 1 that might strike readers as unfamiliar is the addition of "professional" and "practice" roles to the conventional inventory of policy-, system-, and school-level leaders. This is an explicit acknowledgement of the importance of instructional expertise, at both the general professional level and at the level of schools and classrooms. Since this is the task of large-scale improvement, and improvement is about the development and distribution of knowledge, leadership functions engaged in improvement have to include those that explicitly create and engage people in learning new forms of practice. These roles must develop in systems that are engaged in large-scale improvement. Where they don't exist, they will have to be created or redefined from existing roles.

TABLE 1

LEADERSHIP ROLES	LEADERSHIP FUNCTIONS
POLICY Elected, Appointed Officials: Legislators, Chief State School Officers, State Board Members, Local School Board Members	• Set performance targets • Approve standards • Monitor performance • Approve, monitor incentive structures • Monitor design problems, redesign • Adjudicate conflicts over design, performance issues • Administer rewards and sanctions • Buffer noninstructional issues
PROFESSIONAL Distinguished Practitioners, Professional Developers, Researchers	• Develop, vet standards • Develop, pilot new instructional practices • Design preservice, inservice learning • Conduct model professional development • Create benchmarks for content, practice • Develop, pilot new structures
SYSTEM Superintendents, Support Personnel	• Design system improvement strategies • Design, implement incentive structures for schools, principals, teachers • Recruit, evaluate principals • Provide professional development consistent with improvement strategy • Allocate system resources toward instruction • Buffer noninstructional issues from principals, teachers
SCHOOL Principals, Support Personnel	• Design school improvement strategies • Implement incentive structures for teachers, support personnel • Recruit, evaluate teachers • Broker professional development consistent with improvement strategy • Allocate school resources toward instruction • Buffer noninstructional issues from teachers
PRACTICE Teachers, Professional Developers	• Design, conduct, participate in professional development • Participate in recruitment, hiring of new teachers • Evaluate professional development • Consult, evaluate professional practice of colleagues • Evaluate student work • Participate in development of new professional development practices

Notice also that there is a role for leaders in moving non-instructional issues out of the way to prevent them from creating confusion and distractions in school systems, schools, and classrooms. The principle of buffering here is the inverse of the principle of buffering under loose-coupling. In a loosely coupled system, administrators buffer instructional practice from outside interference. In a distributed leadership system, the job of leaders is to buffer teachers from extraneous and distracting non-instructional issues so as to create an active arena for engaging and using quality interventions on instructional issues.

Overall, then, Table 1 presents a model of how one might go about reconstructing roles and functions around the idea of distributed leadership in the service of large-scale instructional improvement. The exact design of roles and functions is less important than the underlying principles of distributed expertise, mutual dependence, reciprocity of accountability and capacity, and the centrality of instructional practice to the definition of leadership roles. Policy leadership, in this model, focuses on translating diverse political interests into coherent standards of content and performance, adjudicating conflicts around the nature of goals, exercising discipline in the design and redesign of accountability systems, and keeping the system focused on its core functions and their consequences for students. Professional leadership—stemming from the research community, professional associations, and knowledgeable experts in content, pedagogy, and professional development—focuses on creating external benchmarks for content and pedagogy that represent the best available knowledge at any given time. Administrative leadership at the system and school levels designs strategies of improvement that align these with practice using resource allocation, hiring, evaluation, retention, and accountability measures. The job of leaders of instructional practice is to extend professional leadership into schools and school systems, drawing upon the differential expertise of educators at each level. Those who have a higher degree of knowledge, skill, and comp ence should be expected to spend some portion of their work en-
the improvement of practice across schools and classrooms.
s of such a framework depends as much on the transactions
—the creation of mutual dependency and reciprocity—as it
ing the core responsibilities of the roles themselves.
th emphasizing again that this model of distributed lead-
from the dominant institutional structure of most pub-

lic schools and school systems. It confronts the impulses for privacy and for idiosyncratic instructional practice. It challenges the conventional roles of policy and administrative leaders in buffering that practice from outside interference. It posits instead a model in which instructional practice is a collective good—a common concern of the whole the institution—as well as a private and individual concern. It posits a theory of leadership that, while respecting, acknowledging, and capitalizing on differences in expertise, predicts failure in the social isolation of practice and predicts success in the creation of interdependencies that stretch over these differences.

Many well-intentioned reformers argue that large-scale improvement of schools can be accomplished by recruiting, rewarding, and retaining good people and releasing them from the bonds of bureaucracy to do what they know how to do. Schools get better, in this view, by attracting and empowering good people. It's not hard to see why this view is so widely held among educators. It accords well with the existing institutional structure. The properties of a system inhere in the personal qualities of the people in it, not in the system itself. To the minds of these reformers the job of the system is to stay out of the business of the gifted practitioners who work in it and to keep the outside world at bay. The problem with this view, of course, is that it produces "good" practice and performance only from those people who already embody the personal attributes and characteristics that make good practice and performance possible. We know that this proportion seldom grows larger than about one-quarter or one-third of the total population of classrooms, schools, or systems.

What's missing in this view is any recognition that improvement is more a function of *learning to do the right things* in the setting where you work than it is of what you know when you start to do the work. Improvement at scale is largely a *property of organizations,* not of the preexisting traits of the individuals who work in them. Organizations that improve do so because they create and nurture agreement on what is worth achieving, and they set in motion the internal processes by which people progressively learn how to do what they need to do in order to achieve what is worthwhile.

Importantly, such organizations select, reward, and retain people based on their willingness to engage the purposes of the organization and to acquire the learning that is required to achieve those purposes.

Improvement occurs through organized social learning, not through the idiosyncratic experimentation and discovery of variously talented individuals. Experimentation and discovery can be harnessed to social learning by connecting people with new ideas to each other in an environment in which the ideas are subjected to scrutiny, measured against the collective purposes of the organization, and tested by the history of what has already been learned and is known.

The idea of learning to do the right thing—collectively, progressively, cumulatively over time—is at the core of the theory of standards-based reform. Such reforms must set content and performance targets, open school performance up to public scrutiny and discourse, and, over time, calibrate rewards and sanctions based on the degree to which schools and school systems engage in sustained improvement. There are, to be sure, major problems with the design of most state standards and accountability systems, problems of the sort one would expect with new policies that are discontinuous with past policies and that deal with inherently complex processes and institutions. As noted in the previous section, the success of these policies will depend, in large part, on the willingness of policymakers to model the kind of learning they are expecting from educators—to scrutinize their own actions and consequences and to modify policies based on their impact on practice and performance.

As important as the problems of policy design and implementation are, the problems of institutional design and educational practice embedded in standards-based reform are much, much larger. One can "make" policy by stitching together coalitions of political interests. Redesigning institutions and improving educational practice are massively more complex. As noted earlier, they involve changes of the most fundamental kind in the norms and values that shape work in schools, in the way the resources of the system get used, in the skills and knowledge that people bring to their work, and in how people relate to each other around the work of the organization. If the theory of distributed leadership outlined in the previous section is correct, these problems of institutional design and practice cannot be solved through policymaking alone. Policy can set the initial expectations and conditions within which large-scale improvement will occur, it can set targets for practice and performance, it can open and stimulate public discussion about content and performance in schools, and it can alter the incentives under which schools and school systems work. The closer policy gets to the in-structional core—how teachers and students interact around content—the more policymakers lose their comparative advantage of knowledge and skill, the more they become dependent on the knowledge and skill of practitioners to mold and shape the instructional core, and the more—again, in the words of distributed cognition—knowledge of policy and practice have to be "stretched over" each other in order to be com-plementary.

Issues of institutional design and practice in large-scale improvement are the domains where our collective public knowledge is weakest. There is strong suggestive evidence, both in early research on effective schools and districts and in recent research on the effects of standards-based reform, that some schools and districts are systematically better at the tasks of large-scale improvement of instruction and performance than others. Murphy and Hallinger, in a study of instructionally effec-tive school districts in California—school districts that showed high per-formance on student achievement measures relative to others, control-ling for student composition—found evidence of common strategic elements in the way these districts managed themselves.

Their superintendents were knowledgeable about, and the key initia-tors of, changes in curriculum and teaching strategies. Superintendents and system-level staff were active in monitoring curriculum and instruc-tion in classrooms and schools, as well as active in the supervision, eval-uation, and mentoring of principals. Superintendents in high-perform-ing districts were also more likely to dismiss principals on the basis of their performance. These districts showed a much greater clarity of pur-pose, a much greater willingness to exercise tighter controls over deci-sions about what would be taught and what would be monitored as evi-dence of performance, and a greater looseness and delegation to the school level of specific decisions about how to carry out an instructional program.

Despite strong leadership, these districts were less bureaucratic than their counterparts. They tended to rely more on a common culture of values to shape collective action than on bureaucratic rules and con-trols. The shared values typically focused on improvement of student learning as the central goal, evidence of steady, sustained improvement, a positive approach to problem-solving in the face of unforeseen difficul-ties, a view of structures, processes, and data as instruments for improvement rather than as ends in themselves, and a heavy internal focus by administrators on the demands of instruction, rather than a focus on events in the external environment (Murphy, Hallinger et al., 1987; Murphy & Hallinger, 1988).

Spillane's more recent work on the district role in the implementation of reform in mathematics instruction points to the pivotal role that district personnel, including administrative leaders, play in shaping discourse about the purpose of changes in instruction, in setting expectations about what will happen in classrooms, and in modeling the active construction of new knowledge, both about the teaching of mathematics and about the learning of new conceptions of content and pedagogy. Spillane's theory focuses on the parallel processes of cognitive change that must occur across levels of the district in order for new ideas to reach into the instructional core, again pointing to the importance of a common normative frame in shaping instructional change on a large scale (Spillane, 2004; see also Spillane, 2002, p. 17).

Knapp and his colleagues (1995), in their study of high-quality instruction in high-poverty classrooms, found that the modal pattern of district involvement in instructional improvement was either negatively associated with high-quality practice (pushing teachers toward less ambitious, lower-level, more structured practice), or, more commonly, chaotic and incoherent. "Most teachers," they conclude, "received mixed signals [from the district] about what to teach." Furthermore, they found that the instruments that most districts use to influence instruction—guidelines, textbook adoptions, testing and assessment, scope-and-sequence requirements by grade level, etc.—were almost entirely disconnected from the learning that teachers had to do in order to master more ambitious instructional practices. Districts were, in their words, long on pressure and short on support (knowing what support to offer takes instructional sophistication), with the predictable effect that much of the learning that did occur around ambitious instructional practice was idiosyncratic by school and classroom (Knapp, Shields et al., 1995). This research tracks with earlier work on the determinants of content and pedagogy in a large sample of schools, which concluded that, for the most part, district influences on instructional practice were diffuse and ineffectual, usually not reaching deeply into teachers' decisions about what to teach or how (Floden, Porter et al., 1988).

With an explicit focus on standards-based reform, Grissmer and Flanagan (1998) have attempted to explain the reason for larger than expected gains in achievement on the National Assessment of Educational Progress (NAEP) and on state-administered performance measures in Texas and North Carolina, two states with very diverse student populations and with relatively well-developed standards-based reform policies in place. They demonstrate that the achievement gains are, in fact, larger than one would predict based on performance of similar students in other states, and that the achievement gains seem to be occurring disproportionately among traditionally low-performing students. They offer as explanations for these gains a number of factors, including clearly stated content and performance standards, an incentive structure that focuses on the performance of all students, not just on average school performance, consistency and continuity of focus among political leaders, clear accountability processes, and a willingness to give flexibility to administrators and teachers in crafting responses to the accountability system. They also observe that "both states have built a substantial infrastructure for supporting a process of continual improvement, . . . jointly funded through the public and private sectors" that uses research and technical assistance around research on effective practice and professional development.

A parallel study, conducted by the Dana Center in Texas, examined high-performing Texas school districts with diverse student populations.[3] The study found that superintendents in these districts used their positions to create a sense of urgency in their communities that translated into expectations that students could meet demanding new standards. They used data on student performance to focus attention on problems and successes, they built district accountability systems that complemented the state's system, and they forged strong relationships with their boards around improvement goals. They created a normative climate in which teachers and principals were collectively responsible for student learning and in which the improvement of instruction and performance was the central task and other distractions were reduced. Accountability systems in these districts rewarded higher performance with greater discretion and challenged school personnel to develop better solutions to the problems faced by the districts. Superintendents realigned district offices in these systems to focus on direct relationships with schools around instructional issues, and they focused more energy and resources on professional development, much of it delivered in classrooms and schools rather than in offsite locations.[4]

My own work on instructional improvement in New York City's Community School District #2 reinforces many of the themes in these studies. District #2 is, by any standard, one of the highest-performing urban school systems in the country, with, overall, fewer than 12 percent of its students—60 percent of whom are low income—scoring in the lowest quartile of nationally standardized reading tests. A comparable figure for most urban districts is in the 40-50 percent range. The District #2 story is a complex one, as are, I suspect, the stories of all improving school districts.

But the main themes of the story are *continuity* of focus on core instruction, first in literacy and then in mathematics; *heavy investments in highly targeted professional development* for teachers and principals in the fundamentals of strong classroom instruction; *strong and explicit accountability by principals and teachers* for the quality of practice and the level of student performance, backed by direct oversight of classroom practice by principals and district personnel; and a *normative climate in which adults take responsibility for their own, their colleagues', and their students' learning.* At all levels of the system, isolation is seen as the enemy of improvement, so most management and professional development activities are specifically designed to connect teachers, principals, professional developers, and district administrators with each other and with outside experts around specific problems of practice.

Principals in District #2 are directly and explicitly accountable for the quality of instruction and performance in their schools, which means that principals and teachers hold their jobs based on their capacity to learn how to practice at progressively higher levels of accomplishment. Schools operate in very distinct and different communities, they embody very different problems of practice, they include very different student populations, and they are at very different places in their improvement processes. The district applies a strategy of differential treatment to these variations, concentrating more oversight, direction, and professional development on those schools with the lowest-performing students, adapting professional development plans for every school to the particular instructional progress of specific teachers in those schools, and granting high-performing schools more discretion than low-performing schools in both practice and professional development. Principals are the linchpins of instructional improvement in District #2: They are recruited, evaluated, and retained or dismissed based on their ability to understand, model, and develop instructional practice among teachers, and, ultimately, on their ability to improve student performance.

District #2 has also been characterized by an extraordinary level of stability in leadership. Anthony Alvarado, the superintendent who initiated the strategy, was in the district for eight years, and his former deputy, Elaine Fink, who served as the main source of instructional guidance and oversight in the district during Alvarado's whole term, is now superintendent. Similarly, the community school board, which is quite diverse and represents many segments of a very diverse community, has been relatively stable and has served as a stable source of guidance and support for administrative leadership (Elmore & Burney 1997a, 1997b, 1998).

Considering the magnitude of the task posed by standards-based reform for local school districts and schools, there is shockingly little research and documentation of institutional design and practice in exceptionally high-performing school districts. The available work does point to common themes, which I will treat in a moment. But the knowledge base on which to base advice to local districts on the design of large-scale improvement processes is very narrow.

Educators are fond of responding to any piece of research that demonstrates a promising approach, or any seemingly successful example from practice, with a host of reasons why "it"—whatever it is—would never work in *their* setting. *Their* students are much different from those in the example, *their* communities would never tolerate such practices, *their* union contract contains very different provisions that would never permit such actions, *their* teachers are much too sophisticated (or unsophisticated) to deal with such improvements, etc., etc., etc. The institutional environment of public education is, in the default mode, astonishingly, perversely, and ferociously parochial and particularistic; all significant problems are problems that can only be understood in the context of a particular school or community; no knowledge of any value transfers or adapts from one setting to another.[5]

The most effective response to this parochialism, which is a direct outgrowth of the isolation of teaching as a vocation, is to surround practitioners with dozens, perhaps hundreds, of examples of systems that have managed to design their institutional structures around large-scale improvement. The way to get those examples is both to substantially increase the research and documentation of high-performing systems with high proportions of low-income students, and to use policy to stimulate demand for such knowledge by investing in inspection activities among high- and low-performing districts. The states that seem to be stimulating higher proportions of high-performing districts seem to be the ones that have invested in the creation of an infrastructure to capture, examine, and disseminate successes of large-scale improvement (Grissmer & Flanagan, 1998; O'Day, Goertz et al., 1995). Still, in the short term, the fundamental problem is a relative lack of knowledge about the practical issues of institutional design in the face of problems, stimulated by standards-based reform, that require knowledge-intensive solutions.

Based on existing work, however, it is possible to state a few initial guiding principles that can be used to design institutional structures and to stimulate practices that result in large-scale improvement. Table 2 states these principles. Again, the exact form or wording of the principles is less important than the fact that they are an attempt to derive general guidance from practice and research in a form that can be tried in multiple settings and revised and elaborated with experience.

A major design principle is to organize everyone's actions, at all levels of the system, around an instructional focus that is stable over time. Most low-performing schools and systems start, for example, with a single instructional area—literacy, in most cases—and focus on that area until practice begins to approach a relatively high standard in most classrooms and performance begins to move decisively upward. They then add another instructional area—typically mathematics—and increase the level of complexity they expect of teachers and principals in practice and learning. Even relatively high-performing schools and districts could benefit from this approach, since the purpose of focus is not just to improve practice and performance but to *teach people in the organization how to think and act around learning for continuous improvement.* Presumably, many nominally high-performing schools and districts do well because of the backgrounds of their students and may be just as

TABLE 2

Maintain a tight instructional focus sustained over time

- Apply the instructional focus to everyone in the organization
- Apply it to both practice and performance
- Apply it to a limited number of instructional areas and practices, becoming progressively more ambitious over time

Routinize accountability for practice and performance in face-to-face relationships

- Create a strong normative environment in which adults take responsibility for the academic performance of children
- Rely more heavily on face-to-face relationships than on bureaucratic routines
- Evaluate performance on the basis of all students, not select groups of students and —above all—not school- or grade-level averages
- Design everyone's work primarily in terms of improving the capacity and performance of someone else—system administrators of principals and teachers, principals of teachers, teachers of students. In a well-developed system, the order should be reversed as well.

Reduce isolation and open practice up to direct observation, analysis, and criticism

- Make direct observation of practice, analysis, and feedback a routine feature of work
- Move people across settings, including outsiders into schools
- Center group discussions on the instructional work of the organization
- Model desired classroom practice in administrative actions
- Model desired classroom practice in collegial interactions

Exercise differential treatment based on performance and capacity, not on volunteerism

- Acknowledge differences among communities, schools, and classrooms within a common framework of improvement
- Allocate supervisory time and professional development based on explicit judgments about where schools are in a developmental process of practice and performance

Devolve increased discretion based on practice and performance

- Do not rely on generalized rules about centralization and decentralization
- Loosen and tighten administrative control based on hard evidence of quality of practice and performance of diverse groups of students; greater discretion follows higher quality of practice and higher levels of performance

lacking in organizational resources for learning as low-performing schools. Focus also has to be accompanied by stability—in leadership, in the language that high-level administrators and board members use to describe the goals and purposes of the organization, and in the commitment to monitoring and redesigning policies and structures that are supposed to enable improvement. Most importantly, the principle of tight focus and stability in message should apply to *everyone*. Superintendents and board members should be just as subject to criticism for straying off message as principals and teachers.

Another major design principle has to do with the development and conduct of accountability relationships in schools and school systems. It appears from early research that school systems that improve are those that have succeeded in getting people to *internalize* the expectations of standards-based accountability systems, and that they have managed this internalization largely through modeling commitment and focus using face-to-face relationships, not bureaucratic controls. The basic process at work here is *unlearning* the behaviors and normative codes that accompany loose-coupling, and learning new behaviors and values that are associated with *collective responsibility* for teaching practice and student learning.

People make these fundamental transitions by having *many* opportunities to be exposed to the ideas, to argue them into their own normative belief systems, to practice the behaviors that go with these values, to observe others practicing those behaviors, and, most importantly, to be successful at practicing in the presence of others (i.e., to be seen to be successful). In the panoply of rewards and sanctions that attach to accountability systems, the most powerful incentives reside in the face-to-face relationships among people in the organization, not in external systems. It is the dailiness of life in schools and school systems that sustains loose-coupling. Unless new values and behaviors reach into the dailiness of schools, there will be no change in business as usual.

The early evidence also suggests that low-capacity schools and school systems—schools and systems with weak collective values and atomized organizations—tend to try to find the easiest possible way of solving accountability problems with the knowledge they already have. Schools tend to teach to the test because they have no better ideas about how to improve content and pedagogy. They tend to focus on students who are closest to meeting standards rather than those who are furthest away. They tend to give vague and general guidance about instruction rather than working collectively on learning new instructional practices, etc. Improving school systems override these practices by insisting that the expectations and standards apply to all students, which translates into examining assessment data on individual students in all classrooms and schools, focusing on the particular problems of low-performing students, and avoiding judgments about school performance based on school- or grade-level averages.

A corollary of this focus on all students is that adults in the organization all frame their responsibilities in terms of their contribution to enhancing someone else's capacity and performance. System-level administrators are judged on the basis of how well they contribute to principals' capacities to work with teachers, principals are judged by how well they contribute to teachers, and teachers are judged for their contributions to students. In very well-developed improvement systems, one could imagine the evaluation working the other way too—students being evaluated, in part, on their contribution to improving their teachers' capacities, teachers for principals, principals for superintendents, etc.

One thing is clear: Schools and systems that are improving directly and explicitly confront the issue of isolation embedded in loose-coupling. Administrators—both system-level and school-level—are routinely engaged in direct observation of practice in schools and classrooms; they have mastered ways of talking about practice that allow for nonthreatening support, criticism, and judgment.

Such systems also create multiple avenues of interaction among classrooms and schools, as well as between schools and their broader environment, always focusing on the acquisition of new skills and knowledge. They adjust and adapt the routines of the workplace—teaching schedules, preparation periods, substitute teacher allocations—with the primary purpose of creating settings where teachers, administrators, and outside experts can interact around common problems of practice. In the words of Anthony Alvarado, former superintendent of District #2, all discussions are about "the work," and all nonclassroom personnel are expected to learn and model the practices they want to see in the classroom in their own interactions with other people in the organization. Inquiry-oriented classrooms and working toward high standards of performance require inquiry-oriented administrators and support staff who not only know what a good classroom looks like, but who also consistently use the precepts of instructional practice in their own interactions with others. A corollary of this principle is that if *anyone's* practice is subject to observation, analysis, and critique, then everyone's practice should be. Supervisors should be just as subject to evaluation as those they supervise. The principle of reciprocity applies to all accountability relationships; there can be no demands without attention to the capacity that exists to deliver them. Such reciprocity makes the purpose of getting better at work the common currency of exchange in all relationships.

Improving school systems appear not to have been captured by age-old, largely pointless debate about centralization versus decentralization. Rather, they seem to have developed ways of tailoring systemwide strategies of improvement to differences in communities, schools, and classrooms, without losing the overall coherence of systemwide standards for content and performance. I call this phenomenon differential treatment. Research on school-based management has said for a long time—more than ten years now—that there is no systematic relationship between the degree of centralization in school systems and their overall performance (Drury, 1999; Elmore, 1993; Malen, Ogawa et al., 1990). This should not be a particularly mysterious finding, since decentralization tends to be toward the top of the list of symbolic reforms that most relatively large districts undertake to create the appearance that they are governing schools, even as they seldom, if ever, deal directly with instruction or student performance. And, one might add, these schemes are almost never fully implemented before they are overturned in favor of some other innovation (Hess, 1999).

Indeed, one could argue that certain school-based management reforms are explicitly designed to push instructional decisions off the policy agenda altogether and focus debate instead on the representation of key constituencies in school governance. It seems clear that administrators in the districts that are improving avoid pointless and distracting debates about centralization and decentralization. Instead, they spend a lot of time building a sense of urgency and support in specific schools and communities around issues of standards and performance.

It also seems clear that if they communicate that urgency to principals and teachers, as well as to schools collectively, they will have to accept a high degree of responsibility for the detailed decisions required in managing improvement. In so doing they may need to engage in differential treatment of high- and low-performing schools, varying both the content of their oversight and professional development and the *process* by which they deal with schools, depending on how well a given school is doing on instructional quality and performance. Burney and I have documented this process in some detail in District #2. It is less well documented in other settings (Elmore & Burney, 1997b).

It seems that discretion in decisionmaking about core issues should, in some fundamental sense, be a function of demonstrated capacity and performance in managing an improvement process at the school level. This is the final design principle I would offer. Elsewhere I have called this the issue of "what's loose and what's tight" (Elmore, 1993). That is, strategic administrators seem to have different standards for how much discretion they grant to various units in their systems, based on judgments about how well those units can manage their resources in an improvement process. While high-performance organizations might require high levels of discretion in their operating units, most large school systems are confronted with schools that are either at widely different levels of quality and performance or at uniformly low levels of quality and performance. Starting with a broad-scale grant of discretion to all schools in either of these situations virtually guarantees that those who know what to do will get better and those who don't will stay the same or get worse. So some form of differential treatment, based on judgments of quality and performance, seems to be a requirement of large-scale improvement. Yet differential treatment only makes sense as an administrative strategy when it is embedded in a set of clear expectations and standards of learning that apply to all schools, teachers, and students. Differential treatment is, in other words, not an invitation to return to loose-coupling; it requires careful scrutiny of instructional practice and student performance in schools, as well as detailed knowledge of the conditions that distinguish one school from another in responding to common expectations.

Also, it should go without saying that volunteerism is *not* a strategy of differential treatment. In systemwide improvement, schools don't get to choose whether they participate or not. Participation is a condition of being in the system. Different schools might get to choose how they will participate. Some systems have allowed schools to enter various phases of an improvement process at different times. Some systems allow schools to choose among an array of instructional approaches as the focus for improvement. There are a variety of ways of introducing choice at the front end of an improvement process. But allowing schools to choose *whether* they participate is tantamount to returning to the old principles of loose-coupling, in which improvement occurs in small pockets captured by faithful adherents to some instructional approach and never influences the rest of the system. It is not coincidental, I think, that most of the current examples of improving districts occur in states that have relatively strong standards-based accountability systems in place. Local school systems in those states are at various stages of discovering that, in some fundamental sense, they don't have the option of using volunteerism, since ultimately their performance as a system will be based on the performance of all classrooms and schools in the system.

I have argued that standards-based reform poses problems of the deepest and most fundamental sort about how we think about the organization of schooling and the function of leaders in school systems and schools. The stakes are high for the future of public schooling and for the students who attend public schools. Change, as it has been conceived and carried out in the past, is not an option in responding to these problems. Large-scale, sustained, and continuous improvement is the path out of these problems. This kind of improvement is what the existing institutional structure of public schooling is specifically designed not to do. Improvement requires fundamental changes in the way public schools and school systems are designed and in the ways they are led. It will require changes in the values and norms that shape how teachers and principals think about the purposes of their work, changes in how we think about who leaders are, where they are, and what they do, and changes in the knowledge and skill requirements of work in schools. In short, we must fundamentally redesign schools as places where both adults and young people learn. We are in an early and perilous stage of this process, in which it is not clear whether public schooling will actually respond to the challenge of large-scale improvement or will adapt to this reform in the way it has adapted to others over the past century—by domesticating it into the existing loose-coupled institutional structure.

The pathologies of the existing institutional structure—a normative environment that views all matters of practice as matters of idiosyncratic taste and preference, rather than subject to serious debate, discourse, or inquiry; a structure of work in which isolation is the norm and collective work is the exception; and a managerial philosophy in which it is the job of administrators to protect or buffer teachers from the consequences of their instructional decisions and from any serious discussion of practice—these pathologies are all being addressed, in one way or another, in isolated school systems that are seriously at work on the problems of large-scale improvement.

The question is whether other school systems, operating in an environment of increased attention to student performance and quality of instruction, will discover that they need to learn not just different ways of doing things, but very different ways of thinking about the purposes of their work, and the skills and knowledge that go with those purposes. This shift requires first, a redefinition of leadership, away from role-based conceptions and toward distributive views; and second, a clearer set of design principles to guide the practice of large-scale improvement. Distributed leadership—hardly an original idea with me—derives from the fact that large-scale improvement requires concerted action among people with different areas of expertise and a mutual respect that stems from an appreciation of the knowledge and skill requirements of different roles. Design principles derive from the fact that large-scale improvement processes run directly against the grain of the existing institutional structure of public education, and therefore it is difficult to do anything consequential about large-scale improvement without violating some fundamental cultural or managerial tenet of the existing structure. The problem, then, is how to construct relatively orderly ways for people to engage in activities that have as their consequence the learning of new ways to think about and do their jobs, and how to put these activities in the context of reward structures that stimulate them to do more of what leads to large-scale improvement and less of what reinforces the pathologies of the existing structure.

As I said earlier, I offer these design principles based on my own work on large-scale improvement and from my reading of the little research that exists on the subject. The main point here should be the urgency of learning more about these issues in many school districts and in many different settings. This requires pressing hard for more concrete knowledge about how large-scale improvement processes work.

3

Bridging the Gap between Standards and Achievement

The Imperative for Professional Development in Education

At this writing, schools and districts across the country are struggling to meet the accountability demands of No Child Left Behind (NCLB), the federal government's stringent new law that holds schools accountable for the annual progress of students and prescribes sanctions and remedies for low-performing schools. Never have the demands for new skills and knowledge on the part of teachers and administrators been greater. Never has the gap between these demands and the actual knowledge and skills of educators been greater.

This essay deals with the gap between performance and human capacity in schools and the role of professional development in bridging that gap. Professional development is one of those areas in which our knowledge of what to do and how to do it exceeds our demonstrated capacity to act on that knowledge. The knowledge base for what constitutes effective professional development is far from complete or perfect, but the gap between what we know how to do and what we are actually doing is dangerously large.

This essay focuses particularly on the idea of reciprocity of accountability: For every increment of performance I require of you, I have a responsibility to provide you with the additional capacity to produce that performance. It must be said that the principle of reciprocity is not honored in the design of most accountability systems. It is still an open question whether the ongoing demands from policymakers for greater accountability for student performance will be accompanied by investments in the development of professional knowledge and skills required to produce that performance.

The work of schools is becoming more complex and demanding, while the organization of schools remains, for the most part, static and rigid. If you push hard enough on a rigid structure, eventually it will break and hurt the people in it. This is the perilous state of American public education. The immediate cause of this situation is a simple, powerful idea dominating policy discourse about schools: that students should be held to high, common standards for academic performance, and that schools and the people who work in them should be held accountable for ensuring that students—all students—are able to meet these standards. Accountability schemes come in many forms, including high-stakes student testing, district-led closure or restructuring of low-performing schools, and state takeover of low-performing schools and districts.

The term "accountability" also can refer to many things, including rules and procedures, or to the delivery of certain types of academic content. But in this paper, I use the term only to refer to systems that hold students, schools, or districts responsible for academic performance, since this is the dominant form of accountability in education today. Unfortunately, schools and school systems were not designed to respond to the pressure for performance that standards and accountability bring, and their failure to translate this pressure into useful and fulfilling work for students and adults is dangerous to the future of public education.

The standards and accountability movement is broad-based politically and persistent over time. It involves state legislators, governors, advocacy groups, and professional organizations. It stems from the basic belief that schools, like other public and private organizations in society, should be able to demonstrate what they contribute to the learning of students and that they should engage in steady improvement of practice and performance over time. The accountability movement expresses society's expectation that schools will face and solve the persistent problems of teaching and learning that lead to the academic failure of large numbers of students and the mediocre performance of many more. Over time, if schools improve, increased accountability will result in increased legitimacy for public education. Failure will lead to erosion of public support and a loss of legitimacy.

With increased accountability, American schools and the people who work in them are being asked to do something new—to engage in systematic, continuous improvement in the quality of the educational experience of students, and to subject themselves to the discipline of measuring their success by the metric of students' academic performance. Most people who currently work in public schools weren't hired to do this work, nor have they been adequately prepared to do it, either by their professional education or by their prior experience in schools.

Schools as organizations aren't designed as places where people are expected to engage in sustained improvement of their practice, where they are supported in this improvement, or where they are expected to subject their practice to the scrutiny of peers or the discipline of evaluations based on student achievement. Educators in schools with the most severe performance problems face truly challenging conditions for which their prior training and experience have not prepared them—extreme poverty, unprecedented cultural and language diversity, and unstable family and community patterns. To work effectively under these conditions requires a level of knowledge and skill not required of teachers and administrators who work in less demanding situations, yet accountability systems expect the same level of performance of all students, regardless of social background. Hence, given the conditions of their work, some school staff regard demands for performance-based accountability as unreasonable. Throughout much of society and the economy, however, there has been a discernible shift toward performance and value-added measures of success triggered by the economic crisis of the late 1970s and early 1980s. In other high-skill, knowledge-based occupations—research and development, engineering, health care, even social services—some system of evaluation and accountability has been an important part of professional life for at least two decades. So when educators claim that they are being unfairly treated by a hostile accountability system, it's not surprising that people who work in other knowledge-intensive sectors are not particularly sympathetic.

The organization and culture of American schools is, in most important respects, the same as it was in the late nineteenth and early twentieth centuries. Teachers are still, for the most part, treated as solo practitioners operating in isolation from one another under conditions of work that severely limit their exposure to other adults doing the same work. The work day of teachers is still designed around the expectation that teachers' work is composed exclusively of delivering content to students, not, among other things, to cultivating knowledge and skill about how to improve their work.

The prevailing assumption is that teachers learn most of what they need to know about how to teach before they enter the classroom—despite massive evidence to the contrary—and that most of what they learn after they begin teaching falls into the amorphous category of "experience," which usually means lowering their expectations for what they can accomplish with students and learning to adjust to an organization that is either hostile to or unsupportive of their work. This limited view of what teachers need to know and do demands little educational leadership from administrators. And, since administrative work currently has little to do with the content of teaching, much less its improvement, it may actually act to protect teachers from various external intrusions on their isolated work.

The learning that is expected of teachers and administrators as a condition of their work also tends to be predicated on the model of solo practice. In order to advance in rank and salary, individual teachers and administrators are expected to accumulate academic credit for the university courses they take, any or all of which may be totally unconnected to their daily work. Most workplace learning also mirrors the norms of the organization—it takes the form of information about policies and practices delivered in settings disconnected from where the work of the organization is actually done.

It would be difficult to invent a more dysfunctional organization for a performance-based accountability system. In fact, the existing structure and culture of schools seems better designed to resist learning and improvement than to enable it. As expectations for increased student performance mount and the measurement and publication of evidence about performance becomes part of the public discourse about schools, there are few portals through which new knowledge about teaching and learning can enter schools; few structures or processes in which teachers and administrators can assimilate, adapt, and polish new ideas and practices; and few sources of assistance for those who are struggling to understand the connection between the academic performance of their students and the practices in which they engage. So the brutal irony of our present circumstance is that schools are hostile and inhospitable places for learning. They are hostile to the learning of adults, and because of this they are necessarily hostile to the learning of students. They have been this way for some time. What's new about the current situation is that the advent of performance-based accountability has made the irony more visible—and may ultimately undermine the legitimacy of public education if something isn't done to change the way schools work.

Accountability must be a reciprocal process. For every increment of performance I demand from you, I have an equal responsibility to provide you with the capacity to meet that expectation. Likewise, for every investment you make in my skill and knowledge, I have a reciprocal responsibility to demonstrate some new increment in performance. This is the principle of "reciprocity of accountability for capacity." It is the glue that, in the final analysis, will hold accountability systems together (Elmore, 2000). At the moment, schools and school systems are not designed to provide support or capacity in response to demands for accountability. The imperative here is for professionals, policymakers, and the public at large to recognize that performance-based accountability, if it is to do what it was intended to do—improve the quality of the educational experience for all students and increase the performance of schools—requires a strategy for investing in the knowledge and skill of educators. In order for people in schools to respond to external pressure for accountability, they have to learn to do their work differently and to rebuild the organization of schooling around a different way of doing the work. If the public and policymakers want increased attention to academic quality and performance, the quid pro quo is investing in the knowledge and skill necessary to produce it. If educators want legitimacy, purpose, and credibility for their work, the quid pro quo is learning to do their work differently and accepting a new model of accountability.

THE KNOWLEDGE GAP IN PROFESSIONAL DEVELOPMENT: THE IDEAL AND THE REAL

Professional development is the label we attach to activities that are designed in some way to increase the skill and knowledge of educators (Fenstermacher & Berliner, 1985). In professional discourse, "professional development" is distinguished from "preservice" education by the fact that it occurs after teachers and administrators are on the job, during the routine course of their work. However, as we shall see later, this distinction is problematical in designing comprehensive approaches to the development of skill and knowledge. In practice, professional development covers a vast array of specific activities, everything from highly targeted work with teachers around specific curricula and teaching practices to short, "hit-and-run" workshops designed to familiarize teachers and administrators with new ideas or new rules and requirements, to off-site courses and workshops designed to provide content and academic credit for teachers and administrators.

So, to say that we should invest more money in professional development in the present context is not to say anything very meaningful. The connection between professional development as presently practiced and the knowledge and skill of educators is tenuous at best; its relationship to the imperative of improving instruction and student performance is, practically speaking, nonexistent (Feiman-Nemser, 1983, p. 163). Spending more money on existing professional development activities, as most are presently designed, is unlikely to have any significant effect on either the knowledge and skill of educators or on the performance of students.

Yet, much of the literature written by researchers and practitioners about professional development seems quite sensible and useful in thinking about how to design and operate professional development activities that have some likelihood of improving teaching and learning. The research is rarely grounded in hard empirical evidence about its effects on practice or on student learning, but it certainly provides an ample basis for designing activities that could be subjected to empirical testing.

Consensus on Effective Professional Development

Educators' professional literature and academic research reflect a broad consensus on the main features of effective professional development. Exhibit 1 presents one summary of this consensus. This account of the consensus view draws heavily on the original standards for professional development adopted by the National Staff Development Council in 1995 (Sparks & Hirsch, 1997; Sparks, 1995). In this view, effective professional development is focused on the improvement of student learning through the improvement of the skill and knowledge of educators. In a given school or school system, specific professional development activities would follow from a well-articulated mission or purpose for the organization, and that purpose would be anchored on some statement about student learning. So, for example, a school or system might say that its objective over a period of time would be to improve students' demonstrated knowledge and skill in reading, writing, and mathematics, as measured by portfolios of student work, curriculum-based assessments, and state- or district-administered examinations. From this broad statement of purpose, the school or district might derive expectations focused more specifically on certain settings—for example, basic reading and writing skills among students with learning problems in the primary grades, inferential and problem-solving skills in algebra in the middle grades, interpretation and analysis of expository and technical writing in the upper grades.

The point here is that professional development, if it is to be focused on student learning, at some point must be tailored to address the difficulties encountered by real students in real classrooms as well as broader systemic objectives. Similarly, effective professional development is connected to questions of content and pedagogy that educators are asking—or should be asking—about the consequences of their instructional practices on real students, as well as to general questions about effective teaching practice.

Professional development brings the general and the externally validated in contact with the specific and the contextual. So, for example, an elementary school with persistently low reading scores and many students who have basic decoding and comprehension difficulties might focus its professional development activities on instructional strategies to improve students' skills in those domains—especially those that work well in concert with the schools' specific reading program. Or, a secondary school struggling with the introduction of a new requirement that all students demonstrate a knowledge of basic algebra might focus its professional development efforts on strategies to engage students who previously would not have been expected to master this level of mathematics.

According to the consensus view (see Exhibit 1, p. 96), the practice of professional development, however focused and wherever enacted, should embody a clear model of adult learning that is explained to those

EXHIBIT 1   Professional Development: The Consensus View

- Focuses on a well-articulated mission or purpose anchored in student learning of core disciplines and skills
- Derives from analysis of student learning of specific content in a specific setting
- Focuses on specific issues of curriculum and pedagogy
- Derives from research and exemplary practice
- Connects with specific issues of instruction and student learning of academic disciplines and skills in the context of actual classrooms
- Embodies a clearly articulated theory or model of adult learning
- Develops, reinforces, and sustains group work
- Ensures collaborative practice within schools
- Networks across schools
- Involves active participation of school leaders and staff
- Sustains focus over time—continuous improvement
- Provides models of effective practice
- Is delivered in schools and classrooms
- Practice is consistent with message
- Uses assessment and evaluation
- Actively monitors student learning
- Provides feedback on teacher learning and practice

who participate. Those who engage in professional development should be willing to say explicitly what new knowledge and skill educators will learn as a consequence of their participation, how this new knowledge and skill will be manifested in their professional practice, and what specific activities will lead to this learning.

Professional development, in the consensus view, should be designed to develop the capacity of teachers to work collectively on problems of practice within their own schools and with practitioners in other settings, as much as to support the knowledge and skill development of individual educators. This view derives from the assumption that learning is essentially a collaborative rather than an individual activity—that educators learn more powerfully in concert with others who are struggling with the same problems—and that the essential purpose of professional development should be the improvement of schools and school systems, not just the improvement of the individuals who work in them. The improvement of schools and school systems likewise has to engage the active support and collaboration of leaders, not just their tacit or implicit support, and this support should be manifested in decisions about the use of time and money.

Professional development in the service of improvement requires commitment to consistency and focus over the long term. The broad mission and goals that shape professional development should reflect a path of continuous improvement in specific domains of student learning. The activities should be continuous from one year to the next. As schools reach one set of objectives they should move on to more ambitious ones, and educators should demonstrate continuity and consistency in the improvement of their practice in specific domains from one year to the next. So, for example, a school district might frame broad goals for the improvement of student learning in basic academic content areas. It would then work out with each school a more specific plan of action based on the profile of that school's student population and patterns of student performance—adjusting performance expectations upward each year as the school advances.

The focus of professional development on enacted practice—the combination of academic content and pedagogy into classroom delivery that is responsive to issues of student learning in specific settings—requires that the physical location of the learning be as close as possible to where the teaching itself occurs. Hence, successful professional development is likely to occur in schools and classroom settings rather than off site, and it is likely to involve work with individual teachers or small groups around the observation of actual teaching. Proximity to practice also requires that the pedagogy of professional developers be as consistent as possible with the pedagogy that they expect from educators. It has to involve professional developers who, through expert practice, can model what they expect of the people with whom they are working.

Finally, successful professional development—because it is specifically designed to improve student learning—should be evaluated continuously, and primarily on the basis of the effect it has on student achievement.

Potential Areas of Conflict and Disagreement

Within this broad consensus on the essentials of effective professional development there is plenty of disagreement. Associations that represent coalitions of practitioners, such as the National Staff Development Council (NSDC), tend to present their recommendations as voluntary and consensual. They view a school system's process of creating a professional development strategy as consensus-building—between the system and its community and among teachers and administrators within schools. In their words, "Everyone works together to identify strategies and develop action plans consistent with the district's overall mission" (Sparks, 1995). In reality, deciding on who sets the purpose and focus of professional development is often conflict-ridden, especially in systems with high proportions of low-performing students. Student learning is a function, in part, of adult expectations; when educators work in schools where expectations for student achievement are chronically low or where expectations are highly differentiated, a consensus professional development plan may only institutionalize mediocrity and low performance. Hence, connecting professional development to the overall improvement of student achievement is likely to raise key issues about teaching and learning that may never arise through a process of simple consensus-building.

Similarly, the idea of voluntarism raises the question of whether teachers should be able to choose to participate in professional development activities in their schools, whether schools should be required to participate in an overall process for determining which professional development activities should be present in their schools, and whether there should be a system-wide instructional improvement process that limits and focuses professional development activity within schools. There are two fundamental principles in tension here: The first suggests that professional development should be focused on systemwide improvement, which leads to limiting individual and school discretion; the other suggests that educators should play a major role in determining the focus of professional development, both for themselves and for their schools. These principles can be difficult to reconcile, especially in the context of an accountability system that emphasizes measurable student performance.

Another difficult issue arises out of the relationship between professional development and personnel evaluations. If professional development occurs in close proximity to practice, then professional developers are likely to know a great deal about the strengths and weaknesses of the teachers with whom they work. Also, if principals are closely involved with the planning and implementation of the school's professional development activities, they will tend to treat the knowledge they gain from observing teacher practices as useful in their responsibility for evaluating those teachers. One possibility is that the learning objectives of professional development are corrupted by the possibility that they will be used for evaluation. Another possibility is that, in a well-functioning school, professional development is part of a seamless process of instruction and improvement for adults and children, and that it is almost impossible to pull the two apart. Whichever view you take, active pursuit of professional development is likely to create conflict around its relationship to teacher evaluation.

Finally, guidance about successful professional development fails to resolve an important issue of content versus process. In general, advocates of thoughtful, systematic approaches to school improvement (see Fullan, 1991) stress that to change their schools educators need to develop skill and knowledge about the fundamentals of group problem-solving and interpersonal skills. At the same time, professional development that improves student learning must involve hard, detailed work on the fundamentals of content and pedagogy. In principle, there is no conflict between these purposes. In practice, they are likely to be in constant tension. In some senses, it is easier for educators to focus on issues of process—at the expense of issues of content and pedagogy (see below, and Little, 1990)—because process can be framed so as to avoid difficult questions of teacher autonomy and control. For example, we can agree as a matter of process to treat all issues of pedagogy as matters of personal taste. But doing so would mean that decisions about professional development would be largely personal also, disconnected from collective knowledge about best practice in the improvement of student learning. Thus, the prospects for large-scale improvement would remain dim.

THE PRACTICE OF PROFESSIONAL DEVELOPMENT

While there is evidence that the consensus about effective professional development has influenced the way professional associations and researchers portray the field, there is little evidence that this consensus has had a large-scale effect on the practices of schools and school systems. School systems use a more or less standard model for handling issues of professional development, and this model is largely, if not entirely, at odds with the consensus about effective practice. Few school districts treat professional development as part of an overall strategy for school improvement. In fact, many districts do not even have an overall strategy for school improvement. Instead, districts tend to see staff development as a specialized activity within a bureaucratic structure. In some instances, there are particular people with assigned roles who work with teachers and principals around content. In other instances, professional development is a function of certain categorical programs designed to serve special student populations, such as English-language learners, poor students, students with disabilities, or the gifted and talented. In many cases, individual teachers—and sometimes whole schools—are required to have a coordinated professional development plan. Yet these plans are often nothing more than a collection of teachers' individual activities over the course of a year, without a general design or specific focus that relates particular activities to an overall strategy or goal (Little, 1993).

Most school systems organize formal professional development around specified days. Teachers are relieved from their regular duties to participate in activities that are usually unrelated to instructional practice, except in the broadest sense of that term. Designed to serve the widest possible audience, systemwide professional development is usually focused on specific and disconnected topics—student discipline, test preparation, district and state policy changes—and typically occurs in large-group settings away from classrooms and schools. Often these days are specified contractually through local collective bargaining agreements, so that professional development becomes associated with a specific number of discrete days disconnected from any focused strategy to equip teachers with the knowledge and skill they need to improve student learning in specific domains. More importantly, the incentive structures under which most teachers work reward them with salary increases for the courses they take on their own time and largely outside of the schools and systems in which they work, either through private vendors or colleges of education. There is usually no incentive and little guidance for aligning these courses with school and district priorities. Thus, most courses are determined by individual teacher preference.

The Gap

Whatever else one might say about the consensus view of effective professional development, it is, at the very least, a reasonable working theory for the design of large-scale professional development activities. In response to demands for accountability, it rightly aims to improve teaching practice and student learning. The main elements of the consensus view—a strong focus on systemwide and schoolwide performance goals, heavy emphasis on teachers' content knowledge and the pedagogical skills that go with effective instruction, explicit theories of adult learning, use of group settings, moving learning close to the point of practice, etc.—are all things that could be operationalized, evaluated, and studied for their effectiveness in improving practice. The terms of the consensus view are sufficiently clear to be broadly communicated.

The guidance of the consensus view is sufficiently broad to be applicable in a variety of settings and adaptable to a variety of contexts. And, finally, the potential conflicts that arise out of the consensus view are problems that can be understood and anticipated. The knowledge gap, then, is not so much about knowing what good professional development looks like; it's about knowing how to get it rooted in the institutional structure of schools. The problem is connecting the ideal prescriptions of the consensus model with the real problems of large-scale improvement and accountability.

Exhorting schools and school systems to engage in more enlightened professional development practices, even under the pressure of performance-based accountability, is unlikely to have much effect without more explicit guidance about how to bring these more enlightened practices into the mainstream of school life. This knowledge gap requires more explicit attention to the practice of improvement.

The Varieties and Costs of Failure

As noted above, the relationship between professional development and accountability is essentially reciprocal. It is an investment in knowledge and skill in order to achieve an end. Those who are being "developed" must consent to learning what they are being asked to do and how to do it; those who are demanding results must understand that school personnel are being asked to implement practices they currently do not know how to do. Both parties should understand that most learning occurs through experimentation and error, not through a straight linear process. It is in this domain of reciprocity that failures are most likely to occur.

Judith Warren Little (1993) suggests that the traditional "training model" of professional development—which assumes that a clearly defined body of skills can be transferred from trainers to teachers through a well-specified process—is largely inappropriate, given the complexity of the tasks that are required for all schools to help students meet high academic standards. She recommends a variety of approaches that take explicit account of the difficult work required of teachers to meet new expectations, the level of commitment and energy they will need to learn and develop effective new practices, and the uncertainty about whether externally developed solutions will work in their specific classroom contexts.

More direct linkages between professional development and accountability will fail—or at the very least will be relatively ineffective—to the extent that they turn professional development into a tool for control. They will succeed to the degree that they engage teachers and administrators in acquiring knowledge and skills they need to solve problems and meet expectations for high performance. To the degree that people are being asked to do things they don't know how to do, and at the same time are not being asked to engage their own ideas, values, and energies in the learning process, professional development shifts from building capacity to demanding compliance.

The avenues for failure are many: Administrators can construct professional development as training in discrete skills that teachers feel have limited or no applicability to their real work. The level of support for teachers and administrators in learning new practices can be too weak relative to the demands that learning and implementing the new practices will make on them. Problems in connecting new practices to the specific demands that teachers face can be ignored or pushed aside by administrators or professional developers. Or, the new practices themselves may simply not work as intended.

The costs of these failures may be high: the loss of credibility for professional development as an essential activity in the organization; the loss of commitment to building the knowledge and skill that teachers and administrators need to be effective; and an undermining of the premise of improvement—that is, the premise that investment in educators' skills and knowledge can be connected to improvement in student achievement. Later, I will speak to these issues under the heading of capacity-building. For now, it is important to reinforce the idea that professional development and accountability are reciprocal processes demanding high engagement in both policy and practice, and that the long-term objective of investing in educators' skills and knowledge is to increase the capacity of schools to solve pressing problems through the application of best practice, not just to implement someone else's solutions.

THE PRACTICE OF IMPROVEMENT: GETTING FROM HERE TO THERE

In its simplest form, the practice of large-scale improvement is the mobilization of knowledge, skill, incentives, resources, and capacities within schools and school systems to increase student learning. Strictly speaking, the practice of improvement is the sharing of a set of proven practices and their collective deployment for a common end. It is not the property of any one individual or any incumbent in any specific job. It is not the property of teachers or administrators or professional developers. It is a common set of practices shared across the profession, irrespective of roles.

Large-scale improvement intends to reach *all* students in *all* classrooms and *all* schools through the daily work of teachers and administrators. The idea of improvement means measurable increases in the quality of instructional practice and student performance over time. Quality and performance are on the vertical axis; time is on the horizontal axis; and improvement is movement in a consistently northeasterly direction.

Improvement, as we will use the term here, means engagement in learning new practices that work, based on external evidence and benchmarks of success, across multiple schools and classrooms, in a specific area of academic content and pedagogy, resulting in continuous improvement of students' academic performance over time. Improvement is *not* random innovation in a few classrooms or schools. It does *not* focus on changing processes or structures, disconnected from content and pedagogy. And it is *not* a single-shot episode. Improvement is a discipline, a practice that requires focus, knowledge, persistence, and consistency over time. Notice that the term "change" does not occur in any of these definitions. Change in the discourse of education is overused and underdefined. Change is generally regarded as positive, even when it achieves no discernible results. Schools are accustomed to changing—promiscuously and routinely—without producing any improvement. When I use the term "change" (which is rarely), I use it only to refer to specific alterations of existing structures, processes, or practices that are intended to result in improvement. In other words, change, in my vocabulary, is motivated and judged by the standard of student learning.

The practice of large-scale improvement is the process by which external demands for accountability are translated into concrete structures, processes, norms, and instructional practices in schools and school systems. Professional development is the set of knowledge- and skill-building activities that raise the capacity of teachers and administrators to respond to external demands and to engage in the improvement of practice and performance.

In this context, professional development is effective only to the degree that it engages teachers and administrators in large-scale improvement. This is an intentionally narrow and instrumental view.[1] Professional development, as it is typically practiced, confuses the individual's personal growth and learning with the growth and learning of the individual that contributes to organizational performance. When teachers present individual professional development plans, for example, it is often unclear which activities are designed to enhance their individual growth and which are designed to improve their practice as teachers in a particular organization with clear goals. Likewise, courses and workshops that are offered for academic credit are often focused on the individual interests of teachers and administrators more than on the development of a shared body of skills and knowledge, necessary for schools and districts to implement a common set of successful practices.

Professional development, as I will use the term in the context of large-scale improvement, is a collective good rather than a private or individual good. Its value is judged by what it contributes to the individual's capacity to improve the quality of instruction in the school and school system.

HOW PROFESSIONAL DEVELOPMENT CAN WORK
TO IMPROVE SCHOOLS

Whether professional development improves instructional quality and academic performance depends as much on the characteristics of the organization it serves as on the characteristics of the professional development activity itself. The features of effective professional development, as described in Exhibit 1, embody some very heroic assumptions about the organizational context in which the activity occurs. For example, focusing professional development on a well-articulated mission or purpose anchored in student learning assumes that leaders know what purposes the system is pursuing and can articulate them specifically enough to identify the particular professional development activities that are needed to support them. Deriving professional development from an analysis of what is needed to improve student learning assumes that the system has the capacity to capture useful, accurate information about student learning and that the people in the system have the capacity to apply that information to decisions about instructional content and professional development. Developing and sustaining group work assumes that there is time in the instructional day and that teachers and administrators have the norms and skills that are required for productive group work. And so forth down the list. At this point, one is reminded of the saying, "If we had some ham, we could have some ham and eggs—if we had some eggs." It does little good to know what quality professional development might look like if schools and school systems are incapable of supporting it.

In summary, the practice of improvement is largely about moving whole organizations—teachers, administrators, and schools—toward the culture, structure, norms, and processes that support quality professional development in the service of student learning. In addition, the practice of improvement at the individual and organizational levels involves mastery in several domains (see Exhibit 2, p. 106): knowledge and skill, incentives, and resources and capacity. The knowledge and skill domain asks what people need to know in order to improve the quality and effectiveness of their practice, and under what conditions they are most likely to learn it. The incentives domain asks what kinds of encouragements and rewards people should receive for acquiring this knowledge and using it to enhance performance and support improve-

EXHIBIT 2 Domains in the Practice of Large-Scale Improvement

- *Students' Knowledge and Skill* What do students need to know and be able to do? Under what conditions will they learn it?
- *Educators' Knowledge and Skill* What do educators need to know and be able to do to help all students succeed? Under what conditions will they learn it?
- *Incentives* What rewards and penalties encourage large-scale improvement? Who will receive these incentives, and who decides, using what criteria?
- *Resources and Capacity* What material supports lead large-scale improvement?

ment. The resources and capacity domain asks what level of material support and what kinds of capacities—organizational and individual— the system needs to ensure that professional development leads to large-scale improvement.

Knowledge and Skill

The practice of improvement involves the acquisition of new knowledge, connecting that knowledge with the skills necessary for effective practice, and creating new settings where learning can occur. As an illustration, take what has become a central problem of performance-based accountability in secondary schools—teaching algebra to all secondary school students.

This seemingly reasonable goal raises a formidable array of practical problems. By the time students reach the ninth or tenth grade, their range of mathematics performance is usually quite wide. Historically, algebra was taught largely to college-bound students who represent the upper range of performance and, perhaps, have a higher level of motivation to master the new subject matter. The new focus on increasing the number of students taking algebra means more algebra classes, which means more algebra teachers—all in a market where mathematics teachers are in short supply.

Most secondary schools solve this problem by drafting teachers with inadequate math skills into teaching the additional classes, typically assigning them to the classes with the lowest-achieving students. In addition, most secondary schools will continue to teach every algebra class with the methods that have always been used to teach well-prepared college-bound students, just adding sections. Using teachers whose main expertise may not be in mathematics instruction, they also layer on remedial classes—conducted after school, by extending class periods during the regular day, or during summer sessions—to accommodate the students who fail to master the content, either because they have difficulty with math or because their algebra classes were badly taught the first time around.

In other words, the school's response to the requirement that all students learn algebra is to make marginal adjustments in organizational structure (remedial classes, more sections), while leaving teachers' knowledge and skill essentially untouched. What this approach ignores, of course, is that the algebra requirement presents an instructional problem that few schools have faced before—how to deal with a broad range of mathematical skill and knowledge among students and teachers. Addressing this instructional problem will require that everyone involved in teaching algebra learn something new about both the content and the pedagogy required to reach students with a wide range of skill and preparation levels.

There are many other, similar examples: students in the early grades being expected to demonstrate mastery of written text in a language they don't yet comprehend; students arriving in the eighth or tenth grade who are expected to provide written interpretations of text that they don't have the literacy skills to understand; students in secondary school who perform well on tasks that involve factual recall, but who have not been taught to answer questions that require interpretation and analysis. These problems all have a common structure. In fact, at some level, they are the same problem: They all involve a fundamental issue of practice that challenges the existing structure of schools, and they all require more knowledge and skill of the people who work there. They all require people in the organization not just to do their work differently, but to think differently about the nature and purpose of their work. And, they all require a high degree of cooperation among people with diverse roles in deploying the skills and knowledge that are necessary to help students with very different levels of interest prepare to meet common, high expectations for learning. These problems also expose the weakest aspects of schools and school systems as organizations. Their solution requires traditionally isolated teachers to act in concert with each other around common issues of content and practice, and they require administrators to play a much more active role in the provision and improvement of instruction. Interestingly, though, these problems lie in a domain about which we know a considerable amount. Here, in summary, is what the research says about the issues of knowledge and skill in the improvement of practice:

Expertise in teaching exists. It can be identified and it can be enhanced through professional development, but it doesn't necessarily support improvement in student achievement.

The knowledge necessary for successful teaching lies in three domains: 1) deep knowledge of the subject matter (i.e., history and mathematics) and skills (i.e., reading and writing) that are to be taught; 2) expertise in instructional practices that cut across specific subject areas, or "general pedagogical knowledge"; and 3) expertise in instructional practices that address the problems of teaching and learning associated with specific subjects and bodies of knowledge, referred to as "pedagogical content knowledge."

Novice teachers differ markedly from expert teachers in their command of these domains and their ability to use them. For example, they differ in the array of examples and strategies they can use to explain difficult concepts to students, in the range of strategies they can employ for engaging students who are at different performance levels, and in the degree of fluency and automaticity with which they employ the strategies they know. Professional development that results in significant changes in practice will focus explicitly on these domains of knowledge; engage teachers in analysis of their own practice; and provide opportunities for teachers to observe experts and to be observed by and to receive feedback from experts. One aspect of expertise, however, sometimes works against improvement. When the deeply embedded practices of experienced teachers run against new models of practice, when teachers are asked to challenge what they think about the range of student knowledge and skill they can accommodate in a given classroom, entrenched beliefs can work against the acquisition of new knowledge. Thus, one aspect in improving the quality of teaching is often *un*learning deeply seated beliefs and implicit practices that work against the development of new, more effective practices (Borko & Putnam, 1995; Clark & Peterson, 1986; Feiman-Nemser, 1983).

So while expertise exists, matters, and can be improved, it is not true that experience equals expertise. That is, deep knowledge in the domains necessary to become a powerful and fluent practitioner does not automatically, or even reliably, come as a result of continuous practice. In fact, the evidence is substantial that the early socialization of teachers, coupled with the isolation of teaching, rather quickly socializes novices into what Feiman-Nemser (1983) calls a "utilitarian" view of teaching, characterized by narrow focus and routinization rather than active learning and the deepening of knowledge. The disjunction between experience and expertise is an issue to which I will return, but it is important to acknowledge that, in a system that values expertise and its dissemination, it may be necessary to make judgments about who has it that are at odds with the conventional view that experience inevitably leads to expertise.

Learning is both an individual and a social process. Capturing individual learning for the benefit of the group enterprise depends on structures that support interdependence in serious, substantive ways.

It is now commonplace to argue, as does the consensus view of professional development, that teachers learn through social interaction around problems of practice and that the enhancement of teacher learning requires support for collegial interaction where teachers can work on new practices. A substantial part of the research in this domain takes its conceptual guidance from the idea of "communities of practice"; that is, informal social networks of people who share concrete ideas, values, and norms about their work (Lave & Wenger, 1991; Wenger, 1998). While it is clear that the creation of social networks can have a significant effect on the development of new practices among experienced teachers (e.g., Stein, Smith, & Silver, 1999), it is also clear that certain forms of collegiality work against improvement. Mandated activities that have little or no purpose or utility, activities that stress the social aspects of collegiality over the use of collegiality to enhance instructional practice, and forms of interaction that aren't grounded in the quest to improve student achievement—all these forms of collegiality are likely to sidetrack cooperative work away from improvement (Bird & Little, 1986; Brown, Collins, & Duguid, 1989; Hargreaves, 1991; Huberman, 1995; McLaughlin & Yee, 1988). In general, the existing school structure, which is organized to reinforce isolated work and problem-solving, makes collaboration very expensive. Thus, collaborative professional development activities that are not engaging and demonstrably useful to teachers and administrators can lead quickly to cynical compliance or outright resistance.

Practice and values change in concert. Both are important and both should be the focus of new learning for teachers and administrators.

I began by stating that performance-based accountability systems are asking the people who work in schools to do things they currently don't know how to do. They are also asking many people to do things they don't think are possible and may not even believe are desirable. Experienced teachers often have very strong, fixed ideas about which students can master high academic standards and which can't. They also have very strong ideas about which kinds of practices will work for their students and which won't. These ideas are formed from experience, personal values, and knowledge of pedagogy and content. By virtue of their working conditions, most teachers deal with issues of practice in a very particularistic way. Thus, more likely than not, broad guidance about instructional practice or even very specific guidance without a strong connection to the particular circumstance or specific curriculum that must be taught will have little or no effect on practice.

Improving instructional practice requires a change in beliefs, norms, and values about what it is possible to achieve, as well as in the actual practices that are designed to bring achievement. In other words, improvement requires a theory of individual learning. This is a domain in which there is not likely to be a high level of disagreement about the right working theory. In the short run, it is probably more important to have an explicit working theory than it is to have any one particular working theory. One example of a well-specified and tested theory of individual learning and improvement is Guskey's (1989) theory of attitude and perceptual change in teachers. He argues that practice changes attitudes rather than vice-versa. Rather than exhorting teachers to believe that students can learn differently, or that different students can learn at higher levels, then showing teachers the practices that go with these beliefs, Guskey argues that teachers must actually try these new practices with the students for whom they believe the practices are problematical. If the new practices succeed with those students, then teachers have the opportunity to reflect on their values and attitudes and on the changes in them that are required as a result of this experience. Guskey found that teachers who were able to use certain practices successfully "expressed more positive attitudes toward teaching and increased personal responsibility for their students' learning" (p. 444). He concludes that changes in attitudes and beliefs generally follow, rather than precede, changes in behavior.

An important implication of Guskey's (1989) theory is that instruction itself is probably the most potent form of professional development available to schools. This organizational reality can operate both for and against improvement. Guskey puts it this way:

> The instructional practices that most veteran teachers employ are fashioned to a large extent by their experiences in the classroom. Practices that are found to 'work,' that is, those leading to desired learning outcomes, are retained; others are abandoned. Hence, a key determinant of enduring change in instructional practices is demonstrable results in terms of students' performance. Activities that are demonstrably successful tend to be repeated while those that are not successful, or for which there is no tangible evidence of success, are dropped. (p. 445)

It follows that, if most of what teachers learn about practice they learn from their own practice, it is imperative to make the conditions and context of that practice supportive of high and cumulative levels of achievement for all students. Which leads to the last principle under knowledge and skill, which is . . .

Context matters.
Improvement requires a more or less specific understanding or theory about what matters in a given context—a classroom, a school, a school system—in line with the overall purposes and standards by which performance is being judged. Any accountability system, any system of improvement, any professional development strategy must relate the particularities of the student body, the classroom, the school, and the system to the overall demands being made on the entire school system.

The level of expertise among teachers is important. It determines the starting point for work on instructional issues and, hence, the professional development capacity of schools and school systems. Teachers' level of experience, knowledge of subject matter, and facility with collaborative work form the bedrock for developing group norms and forms of collaboration around specific instructional practices. The students, their prior knowledge and skill, their family and community contexts, and their previous educational experiences influence teachers' attitudes, expectations, and practices. The norms, values, and expectations that teachers hold about student learning and their own practice guide teachers' focus on new practices that they see as useful to their daily work. While it's possible, indeed necessary, to have broad standards of quality and performance for teaching practice and even specific priorities for which content areas and which grade levels are the priorities for professional development, this broad guidance takes complicated translation for specific schools and teachers to use it to improve the system as a whole.

In general, knowledge and skill are at the core of school improvement. If you don't know what kinds of knowledge and skill are required to improve student learning, if you can't recognize different levels of expertise in that core knowledge, and if you don't have a working theory for how to build greater expertise in teaching practice, then it's unlikely that more resources spent on professional development will make any difference to student learning.

Incentives

Any plan of improvement has to address the motives of individuals and of groups, their willingness to pursue a common purpose through collaborative activity that is likely to entail great effort, uncertainty, and alteration in established norms and habits. The question of motive is especially significant for the typical school, where most people experience their work as difficult and complex without the additional burden of collaborative effort. Few people willfully engage in practices that they know to be ineffective; most educators have good reasons to think that they are doing the best work they can under the circumstances. Asking them to engage in work that is significantly different from what they are already doing requires a strong rationale and incentive. This is probably the aspect of performance-based accountability and improvement that has received the least attention.

In general, the theory of performance-based accountability is that providing communities, parents, teachers, and administrators with evidence of student performance, coupled with rewards and sanctions for high and low performance, will stimulate schools and school systems to focus on doing what is necessary to improve student learning. We now know, of course, that there are serious problems with this theory: People in schools often don't know what to do to fix the problems and don't have access to the resources that are necessary to learn. Schools and school systems often do things—teaching test items rather than real content, for example—that manifestly are bad educational practice but that help them raise test scores quickly. And, under the new performance-based system, schools often compete for the students who are most likely to succeed rather than learning how to succeed in educating the students that they have.

Ideas about the use of incentives to accompany performance-based accountability are also underdeveloped. The incentives that are available to policymakers are fairly blunt instruments: publication of test scores; student promotion, retention and graduation; identification and classification of schools by performance levels; cash awards to individuals or schools; and the takeover or reconstitution of failing schools. The characteristic that all of these incentives share is that they have virtually no relationship to the knowledge and practice of improvement. The data, the penalties, the administrative drama of designating failure or placing blame—none of these tells school staff anything about how to advance student and adult learning. In other words, the important question for the design of an effective improvement process is not so much which external incentives are available to press schools for higher levels of performance, but rather what *responses* by schools and school systems are most likely to increase learning and performance.

In fact, while there are many problems with the design and implementation of performance-based accountability systems, the most serious difficulty lies with the inadequacy of the responses that schools and school systems have made to the policies. And it is mostly not their fault. Most schools are unprepared to respond effectively to any performance-based accountability system, whether well designed or poorly designed. Since school preparedness is so central, it makes sense to look at the improvement process at the classroom and school levels, then from the perspective of the broader system. What kinds of incentives are likely to engage teachers and administrators in professional development that improves practice? The research gives us some useful guidance on this question.

Internal accountability precedes external accountability and is a precondition for any process of improvement.

Schools do not "succeed" in responding to external cues or pressures unless they have their own internal system for reaching agreement on good practice and for making that agreement evident in organization and pedagogy. We know this from the many studies of effective schools —that is, the schools that have the most effective professional development programs and the schools that accommodate accountability most successfully. These schools have a clear, strong internal focus on issues of instruction, student learning and expectations for teacher and student performance. In academia, we call this a strong internal accountability system. By this we mean that there is a high degree of alignment among individual teachers about what they can do and about their responsibility for the improvement of student learning. Such schools also have shared expectations among teachers, administrators, and students about what constitutes good work and a set of processes for observing whether these expectations are being met (Little, 1993; Newmann & King et al., 2000).

No externally administered incentive, whether it be reward or sanction, will automatically result in the creation of an effective improvement process inside schools and school systems. Nor will any incentive necessarily have a predictable effect across all schools. The effect of incentives is contingent on the capacity of the individual school or school district to receive the message the incentive carries, to translate it into a concrete and effective course of action, and to execute that action. Incentives have a differential effect, depending on the capacity of the settings in which they work, with the differential effects of accountability systems being relatively predictable. Schools with weak internal accountability systems are likely to respond to external incentives in fragmented, incoherent, and ineffective ways. Schools with relatively strong internal accountability systems are likely to respond in more effective and coherent ways.

The most direct incentives are those embedded in the work itself; the further away from the work, the less powerful and predictable is an incentive's effect.

School personnel are more likely to work collaboratively to improve performance if the work itself is rewarding and if the external rewards support and reinforce work that is regarded as instrumental to increased quality and performance. Kelley, Odden, and their colleagues (Kelley, Odden, Milanowski, & Heneman, 2000) studied the effects of school-based performance award systems—systems that provide monetary awards to schools for gains in student achievement. They found that the actual monetary reward was often cited by teachers for its importance, but that teachers also valued their own personal satisfaction in seeing improved student achievement, opportunities to work with other teachers on instructional problems, a sense of solidarity in achieving schoolwide goals, and public recognition of their success. Teachers also engaged in their own cost/benefit analysis of external performance incentives. They actively calculated the value of the rewards, tangible and intangible, against the increased pressure and stress that came with performance-based accountability, expressing doubt about the likelihood that policymakers would actually meet their commitments if schools demonstrated widescale improvement.

Given the atomized structure of most schools, it seems improbable that external rewards will, in and of themselves, transform these organizations into coherent, supportive environments for student and adult learning. A more likely scenario, in parallel with the Guskey (1989) argument, is that teachers and administrators will learn the value of successful collaboration from experience, then make the connection between this work and any external rewards or sanctions. It also seems probable that, within the work, visible evidence of student learning will be the most immediate motivator for continued improvement. Certainly it also makes sense to assume that teachers and school leaders will view stability in the level of resources committed to improvement as a basic condition for the investment of their own increased effort. The work itself, then, is the primary motivator for learning and improvement. If the work is not engaging and if it is not demonstrably beneficial to student learning, then any incentives are likely to produce weak and unreliable effects.

Both individual and collective incentives, skillfully designed, can support professional development and large-scale improvement.

School-based incentives are collective rewards; they accrue to the school as a whole or to the individuals who work in the school on the basis of their collective performance. What about individual rewards—rewards that accrue to particular teachers and particular administrators based on their individual work? There is reason to worry that individual incentives might reinforce the existing atomization of schools. As previously stated, individual teachers accumulate points toward salary and step increases by accumulating academic credits from courses that may have no relationship to their school's performance. Many districts also offer professional development activities on a space-available basis for which teachers sign up as individuals, usually disconnected from any school-improvement plan or schoolwide priority. The large-group workshops and school-level meetings that are typical of professional development days also tend to be only loosely related to actual classroom needs. Thus, the structure of professional development reflects and reinforces the atomized, individual incentive structure of schools and school systems. This in turn undermines the possibility of using collective resources—the time of teachers and administrators and the money that is used to purchase outside expertise—to support a coherent and collective improvement of practice. In this instance, individual rewards and incentives work against the objective of overall improvement.

Yet it may be possible to design a system of individual rewards that reinforce large-scale improvement. Not all incentives for large-scale improvement have to be collective, and it's possible for individual incentives to play a powerful role in an overall improvement process. Kelley and Odden (1995), for example, have proposed a knowledge- and skill-based compensation system that ties individual salary increments, step increases, and bonuses to professional development activities and demonstrated competencies in domains of practice that are important to school and systemwide improvement. Thus, teachers could be rewarded for gaining and demonstrating knowledge and skill in new instructional strategies for literacy or mathematics that are tied to the school's and/or school system's performance goals. A similar but broader incentive would be to give increased compensation and responsibility to teachers who successfully complete the performance-based certification process of the National Board for Professional Teaching Standards (NBPTS), an independent professional organization that focuses on the certification of teachers for advanced levels of competency. The design of the incentive structure and uses of incentives are probably more important than the types of incentives that are used.

It seems improbable, however, that a large-scale improvement process could work without strong, stable, and consistent collective incentives for the improved knowledge and skill of individual educators, as well as for the school's development of a more coherent internal accountability system. The addition of an external accountability system could send a strong signal that society expects school personnel to work in concert to improve student achievement. Currently, many schools are not much more than organizational fictions—places where adults interact with students in the classroom, but which have little adult interaction and a weak organizational identity in the lives of the those who work there. Such organizations are not designed to engage in systematic, cumulative, collective learning about how to reach progressively higher levels of quality and performance. Thus, the fundamental problem of incentives is how to engage school personnel in work that is rewarding in some immediate, personal way, but that also encourages collaborative work around the shared purposes of the organization.

Capacity

Accountability systems and incentive structures, no matter how well designed, are only as effective as the capacity of the organization to respond. The purpose of an accountability system is to focus the resources and capacities of an organization toward a particular end. Accountability systems can't mobilize resources that schools don't have. School responses to accountability systems vary, depending on how well they manage themselves around collaborative work on instructional improvement. Accountability systems don't cause schools to improve; they create the conditions in which it is advantageous for schools to work on specific problems, to focus their work in particular ways, and to develop new knowledge and skills in their students and staff. The capacity to improve precedes and shapes schools' responses to the external demands of accountability systems.

Most state accountability structures are either blind or relatively ineffectual in regard to the question of capacity. Some states, notably Kentucky and Texas, provide technical assistance to failing schools, but the statewide scope of the capacity problem far exceeds states' commitment of resources to these efforts. Some states also have created networks to provide technical assistance and professional development to teachers and administrators around curriculum content, standards, and performance measurements. However, most states' efforts are uninformed by any particularly powerful models of large-scale improvement. The networks are largely disconnected from the daily, detailed work of schools, and so in some ways may reinforce the isolation that exists within schools. Lack of capacity is the Achilles' heel of accountability. Without substantial investment in capacity-building, all that performance-based accountability systems will demonstrate is that some schools are better prepared than others to respond to accountability and performance-based incentives, namely, the ones that had the highest capacity to begin with. This is not exactly what the advocates of performance-based accountability had in mind (Elmore, 2001).

When experts are asked what they would do about the capacity problem in schools and school systems, they invariably recommend more spending on professional development, as if any increase in professional development activity will automatically increase capacity and student performance. The problem with this prescription is that it confuses cause and effect. If schools and school systems understood the importance of professional development to their overall performance, they would of course already be spending their own money on it and spending it in a targeted and coherent way. The fact that most school systems do not already have a coherent and powerful professional development system is itself evidence that they would not know what to do with increased professional development funding. Investing in more professional development in low-capacity, incoherent systems is simply to put more money into an infrastructure that is not prepared to use it effectively. Thus, the question of capacity precedes and coexists with the question of how much new money should be invested in professional development.

Capacity is defined by the degree of successful interaction of students and teachers around content.

Defining the connection between professional development and capacity requires us to understand what capacity is, how to reach it with professional development, and what resources are available for this. If investments in it are to be directly related to improvement, the definition of capacity has to be rooted in instruction. Cohen, Raudenbush, and Ball (2002) define instructional resources, or capacity, as the knowledge, skill, and material resources that are brought to bear on the interaction among students, teachers, and content. They argue that none of these three elements can be treated in isolation from the others. One cannot, for example, enhance teachers' knowledge and skill without also addressing what teachers know about reaching individual students and the actual curriculum that teachers are expected to teach and students are expected to master. Likewise, you can't insist on the mastery of more rigorous content without also asking whether teachers have the requisite knowledge and skill to teach it, and where students are in their own learning relative to where the content is pitched. Nor can you "improve" student achievement without understanding what students bring to the learning, what teachers understand about student learning and in what content domain, using what curricular materials and resources, teachers and students are expected to function.

This simple, powerful model of capacity relates to the conditions under which instruction occurs. The existence of capacity in a school is evident in the interaction among teachers and students around content. Investments in capacity that do not directly affect this interaction are unlikely to improve either the quality of instruction or student learning. It also suggests that there are three entry points, or portals, for the development of capacity: teachers, students, and content. Professional development works as a capacity-building device to the extent that it enters each of these portals and acknowledges the relationship among them. The model also suggests that all schools and school systems have solutions to the problem of instructional capacity embedded in their existing teaching practices and organizational arrangements, and that enhancing capacity consists of unpacking these existing arrangements, diagnosing how they support or undermine what the school system is trying to accomplish, and changing them to be consistent with collective goals for improvement.

EFFECTIVE USE OF PROFESSIONAL DEVELOPMENT REQUIRES HIGH ORGANIZATIONAL CAPACITY

Returning to the relationship between professional development and organizational capacity, the Cohen et al. (2002) model explains why investment in professional development by low-capacity schools and school systems often has no effect or a negative effect on morale and performance. Professional development affects teachers, that is, its use assumes that giving teachers new skills and knowledge enhances the capacity of teachers to teach more effectively. But, if it consists only of that, it is likely to have a modest to negative effect because the teacher usually returns to a classroom and a school in which the conditions of instruction and the conditions of work are exactly the same as when he or she began the professional development. The students are exactly the same. The content is exactly the same, or only slightly altered by the new materials introduced through the professional development. The teacher begins to teach and discovers that the ideas that seemed plausible during training don't seem to work in the school or classroom context. The "real world," in the language of teachers, overwhelms the new idea, no matter how powerful or well demonstrated in theory. If this professional development cycle is run repeatedly, it produces a negative reinforcement pattern. Teachers become cynical about any new idea when no previous new idea has worked. The low capacity in this situation is the inability of the organization to support the teacher in navigating the complex interactions among the new skills and knowledge he or she has acquired, existing patterns of student engagement, and the modifications to curricula and content that may be necessary to execute the new practices in this particular setting with these particular students.

Under these circumstances, it is a gargantuan task for teachers to actually improve their practice: They would have to assimilate the new knowledge and skill at a relatively high level of understanding (how one does that without actually practicing the skill repeatedly is a mystery, like learning to fly an airplane or play tennis by reading a book or watching a videotape). Immediately, they would have to transfer that knowledge into a setting in which student responses are highly unpredictable, and probably predictably disappointing on the first try. And they would somehow have to invent the curriculum materials that are necessary to align the new skill to the particular classroom: All this in real time. It seems, on its face, absurd to expect anything other than a pro forma response to this kind of professional development.

When you begin to describe the organizational conditions under which professional development actually contributes to instructional capacity in schools, you begin to describe an organization as it rarely exists. Such an organization would only require teachers to learn new skills and knowledge if it were prepared to support their practice of these skills in real classrooms, providing experts to work with teachers as they master these skills and adapt them to their students' responses to the new practices and materials. It would be an organization that offered consistent messages to principals, teachers, and students about what goals are most important and what resources are available to support the work of meeting them. It would be an organization in which administrators, at the school and system level, think their main job is to support the interaction of teachers and students around the mastery of specific content. And, it would be a system in which no judgments about performance, of teachers or students, are made without first ensuring that the conditions for high performance have been met; a system in which no one is expected to demonstrate knowledge and skill that they haven't had the opportunity to learn.

These conditions create a formidable agenda of organizational redesign for most schools and school systems. System officials would have to have considerable expertise about the instructional practices they expect teachers to acquire. That expertise would have to entail not just teaching teachers how to teach differently, but actually working with teachers in their classrooms to solve problems of practice in a way that supports continuous improvement. The system would have to manage its resources to support and fund the work of teachers and professional developers in sustained interaction. It would also have to set priorities, clearly stating which problems of instructional practice are central and which peripheral to overall improvement before deciding how to allocate professional development resources. Schools would have to become learning environments for teachers as well as for students. The instructional day would be designed to facilitate the learning of both groups, and the learning of educators, inside and outside of the classroom, would have to be arranged to avoid any disruption to student learning. And, it would be up to administrators to negotiate with the system at large to secure the resources necessary for implementation. In other words, to use professional development as an instrument of instructional improvement, schools and school systems will have to reorganize themselves in order to make substantial changes in the conditions of work for teachers and students.

Effective professional development requires the development of expertise as an organizational capacity, and this requires differentiated organizational roles.

One of the strongest social norms among school faculty is that everyone is expected to pretend that they are equally effective at what they do. However, most people who work in schools know (or at least claim to know) who the "good" teachers are. Teachers themselves will, under the right circumstances, talk candidly about who the strong and weak teachers are reputed to be. Teachers who threaten this pretence, either by publicly distinguishing themselves as expert teachers or by being singled out as a model within their schools, may have to pay a price in social ostracism.

Yet the entire process of improvement depends on schools making public and authoritative distinctions among teachers and administrators based on quality, competence, expertise, and performance. If everyone is equally good at what they do, then no one has anything to teach anyone else about how to do it better. Thus, educators' pretence of absolute equality is a major impediment to improvement and a significant factor in determining the capacity of schools to engage in effective professional development.

In a previous paper (Elmore, 2000), I argued that developing the capacity to lead instruction requires a differentiated role for "leaders" and a model of distributed leadership in which those with different roles and competencies could work cooperatively around the common task of instructional improvement. This same argument applies to creating and sustaining capacity using professional development. To improve themselves, systems need to be able to identify people who know what to do, to develop the capacity of those in the organization to learn what to do, and to create settings in which people who know what to do teach those who don't. Instructional expertise is a key element of organizational capacity in regard to the use of professional development. One could argue that a school system's capacity to make productive use of professional development is directly related to its willingness to make binding and public judgments about quality and expertise.

One possible source of the presumption of equal competency is the widely held belief that teaching practice cannot be evaluated due to its highly complex, uncertain, and indeterminate nature. It is easy to make mistakes in judgment about better and worse teaching, and it is particularly easy to make egregious mistakes when those who make the judgments know little about what constitutes expert practice. In most systems, the administrators who are assigned the responsibility for evaluating teachers are not selected for their expertise in instruction; indeed, most of their work has nothing to do with instruction. So it's not surprising that teachers distrust proposals for individual assessment of their quality and competence. Their misgivings are well founded.

For distinctions in expertise to be credible among teachers, they have to be rooted in the core issue of instructional capacity. That is, distinctions in expertise probably won't be institutionalized unless they grow out of the work of analyzing and improving student learning. Just as individual teachers are more likely to adopt new practices after powerful improvement in student learning has been demonstrated to them, so too must the distinctions in expertise be observable in actual classroom practice before they will be generally acknowledged.

The good news: The money is probably there. The bad news:
It's already being spent on something else.

Just as it is probably fruitless to spend more money on professional development in schools and school systems that haven't developed the capacity to use it effectively, so too is it problematic to invest more money in professional development if schools and school systems don't know how their current monies are being spent. The purchase of time for teachers to participate in professional development on a large scale, staffing arrangements that permit some teachers to work full or part-time as professional developers, the hiring of outside experts to consult on questions of design and to provide support to teachers and administrators, recruiting and training administrators with deep instructional knowledge, creating time for observation and analysis of students' responses to new types of instruction—all of these activities are very expensive, especially if they are done at scale in all schools and classrooms. The first response of most administrators to these ideas is that they would be happy to try them if someone else would pay for them, usually meaning the next level of government above the one in which they are working. This is the theory of federalism as stated by Daniel Elazar, the renowned political scientist: The appropriate level of government to perform a given function is always the one you're working in; the appropriate level of government to pay for that function is always the one above your own.

But there is a major problem with this theory. School systems that are not spending their own professional development dollars effectively are unlikely to be more effective in spending other peoples' money. More support for professional development from any level of government is unlikely to improve practice unless schools and school districts are already using their own resources effectively.

The evidence is now substantial that there is considerable money available in most district budgets to finance large-scale improvement efforts that use professional development effectively. The money is there. The problem is that it's already spent on other things and it has to be reallocated to focus on student achievement. The sources of revenue are obvious, but using them means tackling the central problem of how schools and school systems are managed. Substantial funding can be found by reducing the staffing demands of specialized programs for teachers and students, carefully tracking differential staff patterns across schools and grade-levels, scheduling larger blocks of instructional time, refocusing categorical and special purpose funding on instructional purposes, reallocating non-instructional administrative funds to serve instructional purposes, and, most importantly, reallocating and focusing existing expenditures on professional development (see, e.g., Miles, 1995; Miles & Darling-Hammond, 1998).

To say that the money is available of course begs the question of why it is not being spent on professional development and improved student achievement already. The answer to that question is that school systems have never had an incentive to evaluate and manage the resources they use around a coherent instructional agenda. Instead, the money that districts spend on instruction tends to be compartmentalized to meet specific external demands and specific incremental decisions at the system and school levels. As with other problems of capacity, the problem of resources can only be addressed by making the improvement of student learning the central priority and then deciding whether the available resources are adequate to the task.

A potential strength of performance-based accountability systems is that they create an incentive system in which schools and school systems are rewarded for developing a coherent focus on teaching and learning, then changing their staffing arrangements and budgets to reflect this. But many schools and school systems are going to need help in understanding what must be done, as well as executing the range of actions they will have to take in order to increase their capacity to use professional development to respond to the new accountability systems. Most people in schools and school systems are not prepared for these changes. People in low-capacity schools and school systems are even less prepared. States and localities need to markedly increase the volume of information and assistance available to schools around organizational capacity issues and to engage in more open experimentation to identify more effective ways of focusing and raising capacity.

CONCLUSION: DEVELOPING THE PRACTICE OF IMPROVEMENT

American public education is leaving a period in which questions of practice and its improvement were essentially pushed into the classroom, where doors were shut and teachers were left to develop their own ideas and practices, largely unsupported by the organizations in which they worked. The next stage of development in American education, propelled by the advent of performance-based accountability, requires the development of a practice of continuous school improvement—a body of knowledge about how to increase the quality of instructional practice and boost student learning on a large scale across classrooms, schools, and entire school systems. At its core is professional development, the process of professional learning for the purpose of improving student achievement.

I have tried to sketch out one view of what theoretical and practical knowledge might constitute a practice of improvement and how professional development fits into that practice. I have argued that the conventional wisdom about effective professional development provides an adequate working theory to guide practice. I have also argued that there are deep organizational and cultural reasons why schools and school systems are not likely, in their present form, to make effective use of professional development. Investing more professional development funds in systems that have not begun a serious practice of improvement is unlikely to produce any discernible increase in student learning. In order for professional development to work as a cumulative learning process, it has to be connected to the practice of improvement. In my view, that practice must entail attention to what knowledge and skill educators require to improve student learning and how people come to master that knowledge, which incentives encourage people to engage in the difficult and uncertain process of changing their teaching and administrative practice, and what resources and capacities are required to support the practice of improvement.

There are several aspects of the idea of a practice of improvement that are counter-cultural to the current organization of American schools. We should acknowledge these conflicts explicitly, rather than pretending that they don't exist. First, the task of improvement is one that schools and school systems are not designed to do and may be one that some people who work in schools think is neither possible nor worthwhile. If you are steeped in a culture in which all practice is essentially invented in classrooms, and in which your daily work life provides you no access to challenging ideas about how to do your work better, it is not surprising that you would think that large-scale improvement is an improbable idea.

Second, existing norms about knowledge and expertise work against improvement. The belief that experience alone increases expertise in teaching, or that those with less experience but more access to knowledge might be qualitatively better teachers than those with more experience and less access to knowledge, works against the possibility that new knowledge can dramatically improve teaching practice. The belief, at least in public, that all teachers are equal in their skill and knowledge and that all teaching practice is the same undermines the possibility that teachers can learn from each other in powerful ways, as well as learning from experts who are not part of their immediate circle of colleagues.

Third, the existing occupational and career structure in schools and school systems is completely inadequate as a basis for improvement. Teaching is a largely undifferentiated occupation, while improvement demands that it become more differentiated—allowing teachers who have developed strong expertise in particular domains to lead the improvement of instruction in those domains by working as mentors, coaches, and professional developers. Administration is a highly differentiated occupation in which the categories of specialization have little or nothing to do with the core function of the organization, which is instruction. Improvement requires a less differentiated administrative structure with more focus on the skills required for the practice of improvement. Mobility among roles is presently limited, while the practice of improvement requires flexibility and movement, so that people with expertise can move into places where their knowledge and skill can be connected to practice more immediately.

Fourth, the design of work in schools is fundamentally incompatible with the practice of improvement. Teachers spend most of their time working in isolation from each other in self-contained classrooms. In most schools and school systems, time away from the direct practice of instruction is considered time that is not spent "working." Hence, learning how to teach more effectively, if it is acknowledged at all in the structure of work, is either done on the teacher's own time through evening or summer courses, or is wedged into short periods of time released from "regular" instructional duties. The problem with this design is that it provides almost no opportunity for teachers to engage in continuous and sustained learning about their practice in the setting in which they actually work, observing and being observed by their colleagues in their own classrooms and in the classrooms of other teachers in other schools confronting similar problems of practice. This disconnect between the requirements of learning to teach well and the structure of teachers' work life is fatal to any sustained process of instructional improvement.

Fifth, the culture of passivity and helplessness that pervades many schools works directly against the possibility of improvement. Schools with weak internal accountability structures assign causality for their success or failure to forces outside their control: the students, their families, the community, the "system." Schools with strong internal accountability assign causality for their success or failure to themselves: to the knowledge and skill they bring to their work, to the power of shared values, and to the capacities of their organizations. The historic absence of clear guidance for schools around issues of performance and accountability has spawned an extensive and resilient culture of passivity, while the practice of improvement requires a culture of coherence and responsibility.

Teachers and administrators learn this culture of passivity and helplessness as a consequence of working in dysfunctional organizations, not as a consequence of choosing to think and behave that way. Improving the organization will change what adults learn.

In developing a practice of improvement, it is possible to confront these contradictions more or less directly, with more or less tactical and strategic skill, but it is not possible to avoid them altogether. Grace, humility, and humor are virtues well suited to this work. The creaking and grinding sounds emerging from schools and school systems over the foreseeable future are the sounds of a nineteenth-century structure passing quickly through the twentieth century in order to confront the demands of the twenty-first. This will not always be a beautiful and edifying process. It will often look exactly like what it is, a wrenching undertaking that involves large numbers of people learning how to do something they previously did not know how to do and developing increasingly high levels of expertise.

So the practice of improvement is about changing three things fundamentally and simultaneously: 1) the values and beliefs of people in schools about what is worth doing and what it is possible to do; 2) the structural conditions under which the work is done; and, 3) the ways in which people learn to do the work. A powerful principle that I think derives from research and practice is that this kind of difficult, contingent, and uncertain learning is best done in close proximity to the work itself. And the work of schools is instruction.[2] Teachers acquire different values and beliefs about what students can learn by observing their own students and students like theirs in other settings, learning things that they, the teachers, might not have believed possible. Teachers and administrators learn how to connect new knowledge and skill to practice by trying to do specific things in the classroom and by asking themselves whether there is evidence that, having done these things, students are able to do things they were not able to do before. School administrators and teachers learn to change the conditions of work by trying new ideas in the context of specific curriculum content and specific instructional problems, grade-level conferences, and observations around particular problems of math or literacy instruction, for example. System administrators learn to change structures and resource-allocation patterns by observing what effective practice in schools looks like and trying to figure out how to support it. Learning by these adults that is not anchored in the work is unlikely to lead to durable and supportive changes in the conditions under which the work is done.

Essentially, the practice of improvement is a discipline of understanding how good work, and the learning of good work, can be supported and propagated in schools and school systems. It is fashionable among people who work on problems of "change" and improvement in schools to argue that a deep transformation of schools will require a long time and much more money. All things in education seem to require a long time and much more money. I hope my argument in this paper brings a note of healthy skepticism on both counts. First, improvements in instruction have *immediate* effects on student learning wherever they occur, and these effects are usually demonstrable through skillful assessment and observation of students' work. The effects in the short term may not be widespread; certain settings may lag behind others in seeing the effects, and certain classroom and school contexts may present more difficult improvement problems than others.

But, I think it is important to keep in mind that *students learn what they are taught,* when the teaching is done effectively and thoughtfully. So we should not peg our expectations for improvement in student performance on fancy and ambiguous theories about the uncertainty and contingency of educational "change." A central part of the discipline of improvement is the belief that if the teaching is good and powerful, and if the conditions of work enable and support that practice, then we should be able to see immediate evidence that students are learning. If we can't, then we should ask whether the teaching was really as good as we thought it was. A central part of the practice of improvement should be to make the connection between teaching practice and student learning more direct and clear. The present generation of students deserves the best practice we can give them and their learning should not be mortgaged against the probability that something good will happen for future generations.

Improvements should be focused directly on the classroom experience of today's students. I also have argued that the discipline of improvement requires major changes in the way schools and school systems manage the resources they already have—the time of teachers and administrators; the practices reflected in existing staffing patterns; administrative overhead; and the resources already being spent, largely ineffectively, on professional development—before we can tell how much additional money is needed to engage in large-scale improvement. This is more than a low-level accounting exercise; it is fundamental to the entire process of improvement. Adding money to a system that doesn't know how to manage its own resources effectively means that the new money will be spent the same way as the old money. Many foundations and government agencies have learned (or, more likely, haven't learned) this lesson the hard way. Yet there seems to be a kind of eternal optimism in the educational-change establishment that the next time we will get it right, that this new idea we have about *how* to give failing schools and school systems more money will make something happen that we were unable to make happen the last time. What seems clear is that the existing structure and culture of schooling is able to assimilate and deflect just about any attempt to influence it fundamentally using money as leverage. A system without a firm strategy for allocating its own money around the task of instructional improvement is like the carnivorous plant in the musical *Little Shop of Horrors;* it eats whatever it is fed and asks for more. The main work of resource allocation has to occur in schools and school systems, not in the policy and fiscal environment around them.

As this work occurs and as we get to know more about the actual resource requirements of large-scale improvement, it is quite possible that we will discover that it takes more money, maybe much more money, to do what needs to be done. But something fundamental will have changed in this process: We will actually know what the money is being spent on and what improvements in teaching practice and student learning we should expect because of it. I would love to write the paper that says why substantial infusions of new money into schools and school systems for professional development will produce higher-quality instruction and higher levels of student learning. I cannot write that paper now.

Professional development is at the center of the practice of improvement. It is the process by which we organize the development and use of new knowledge in the service of improvement. I have taken a deliberately instrumental view of professional development, that it should be harnessed to the goals of the system for the improvement of student achievement, rather than driven by the preferences of individuals who work in schools. There is disagreement in the field on this point. Many people who are knowledgeable about teaching and teacher professional development argue that teachers, as professionals, should be given much more discretion and control as individuals and in collegial groups in deciding the purpose and content of professional development. Indeed, their most powerful critiques of existing professional development practices follow from the insight that mandated teacher learning is an oxymoron (Hargreaves, 1991; Little, 1993). Poorly organized and bad professional development can be, as many educators will testify, a deeply insulting experience.

The use of professional development for purposes of large-scale improvement raises difficult questions of authority, autonomy, and control in school organization. We should not minimize these issues. It will require deep thought and skill to address them. My bias toward an instrumental view of professional development grows out my analysis of the pathologies of the existing structure and culture of schooling, as well as the knowledge that public school teachers and administrators are public professionals who are accountable for the effectiveness of their practice to public authorities and the tax-paying community, as well as to their clients. Hence, it is not a threat to their professional status to argue that their publicly funded professional development should be organized around a common agenda.

This said, however, I think it wise to take a developmental view on issues of authority, autonomy, and control in decisions about professional development. The practice of improvement should create more differentiated and flexible organizations in schools and school systems. The development and distribution of competence and expertise should result in more knowledgeable and powerful people operating in "boundary roles" as mentors, teacher leaders, and professional developers, as well as more knowledgeable and powerful people in the ranks of the teaching force and administration. This distribution of expertise and leadership means that schools and school systems will have to become more consensual in the way they make decisions about issues of professional practice, including professional development. And, I have argued, issues of accountability are essentially reciprocal anyway, since I can't meet your expectations for performance unless you support my learning. So, while professional development will continue to be instrumental to improvement, I expect that it will necessarily become much more consensual in its structure of authority. Knowledge-based organizations, which is what schools will become through the practice of improvement, are organizations designed around the authority of expertise, rather than the authority of position. What you know and the effect of what you know on student learning are more important than whom you know or what your title is.

As I said at the beginning, the development of the practice and discipline of large-scale improvement is a matter of some urgency. The consequences of performance-based accountability can be disastrous (at least for some schools and deleterious for others) if schools and school systems respond to demands for increased performance by pushing harder on the existing structure of schooling and demanding more from school personnel without acknowledging that few, if any, people actually know how to do the improvement work that must be done. We are now at the stage of understanding that schools and school systems have very different responses to pressure for performance, depending on the knowledge and skill embodied in their teaching and administrative staffs, their capacity to create a strong normative environment around good teaching, and their ability to muster and manage the resources required to begin the long process of raising the level of practice. The issue is what we will do with this knowledge, whether we will use it to, once again, affirm the self-fulfilling prophecy that some schools and the students in them are "better" than others, or whether we will enable all schools to become competent and powerful agents of their own improvement.

When Accountability Knocks, Will Anyone Answer?*

Most research on accountability in education is premised on the definition of accountability as something that exists only when it is imposed on schools by external authorities. From this perspective, the study of accountability consists of examining the effects of external accountability systems on how schools operate or how schools implement the requirements of externally imposed accountability systems.

When my colleagues and I undertook a large-scale accountability study under the auspices of the Consortium for Policy Research in Education (CPRE), we found this view of accountability to be suspect. It seemed presumptuous, we thought, to assume that schools had no idea to whom they were accountable, for what, or how, unless and until they were told so by external authorities. It seemed just as plausible to assume that all schools must have had to solve the problem of accountability simply in order to function, and that their solutions to the problem, whether explicit or implicit, would play an important role in determining how they would respond to the requirements of externally imposed accountability systems.

This essay examines the variety of ways in which schools decide to whom they are accountable, for what, and how. We develop a construct we call internal accountability to describe this array of solutions to the accountability

*This chapter was coauthored by Charles H. Ablemann, with Johanna Even, Susan Kenyon, and Joanne Marshall.

problem. And we hypothesize that schools will vary in their responses to external accountability requirements depending on their solutions to the internal accountability problem.

One essential lesson of this research, borne out by our later work as well as that of other researchers, is that schools with strong internal accountability—a high level of agreement among members of the organization on the norms, values, and expectations that shape their work—function more effectively under external accountability pressure. Likewise, schools with weak internal accountability—low agreement and atomization—tend not to do well. These lessons are played out across our subsequent work in high schools.

The major implication of this view is that strong internal accountability is a condition that precedes and determines a school's response to external accountability. Thus, investments in internal accountability must logically precede any expectation that schools will respond productively to external pressure for performance. Otherwise, schools will implement the requirements of external accountability systems in pro forma ways without ever internalizing the values of responsibility and efficacy that are the nominal objectives of those systems.

Pressure for increased school accountability is a distinctive hallmark of the present period of educational reform. Accountability, as presently defined in state and local educational policy, includes four major ideas: the school is the basic unit for the delivery of education and hence the primary place where teachers and administrators are held to account; schools are primarily accountable for student performance, generally defined as measured achievement on tests in basic academic subjects; school-site student performance is evaluated against externally set standards that define acceptable levels of student achievement as mandated by states or localities; and evaluation of school performance is typically accompanied by a system of rewards, penalties, and intervention strategies targeted at rewarding successful schools and remediating or closing low-performing schools (Ladd, 1996).[1]

These accountability policies are typically directed toward individual schools or teachers and, increasingly, students, as in Texas, New York, Virginia, and Florida, where exit exams or proficiency requirements are central to educational reform policies. Coupled with these new accountability systems, states and localities are often pursuing policies such as charter schools and choice programs that move schools outside the existing bureaucratic structure and are intended to sharpen the focus on academic quality and student performance. Growing political and fiscal pressure on schools lies behind this conception of accountability. The political pressure stems from the increasing visibility of school performance as a policy issue at the state and local levels and the increasing capacity of states and localities to measure and monitor student achievement. The fiscal pressure derives from heightened awareness about educational expenditures as a component of state and local budgets. Further, the results of the Third International Mathematics and Science Study (TIMSS) and the National Assessment of Educational Progress have fueled public concern over what American students are taught and know, in comparison with students from other countries.[2] Taken together, these pressures have created strong incentives for elected state legislators and local school board members as well as local administrators to take a continuing interest in school performance.

Nested within these developing external accountability systems are real schools: schools that have their own distinctive organizational characteristics and problems; schools that have unique student populations; schools situated in diverse and particular communities; and schools with their own institutional histories. The reality of particular schools belies the pressure for uniformity behind the emerging external accountability systems. External accountability systems assume a world in which *all* schools are held to the same expectations for student performance. The world that school administrators and teachers see, however, is bounded by their particular settings, by their own conceptions of who they are, who they serve, what they expect of students, and what they think of as good teaching and learning.

The long-term fate of educational reform, as it is presently conceived, lies largely in this tension between the uniform requirements of external accountability systems and the particularities of real schools. The new educational accountability systems will succeed or fail to the degree that they are designed with knowledge of how schools vary in their own conceptions of accountability. Part of what we hoped to learn in this study, the first phase of a five-year research project, was the language of accountability as it is used and operationalized in schools.

Therefore, we have chosen not to adopt the more precise definitions of accountability present in the literature on school reform, but to leave the definitions as open as possible.

This study is focused primarily on schools and how they construct their own conceptions of accountability. We chose this focus for conceptual and practical reasons. First, we are interested in understanding how teachers, administrators, students, and parents think about and behave toward accountability issues in schools, apart from how they respond to new external accountability systems. Schools function, in part, as accountability systems in their own right, and these systems are worth understanding in and of themselves. Second, we are interested in learning, from the variations we observe among schools, about the range of responses that schools of various types formulate to the problem of accountability. To the degree that schools vary in their responses to the accountability problem, we learn something about how conceptions of accountability are formed and how they change in the daily life of schools. Third, we are ultimately interested in joining our research on school-level accountability with research on external accountability systems to understand the sources of school-site variation in response to state and local accountability structures.

A WORKING THEORY OF SCHOOL-SITE ACCOUNTABILITY

Our research on school-site accountability was exploratory and formative in nature.[3] Our objective was to learn as much as we could about how people in schools actually think about accountability in their daily work. To do this, we conducted case studies in a diverse sample of twenty schools, roughly half located in a major metropolitan area on the east coast of the United States and roughly half located in another metropolitan area on the west coast. The school sample was intentionally constructed to maximize the likelihood that schools would vary in their conceptions of accountability. For example, we chose public comprehensive elementary and secondary schools, Catholic parochial elementary and secondary schools, independent private schools, charter schools, and public schools operating under special administrative arrangements. We also chose schools on the basis of variations in communities—schools serving predominantly affluent or poor communities, as well as urban and suburban locations. And we chose schools on the basis of their size and the diversity of their student population. It is important to note that none of these schools was located in a strong external accountability environment. In this exploratory study, we looked at schools in states and districts where strong accountability was just coming on line.

We spent the equivalent of two weeks in each school. Two researchers at each site observed classes, conducted focus groups with parents and students, and interviewed teachers and faculty. The interview protocol we used in conversations with teachers and administration was based upon a working theory described below. The protocol includes direct, indirect, and hybrid questions labeled according to how explicitly the accountability issue is addressed. In general, researchers relied upon the indirect and hybrid questions and found that responses to these questions flowed more freely than with the direct line of questions. Interviews with teachers were preceded by observation of a math or English lesson. This common point of departure provided the basis upon which to ask teachers, "To whom, for what, and how are you accountable in your daily teaching practice?"

To structure our field research in these case study schools, we developed a relatively simple working theory that we have continued to elaborate over the course of our research.[4] It continues to be a working theory in the sense that we will rework it as we understand more about how schools grapple with accountability.

The working theory begins from a set of four key premises. The first premise is that schools actually have conceptions of accountability embedded in the patterns of their day-to-day operations, whether they acknowledge these patterns explicitly or not. In order for schools to function, in other words, they have to establish channels, both formal and informal, through which individuals and the school as a whole may provide an account of behavior.

How, for what, and to whom this account is given may vary from school to school. The second premise is that these school-site conceptions of accountability are organic; they are built out of the raw material of human interactions around the work of teaching and learning and running an organization. Though it may not be explicitly articulated, we assume that basic notions of what it means to be a school—assumptions about how schools, in the most general sense, operate—influence teachers', administrators', parents', and students' conceptions of accountability in their particular context.[5] Schein (1992) describes this group culture as "a pattern of basic, shared assumptions that the group learned as it [solved] its problems of external adaptation and internal integration." A school's conception of accountability, then, can be revealed in the way teachers, administrators, students, and parents talk about fundamental issues of schooling. The third premise is that participants in schools are active agents in the creation of the conceptions of accountability under which they operate, and they can be active agents in changing these conceptions. Whether consciously aware of it or not, teachers, administrators, students, and parents act out their conceptions of accountability in their daily work; these conceptions, while relatively stable, can be changed, either in response to external pressure or out of intentional action at the school level. A fourth premise is that formal, *external* accountability systems are only one among many that influence a school's *internal* conception of accountability.

Schools form their conceptions of accountability from a variety of sources, including individual teachers' and administrators' beliefs about teaching and learning, their shared conceptions of who their students are, the routines they develop for getting their work done, and external expectations from parents, communities, and the administrative agencies under which they work.

Our working theory posits a set of relationships among three factors: individual conceptions of *responsibility*; shared *expectations* among school participants and stakeholders; and *internal and external accountability* mechanisms. An individual school's conception of accountability, in our view, grows from the relationship among these three factors (Wagner, 1989).

Responsibility

Individuals who are parties to schooling—teachers, administrators, students, and parents—have their own personal values that define their responsibilities toward others. Teachers, for example, may have strong views about their personal responsibility for student learning or the degree to which students and their families share this responsibility. Administrators may feel personally responsible for influencing teachers' instructional practice in particular ways, or they may locate responsibility for instructional practice primarily with teachers. The distinguishing characteristic of responsibility, in other words, is that it is personal and individual in nature and it stems from the values and beliefs of individuals. Individual conceptions of responsibility may come from a number of sources—from the life experience and moral background of the individuals, from their education and training, from their beliefs about the social determinants of student learning, and from their interaction with others. From the perspective of our working theory, we do not assume that individuals' conceptions of responsibility come mainly from their work environment or from formal accountability systems. Instead, subscribing to Lortie's (1975) assertion that teaching occurs primarily in isolation, we assume that organizational and external influences *may* play a part in teachers' perceptions of their role, but that individual values are *certainly* influential.

For example, individual English teachers may have strong beliefs about what constitutes a good essay, what constitutes a good book for students to read, what might be an acceptable number of books for a student to read in a year, or what might be an acceptable amount of homework to assign in a given week. They may also have strong beliefs about the capacities of their students to learn certain things. Further, teachers may include among their responsibilities students' emotional and physical well-being, and in some cases individuals may even perceive this responsibility as taking priority over curriculum requirements. Beliefs may be shared among English teachers, or they might lie in the domain of individual teacher discretion and vary widely among English teachers. To the degree that beliefs lie in the domain of individual discretion and relate to one's individual beliefs about his or her *own* behavior, we call them responsibility.

Expectations

Expectations, by contrast, are collective in nature and they characterize the shared norms and values of school participants developed to get the work of the school done. They are formed out of relationships among individuals, and they operate in often powerful ways to shape individuals' behavior and values. For example, first-grade teachers may have shared conceptions in a given school about how fluently first graders should be reading by the end of the school year. Or, they might have expectations of how much noise is tolerable from their colleagues' adjoining classrooms or of what constitutes good student decorum in the hallways. Parents may expect teachers to treat their children in certain ways in the classroom or to prepare their children for certain post-school futures. And, teachers may have expectations regarding the amount of time parents should spend supervising homework. Teachers and administrators together may form certain expectations about what academic work students from "their" community are capable of doing; these expectations may or may not be shared by students and their families.

The distinctive feature of expectations is that they are collective in nature—shared among individuals—although not necessarily with complete consensus among all the individuals in a given school. Further, expectations are beliefs about *others'* behavior, though individuals may include themselves within the collective for whom they hold these expectations. Certain expectations might be widely shared among all parties—teachers, administrators, students, and parents—or expectations might vary among groups or factions within a school. Different groups of teachers, for example, might have different expectations of what constitutes adequate student performance or decorum in the classroom. Teachers might have one set of expectations for students and parents might have another. So the fact that expectations are shared doesn't necessarily mean that they reflect a consensus among all parties in a given school.

Accountability

Accountability mechanisms are, literally, the variety of formal and informal ways by which people in schools *give an account* of their actions to someone in a position of formal authority, inside or outside the school. Some accountability mechanisms are *internal* to schools. Principals, for example, may require teachers to provide copies of their lessons, to write a daily schedule on the blackboard in their rooms, or to be available for supervisory duty in hallways, playgrounds, or lunchrooms. Some accountability mechanisms are *external* to schools. School districts may administer periodic student assessments, for example, and use the resulting data to influence what teachers teach. Accountability mechanisms, whether internal or external, take a wide variety of forms. They might be explicitly *formal* in character, as when written in a school handbook or district or state policy. They might also be relatively *informal*, as when a principal communicates to teachers that they should keep the noise level down in their classrooms, then engages in explicit monitoring of classrooms.

FIGURE 1 Interactions and Alignment

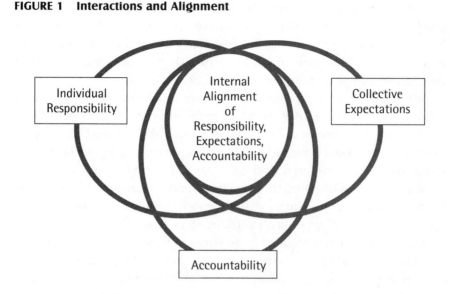

Likewise, accountability mechanisms vary considerably in their consequences for success or failure. The consequences might be communicated, with relatively *low stakes*, such as a principal's approval or disapproval communicated to a teacher for something that happens in that teacher's classroom. Or accountability mechanisms might carry relatively *high stakes*, as when a principal publicly praises or criticizes a teacher for disciplinary practices or when a district publishes in the local newspaper student academic performance data by schools.

In the context of our working theory, accountability carries a specific meaning. When we asked people in schools about accountability, we were interested in three factors: accountability for what; how they were required to give an account of their actions; and the consequences or stakes for failing to do so. In our working theory, responsibility, expectations, and accountability operate in a close mutual and reciprocal relationship with each other, and this relationship takes a variety of forms in different schools. This relationship is captured in Figure 1. Individual conceptions of responsibility may influence collective expectations or, alternatively, collective expectations may influence individual conceptions of responsibility. Similarly, individual conceptions of responsibility or collective expectations may influence formal or informal accountability systems, or vice versa. In Figure 1, we mean to convey that a given school's response to the problem of accountability is the result of how it resolves the tensions, inconsistencies, and complementarities between individuals' personal values, their shared expectations, and the mechanisms by which they account for what they do.

Implicit in the model presented in Figure 1 is the normative view that schools are likely to have more powerful internal accountability systems—formal or informal—if the values and norms embodied in these systems are *aligned with* individual conceptions of responsibility and collective expectations in the school. That is, internal accountability systems are likely to be powerful in their influence over individual actions to the degree that they are consistent with the values represented in individual responsibility and collective expectations.

Alignment can be produced in a variety of ways—for example, by deliberately choosing people who share a common set of values to participate in the school or by deliberately using the structures and processes of the organization to socialize people to a set of common views. To the degree that individual responsibility, expectations, and internal accountability systems are not aligned, one can expect various degrees of incoherence among individual beliefs and collective norms, and relatively weak internal accountability systems. We have said nothing yet in this analysis about *what* individuals or schools consider themselves to be responsible or accountable for. To say that there is a high degree of alignment between responsibility, expectations, and accountability is to say nothing specific about the purposes for which the school is aligned. Schools could, for example, have a high degree of alignment about values that stress student academic performance, or they could have alignment about values that stress order and discipline in the classroom and hallways but little or no agreement on academic goals. Alignment, then, refers to the consistency and strength of agreement inside the school, not the subject of that agreement.

Also implicit in the Figure 1 model is a normative view about the relationship between external accountability systems and the internal life of schools. If the power of internal accountability systems is a function of the alignment of responsibility, expectations, and internal accountability mechanisms, then the power of external accountability systems is a function of the alignment between the norms and values represented in these systems and the internal accountability mechanisms of schools.

FIGURE 2   Phoenix Charter School

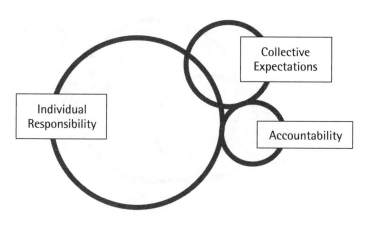

The effect of external accountability systems is mediated by internal accountability mechanisms. Schools might, for example, have a high degree of internal alignment around values and expectations that are quite inconsistent with the requirements of local or state accountability systems. Or, alternatively, schools may not be aligned around individual responsibility, collective expectations, and internal accountability, and, therefore, respond incoherently to relatively clear guidance from local or state accountability systems. In other words, how a school responds to external accountability systems is largely determined not by the details of those external systems but by the degree of alignment between the schools' internal accountability mechanisms and the requirements of the external accountability system.

For example, a school might have relatively weak common expectations for teachers and students and relatively weak internal accountability structures. In such a school, teachers' conceptions of their work would be largely driven by their individual sense of responsibility. As represented in Figure 2, the responsibility area would dominate our Venn diagram, and there would be very little overlap between the circles. Similarly, internal accountability measures, if they exist at all, would have relatively little influence. This school would be atomized; that is, fragmented into individual or very small units. Teachers would form their expectations for students and their ideas about what and how to teach largely out of their individual conceptions of responsibility. This school's response to any external accountability system, we pre-

FIGURE 3   St. Aloysius Elementary

dict, would reflect its internal incoherence. The requirements of the external system would be translated into idiosyncratic values and practices by individual teachers. Another type of school might have relatively strong common expectations about certain shared norms, and these expectations might be aligned closely with teachers' conceptions of personal responsibility. The graphic representation of this scenario is seen in Figure 3. Expectations dominate the diagram, but to a lesser degree than does responsibility in Figure 2, and with a more balanced relationship between the responsibility and expectations areas. A school might arrive at this state by recruiting teachers who already share a common view of teaching and learning and by creating internal structures and processes through which teachers share their personal beliefs and develop common expectations of each other. These shared expectations might be similarly extended to parents and students by recruitment of like-minded clients or active socialization. In some instances, coherence might be achieved by a community actively imposing its values on the school through sustained parent involvement or political influence in the recruitment of teachers and administrators.

Such a school might have either weak or strong internal formal accountability mechanisms. The school might simply operate on a daily basis, and teachers might define their work, based on shared expectations that are aligned with their sense of personal responsibility, with relatively few explicit rules or procedures designed to hold individuals

FIGURE 4 Turtle Haven Pilot School

accountable for their work. Or a school might extend its agreement at the level of responsibility and expectations into a relatively explicit internal accountability system of rules and procedures that provide a basis for teachers and students to account for their actions. This scenario is represented by Figure 4, where the strength of alignment between the three areas, and particularly between responsibility and expectations, functions as an informal accountability system.

This type of relatively cohesive school is characterized by a high degree of alignment between individual responsibility and collective expectations, and can possibly be complemented by a relatively explicit internal accountability system. Such a school might, in our working theory, respond to an external accountability system in a number of ways, including accepting and internalizing it; rejecting it and developing defenses against it; or incorporating just those elements of the system that the school or individuals deem relevant. Response to the introduction of an external accountability system would, we assume, depend upon the degree of alignment between the purposes of the external accountability system and the internal norms of a school.

Accountability for What, to Whom, and How?

A final part of our working theory addresses the issue of the purposes behind accountability systems. Most formal external accountability systems are predicated on the assumption that schools should be held accountable mainly for student academic performance. Viewed from the school level, however, the picture is far more complex. We addressed the issue of purpose by posing, in each of our schools, the question, *For what are you accountable, to whom,* and *how?* Schools are characterized, not surprisingly, by a wide variety of answers to the *for what* question, and the various answers they give to the *for what* question, not surprisingly, have very different implications for how they answer the *to whom* and *how* questions. In some schools, for example, teachers have explicit theories about the relationship between the characteristics of the children and the communities they serve and for what they as teachers are personally responsible or for what they are collectively accountable.

Some teachers, for example, believe that their responsibility and their formal accountability is, and should be, heavily shaped by the socioeconomic background of the children they teach. Children living in poverty, they argue, require social supports in the classroom and in the school that children not living in poverty do not require. When asked for what they are formally accountable, these teachers were apt to rephrase the question using the language of responsibility in place of accountability. Some teachers answered the *for what* question by stating their belief that they are responsible for providing a safe, nurturing environment for children. Other teachers believed that the socioeconomic background of the children they teach should have less importance in determining for what they are responsible or accountable. They answered the *for what* question by stating their belief that they are responsible for students' academic performance or their future success in school. These answers to the *for what* question have very different implications for how teachers answer the *to whom* and *how* questions. Teachers who see themselves as primarily responsible for providing a nurturing environment, for example, are more likely to say they are accountable to the children and their families.

In the following sections, we have organized observations from our first year of exploratory fieldwork into three categories, based upon the schools' responses to the problem of accountability. We reiterate that our findings are limited by the fact that the schools in the exploratory study were not located in strong external accountability environments. Within each section we feature a lead case, followed by several supporting cases that represent variations on the theme of the lead case. The categories are by no means exhaustive of the characteristics we observed in these schools, nor are the distinctions between categories quite so pronounced as they may appear in this format. No school is an absolute case of just one theme, but some are more typical than others in reflecting that theme.[6]

ATOMIZED ACCOUNTABILITY: INDIVIDUAL RESPONSIBILITY DOMINATES

For many teachers, the idea of accountability has little or no tangible reality in their daily work. They operate essentially as solo practitioners in isolated classrooms, relatively detached from the influence of outside forces. In this section, we examine four cases where this daily reality of isolation dominates conceptions of accountability.

The lead case, Phoenix Charter School, which we believe typifies the theme of this section, is a relatively new inner-city elementary school operating under a charter from the state. Phoenix students are disproportionately poor and minority. Phoenix may be unique because of its charter status and its corporate sponsorship, but in many ways it is similar to the other schools in our study that serve urban populations. Figure 2 indicates, by the relative size and independence of individual responsibility, that there is little internal alignment in this category of schools and that individual discretion is the primary mode of accountability.

Gateway, a small urban Catholic K–8 school situated across the street from a housing project, serves, like Phoenix, a heavily minority and disadvantaged student population. Stevens is a large urban middle school with a reputation for being relatively successful with its working-class and disadvantaged student population. Hutchinson is a large nineteenth-century public high school with a once-proud academic legacy and a recent history of student behavior problems. In all of these schools, accountability begins—and usually ends—at the level of individuals, particularly individual teachers.

Phoenix Charter School

To Whom Are You Accountable?
The Teacher-Student Relationship at Phoenix

Proponents of charter schools often claim that they are "the most accountable" kinds of schools. Schools that apply for and are granted charters must persuade their governing agency (the city or state) that they are able to teach children, in return for which they receive funding and autonomy from many state and local regulations. Most charter schools are reviewed annually through site visits and reports, and those who fail to meet the terms of their charter are subject to its revocation. In this sense, some say they exemplify a relatively clear and explicit kind of external accountability—one focused on parent choice and state oversight.

We might therefore expect that teachers at Phoenix would be concerned with this formal accountability, that they would be concerned with making sure their students' test scores increase or with teaching the curriculum mandated by their sponsoring corporation, or with their ongoing evaluation by their administrators. But in the case of Phoenix they are not. Teachers barely mentioned these kinds of formal accountability mechanisms in the course of our interviews. Instead, they spoke with passion and enthusiasm about being most "accountable" to the one group that has no formal power in schools at all—their students. In speaking about their relationships with students, they tended to use the term "accountability" to refer to what we have called personal responsibility. For Phoenix teachers, accountability is largely defined in terms of their individual responsibility toward students, rather than any formal or informal set of rules or procedures by which they account for what they do.

For example, one teacher, when asked to whom he is accountable, responded, "Kids. Twenty-eight kids. . . . That's why I'm here. That's why we're all here. So they can get educated. Get them ready for what they can expect when they get older." Such a response defies the traditional notion of accountability as a reciprocal relationship with consequences, because although teachers claim accountability to their students, students in this and other schools have very little, if any, formal influence. The teacher-student relationship is inherently one where teachers are given authority over their students, a position made fast by the schools' *in loco parentis* function. In return for the authority granted to teachers, teachers accept responsibility for their students. While students may certainly complain about their teacher or act in a way that makes her job easy or difficult, they do not themselves exercise any authority over the teacher or hold her accountable in any meaningful sense of that term, or claim responsibility for the teacher's actions. This most essential of school relationships is thus one-sided: Teachers accept personal responsibility for the students entrusted to them, but that responsibility is unreciprocated.

Students are minors, so society grants authority and responsibility to their parents or guardians. One would therefore expect that parents would represent their children in the teacher-student relationship: Teachers might not be accountable to their students, but they *could* be accountable to their students' parents. Some Phoenix teachers, when asked, did mention students' parents as the people to whom they were accountable, but did not feel that parents were accountable to them in return. While there was a core of very involved parents, most Phoenix teachers expressed frustration with the level of parent involvement. One teacher cited her nonattended parent conferences: "Last year I called them. . . . I would come in on a Sunday and nobody would show up. So that was kind of . . . sad. I just expected parents to care a little bit about their child's education. It's not like I ask them for too much either." Other teachers who said they were accountable to parents said they assumed that parental noninvolvement implied satisfaction. One teacher summarized his relationship with parents: "The fact that I don't really hear from them probably indicates that they're satisfied with what is happening. I make [laughs] that assumption. . . . I don't have the time to call parents when kids are acting up and suspended five days in a row from class. And I wish that they would call me. I mean, it's their kid; they should be calling me and letting me know if they want to know about their kid. They need to call me. So I wish they would call more. But any time I do call them, they're usually pretty supportive."

A Phoenix administrator pointed out that she has learned over the years that public schools cannot hold parents accountable for anything. There are always going to be parents who will be uninvolved, she said. This lack of parental involvement again presents teachers with a one-sided, unreciprocated relationship, which keeps them from being fully accountable to parents and from accepting parental accountability in return: The majority of parents simply aren't there. Because teachers are alone in the teacher-student-parent relationship, they assume more responsibility in it and for it.

Given the primacy of the teacher-student relationship and its one-sidedness, it is not surprising that when we asked Phoenix teachers, "To whom are you accountable?" many answered, "Myself." When we asked one teacher "who checks" to see if she is doing her job, she said, "No one, but *I* know. I don't want them [her students] to be lost." This attitude extends not only to teaching, but also to its auxiliary functions, such as record-keeping, about which one teacher said, "No one has ever checked it, and, to tell you the truth, I'm not very organized about it. I mainly am most accountable to myself. If I am not doing what I am supposed to be doing, then I am failing, and I have a problem with that." Other teachers spoke of self-checks, such as their ability to "sleep at night" or to "look in the mirror." Again, what these teachers were calling "accountability" is what we have defined as their own responsibility.

Based upon the organizational structure of schools, administrators are the obvious people to whom teachers are accountable. Administrators hire, evaluate, and fire teachers; in return, administrators are expected to provide supplies, curricula, and support. However, administrators are excluded from the basic teacher-student relationship upon which the work of schools is founded. Perhaps this outsider status explains why many teachers mentioned being accountable to their administrators only occasionally, and then only after mentioning students, parents, or themselves. This ambivalence is reflected even in attitudes toward evaluation, which one would expect to be the consequence that gives accountability its bite. One teacher said of his administrators' evaluation: "I don't see them [administrators] coming up and saying, 'This is what you need to work on.' I feel I'm doing a good job. The honest truth is that I really don't care [laughs] if they approve or not. I feel what I'm doing is correct." Other teachers told us of quietly disregarding administrative mandates such as curriculum. For example, although the corporation curriculum does not include spelling, one group of four regular classroom teachers and a special education teacher told us that they teach spelling anyway, using materials they purchased themselves. One teacher said, "I'm traditional. . . . They need to learn how to spell. So I start off with things around the room, and science words, and now I've bought a spelling book . . . boring. But they need that. They need that background. They . . . need a stronger way to decipher words."

Another teacher agreed: "Spelling isn't a curriculum in our school. *I* believe children need to memorize ten spelling words a week. So that's something that I do extra, and I give them packets to do it." These teachers also said that there is "no time" to teach spelling, so they send it home with their students even though, one reported, they are "not supposed to." Because teachers have little interaction with administrators other than the evaluations that most of them disregard, and because they *do* have a lot of interaction with their students, it is logical that their accountability to administrators is weaker than is their sense of responsibility to their students. As noted earlier, when there is weak internal accountability and weak expectations of teachers, teachers' sense of responsibility rules.

Teacher Responsibility for What?

When we asked Phoenix teachers for *what* they are accountable, their replies fell into three main categories: students' learning, classroom order, and students' well-being. In answering questions about their accountability, however, teachers frequently referred to their own sense of responsibility for learning, order, and well-being. The extent to which all teachers described feeling responsible for these areas places them in both the individual responsibility and collective expectations categories as defined in our study.

Student Learning: Student learning is the most obvious function of schools, and the school staff mentioned it as a matter of course. Teachers spoke sincerely and eloquently about their work with students, as this Phoenix teacher did: "Mostly I feel like I'm accountable to my students; I'm here to teach them, to make sure that they're learning what they're supposed to learn, and to present it to them in the best way that it's going to get to them." Another teacher said, "I'm supposed to teach them, and I plan to teach them. Like now I'm doing report cards, and when I write something down, I expect to be able to stand behind it and say, 'I did my best to teach this child' and 'I did my best assessing this child' through tests or observation or cooperative learning and everything like that."

And another teacher said, "My job is to teach the curriculum, to suit all the children in my classroom, regardless of their learning ability. So that's my responsibility. I need to find a way to teach everybody so that they . . . [are] basically on grade level."

These three teachers use the language of responsibility. Their comments were very I-centered: "I feel" and "I'm here" and "I plan." There is an implied assumption that they are "supposed" to do this, that the job requires it, and that someone might ask them to stand behind their assessment, but when we asked teachers where they got their ideas of what it means to be a teacher, they spoke not of their administrators or their teacher education programs or their colleagues, but of their own families, their own teachers, and their core values.

One teacher said, "I grew up in a family that was very—I started working when I was fourteen. They believed in work, they believed . . . every summer, every holiday, you went to work with the rest of the family. You did your part. . . . I've always been raised, myself, to . . . do the best at what you do, or don't do it. Find something else to do. . . . So as far as teaching, this is huge. I'm teaching twenty-eight children. . . . You think of it kind of like a privilege. My God, I've got these little minds, little brains, and I can fill them with all this good stuff and hope that they take something with them to the next grade."

Teachers' language revealed their intense desire to find "the best" way to teach "all the children." These teachers' responses were common among Phoenix teachers, so common that they confirmed the observation of another teacher that Phoenix has its own *culture*, one where "The kids are going to progress. And you're going to make sure that happens."

Order in the Hallways and Classrooms: For student learning and progress to take place, everyone at Phoenix believes that order is absolutely necessary, and this is the second area for which teachers claimed responsibility. Their results are immediately noticeable: Phoenix is bright and clean and free of graffiti. Students sit a certain way on rugs (cross-legged), line up a particular way when leaving (each student standing in a square floor tile), and stand a certain way in the halls (arms behind backs). The school has a citizenship program of rewards and punishments, which formalizes the emphasis on student behavior, and most teachers have their own point systems as well. When asked what to look for in a prospective job candidate, most teachers immediately mentioned the candidate's ability to discipline. One teacher elaborated: "I would say it has to start with discipline. I would either just tell [prospective candidates] point blank what we do here about discipline and what our expectations are as far as dress policy; and no talking in the halls; and when someone's talking, pencils are in the pencil holders; and people are not leaving their seats without permission; and using the bathroom all as a class at the same time. I would either just tell them straight up that's what we do, or I would ask them first what their approach to schooling is. And if they start talking about theory and great curriculum and stuff like that, and do not talk about the nuts and bolts of what you have to deal with during the school day . . . then I would probably think twice. . . . I would say, . . . 'This is how we do it. And if you don't like it, then, if you're more . . . touchy feely, and let the kids have this say and that say, then this isn't really going to be the place for you. . . .' Eventually you can get the kids to where they can do that. But initially it's got to be discipline, discipline, discipline."

At times it appears that order becomes an end in itself, rather than a means toward the end of learning. For example, we observed a lesson at Phoenix where directions were given after each math problem— "Chalk down! Chalk up!" —and for each step in clean up— "Collect paper towels. Put your slate in the middle, on top of the box. Bring me the box, go wash your hands." At the end of class the line for lunch had to be redone—lights off, students sent back to their seats, free time at the end of the day taken away, and the line re-formed. Each of these directions takes class time—in giving them and in following them. One could argue that time spent giving and following such directions saves time later, as students learn procedures and can move from task to task efficiently. But the lesson we observed was mid-year, and the directions did not seem necessary to that lesson. There seems to be no reason a lunch line would have to be re-formed except to maintain order as an end in itself.

The expectation that teachers will maintain order is one of the few expectations with which staff associate and anticipate professional consequences. They cited unsuccessful teachers who were not asked to return because their classrooms were "crazy" or administrators had to intervene frequently. By implication, teachers know they are doing a good job if their classrooms are quiet and administrators do not intervene. We asked one of the Phoenix administrators about this emphasis on order, and she offered two explanations. First, such order is necessary in order to maintain safety within the building, especially in case of fire; second, such order teaches children how to behave in society, which is necessary for them to be successful.

Students' Well-Being: Students' well-being is a broad concept that encompasses and depends on academic learning and discipline. That is, student well-being is necessary in order for students to learn, and their learning will improve their well-being. The urban teachers in our study shared what can be called almost a sense of mission to improve their students' lives—a mission that crosses teachers' race, gender, and class lines. Some of the Phoenix teachers worried about their students' survival. One teacher said of his students, "I . . . hope for them to live to see their adulthood . . . by not making a bad decision that will cost them their life. That's what I fear the most because they are inner-city kids." We heard this teacher and others in his cluster repeatedly talk to and about their students in terms of making "good decisions," a phrase usually referring to student behavior. One teacher called this kind of awareness "preparing students for life." We asked him how he would "teach life" in the lesson we observed and he said, "[Today] I didn't go off on a tangent, saying, 'If you don't follow directions, then you'll get fired from a job,' or whatever. Today it didn't really come up. But if there was a conflict there in the class today, then I might have gone off on, 'Well, you handle this situation out on the street, then you might end up dead or you're going to be locked up. If you handle that situation that way on the job, with a coworker or your boss, you might get fired from your job. Or if you're at school, you might get kicked out of school. If you're not turning your work in on time, you're going to get failed; you're going to get F's in college, and you're going to get kicked out of college.' That sort of thing."

Other teachers talked of teaching children "different values from home," such as not resolving a conflict through hitting. Some teachers talked of being role models (especially teachers of color), or of meeting students' emotional needs. At times these responsibilities led to ambiguity about the teacher's role. One teacher spoke of being both an emotional support and a disciplinarian. When asked what her students expect of her, she said: "Too much, actually. They think I'm their friend. They think I'm their mother [she imitates] : 'Ms. Dawson, can you unbutton my . . .' 'Ms. Dawson, can you do that?' And they would feel sick until I would say, 'It's okay, sweetie,' and give them a hug, and then they're fine for the rest of the day. But then it gets in the way of discipline, because when I say, 'Okay, now study for your science test,' they're around me, they're giving me a massage . . . and then I'll go crazy and then I'll start yelling and [she demonstrates]: 'Get in line. I'm not your friend. You need to get in line right now.' [She imitates student]: 'Geesh! I was just doing this!' And then I have a kid, Nikia . . . who writes me letters. . . . I should love her more, and why do I love this other kid? . . . And I say, 'Look, Nikia, I'm your teacher, not your friend.' [She imitates Nikia]: 'You can be my friend and my teacher at the same time.' And I said, 'No, I can't.' . . . I have two kids who lost their mothers . . . and they both . . . desperately need a female somebody."

Another teacher, wishing for more school social workers, talked about the tension between teaching students reading and acknowledging their difficult home lives: "Schools are becoming more than a place to learn. . . . Some of these kids come here at six in the morning, early morning, and they are here until seven-thirty when their parents pick them up and . . . the only time they are going to get counseling or anything is [in] school, and I think the role of school needs to be looked at and how it should be changed. I definitely think more counselors. Half these kids have a parent in jail, or a sibling. They come from neighborhoods where they can't go outside and then they expect them to read these silly books? . . . And I do think it is important for us, as teachers, not to excuse their behavior from where they came from, but to understand it. . . . Why is it important to read this book? What do we want out of it? And to really focus on, What we have gained by doing this? This is really hard for a kid to see." These teachers claimed responsibility for modifying their teaching practice in keeping with their students' needs, whether those needs are academic, social, or psychological.

Gateway Elementary School

One might expect teachers at Gateway, an inner-city Catholic school, to talk about accountability in religious terms: of being accountable ultimately to God or, on a more earthly plane, to the archdiocese. But they do not. Neither is religion an emphasis for learning: The principal reported that teaching students religion is not as important as "educating them so that they'll be able to better themselves in life . . . and sharing values with them."

Perhaps this lack of emphasis on religion is due to the fact that, although the new principal and one teacher are nuns and most of the staff is Catholic, most of the students are not Catholic. In this school where teachers were concerned with their students' very survival—for example, "I pray that they can make it through the summer without getting killed"—the teachers seemed to feel so responsible for their students that they were defensive about anything that referred to their students' poor academic performance, be it low test scores or letter grades. On report-card day, several teachers told their students, "Not everyone is an A student" and "Being average is OK as long as [you] are trying." While these remarks were probably reassuring to students, they did not reflect the priority on learning that the principal desired. At Gateway, when asked about responsibility, every teacher spoke about caring for the children. One teacher said, "I think most of us are here for the welfare of kids." She continued to talk about their welfare: "We are aware of the fact they're here for education. On the other hand, many kids are coming from homes with alcoholism and the last thing they care about is an adjective. So if I get hysterical about an adjective, I'm really doing them harm. So their welfare comes first, before their educational process, [or] whatever. I think we want them to be happy, [to] believe that in an atmosphere of happiness, friendliness, making friends, [and] safety here, that there's not going to be violence in the school yard, that there's not going to be drugs in the building, that they are safe and that they know that there are people here who really care about them, because I would say that we do. We really do. And then, secondly, we want them to succeed in high school and in college."

In the past, reported the principal, Gateway stressed the importance of safety and support rather than teaching and learning. This tension between support and learning was revealed in a story she related about sharing Gateway's low test scores with her staff, and what she perceived to be their response: "Ho-hum. . . . Well, it's an inner-city child who has no family, no motivation, is constantly underfed, tends to sleep in the classroom, and it's very difficult to reach them."

Not only were the teachers more concerned with their students' affective needs, but they also did not believe that the tests were a worthy measure of their students' learning. One teacher commented about the tests: "We don't do anything with them [the tests]. They do not relate to a lot of what these youngsters know. And they [the students] are not readers, so it is very difficult, I think, to have them do as well as they should."

The principal's concern about academic learning was supported by the archdiocese, which provides a formal curriculum and teaching guidelines. But the teachers were unevenly concerned with what the guidelines were or what they were to cover by the end of the year. Gateway is a school with little formal accountability to anyone outside the classroom, very low teacher expectations for academic potential, and very real teacher concerns about students' survival. Teachers seemed to define their roles as that of parent instead of teacher, as responsible for students' well-being and accountable primarily to themselves, with no theory about how to combine attention to affective needs with academic learning.

Stevens Middle School

Stevens is another school with little cohesion among the staff. When asked about accountability, one teacher responded, "[It's] individual all the way." Another teacher, when asked who is accountable to him, said, "I think the students are accountable to me, but who cares? Really, who cares? Except me." Here, too, there was a historical lack of formal accountability. The school has scored well on tests in the past, but the tests have a variable impact on classrooms.

Instead, teachers reported having autonomy over their practice and content. Like other teachers in our study, they said they were accountable to themselves, to their students, or both. There was an emerging sense of formal accountability to the principal because the district's new educational reform plan influences his retention, but this formal accountability was based on the staff's "trust and loyalty for the past twenty years." Administrators and teachers at Stevens agreed that their responsibilities reach beyond the schoolroom door, but there was little commonality in how they felt this responsibility should be met. One staff member said, "Middle school is a special kind of place. . . . We realized that we have to service the whole child because some of the parents can't, they're not able to. We just can't focus on the intellect here, and that's just part of the whole middle school emotional development . . . that's a big part of middle school education . . . just helping them through these years."

Other teachers referred to preparing students academically for high school, teaching organizational skills, and helping students enjoy learning. When asked what influences what she teaches, one teacher commented, "What I want my students to have as background. Their futures, I think, [are] what influence what I teach. I want them to have what they need to succeed beyond me, and if it means doing a lot of rote kinds of things so that in the future when they need to use that kind of information for whatever comes next, they have it." She said that she is preparing students "for the kind of education that [she] expects them to get in high school, based on [her] own experiences at [one of the city's exam schools], which was a very academically oriented program."

If accountability exists at Stevens, it is based on "a set of tacit assumptions that teachers know what to do, that the principal knows what they are doing, *and* that he knows they are doing a good job." Again, when teachers are isolated and there are neither clear expectations nor accountability with consequences, teachers' responsibility rules.

Hutchinson High School

Hutchinson, a large urban comprehensive high school, is similar to Phoenix in that order prevails, but this emphasis at Hutchinson emerged from a recent history of disorder that escalated to fatalities. The teachers expected the administration "to regain control of the hallways, corridors, and classrooms from the ruffians who ran wild about the building," and in return the principal made it clear that teachers were expected to take equal responsibility for "establishing a safe and orderly school environment."

Teachers at Hutchinson spoke explicitly about the importance of order and civility. Their comments about accountability and teaching, however, reflected the same ambiguity and isolation as those of teachers in similar schools. There was a formal teacher handbook, but few teachers or administrators referred to it. The teachers downplayed their accountability to the administrators. One teacher said, "Nobody is going to check to see what I am doing, but the headmaster will check to see if I have adequate control, whatever, more management things and techniques and that type of thing." Another teacher reported "very little collegiality," while still another said, "We impose our own standards." When asked where the standards come from, she said, "They're within us."

In addition to their responsibility for discipline, teachers described responsibility to look after their students in a shepherding manner. Nearly all Hutchinson teachers spoke of their responsibility for students' welfare, defined as "staying out of trouble, staying healthy, and doing what's needed to graduate and either get a job or gain admission to college." One teacher said that his job was to motivate his students and show them that he cared about them. Teachers' perceptions of their students' backgrounds are extremely important, and, when combined with lack of accountability and lack of collegiality, shift the focus to the teacher's personal responsibility.

Teachers claimed responsibility for the welfare of their students both outside and inside the classroom, and spoke of being motivated by their own experiences of good and bad teachers. As at the Phoenix Charter School, when curricular standards interfered with the teacher's sense of what was right for her students, the teacher asserted her own opinion of the students' academic needs. One teacher spoke of a new standard: "There is no way in hell I will teach Algebra II to kids who do not understand general math! . . . All students can learn, I agree with that, but I don't think they can come from middle school and be thrown into a situation where here we're setting them up for failure. Start with the first grade, keep them with us, and maybe they'll succeed."

Summary

The schools described in this section share a common solution to the problem of accountability. They delegate to the individual teacher most decisions about to whom the school is accountable, for what, and how. Accountability in these schools boils down to individual teachers' sense of responsibility. All of the schools had some pro forma internal accountability systems, albeit weak ones, such as teacher handbooks or prescribed curricula. All of the schools existed within some kind of external accountability structure—charter laws, archdiocese curriculum frameworks, or local curriculum standards. But these accountability structures exercised no effective influence over individual teachers' sense of to whom and for what they were accountable.

Teachers in these schools tended to define their sense of accountability entirely in terms of their own sense of personal responsibility to what they perceived as students' needs, both affective and academic. Their responses are as notable for what they do *not* mention as for what they do. They did not mention formal accountability systems, which are what interests most school reformers. Instead they talked about responsibility—to their students and to themselves. They did not mention *how* they were held accountable, because informal or formal systems of accountability, even where they existed, had no reality in their daily lives.

Regardless of recent changes in state and local accountability systems, regardless of teacher evaluations, regardless of parent involvement, even regardless of the charter school law, which is supposed to increase accountability, these teachers were still largely left to decide, based on their own values, what and how to teach. The beliefs of teachers that exercised the greatest influence on their sense of responsibility were those related to the social backgrounds of their students. Teachers in these schools in effect decided on their own what kind of education was appropriate for students from backgrounds they regarded as disadvantaged. They spoke of "these children," with clear opinions as to what was required for children from disadvantaged backgrounds. The teachers stressed order in the classroom and their own conceptions of students' well-being, at the expense of academic performance. These views were unchallenged, either by their colleagues' expectations or by external accountability systems, because these influences were weak relative to the teachers' personal values.

THE EMERGENCE OF COLLECTIVE ACCOUNTABILITY: EXPECTATIONS INFLUENCE RESPONSIBILITY

In the previous section we focused on schools where individuals' conceptions of responsibility dominated collective conceptions of accountability. Our sample of schools also included schools where teachers' work was heavily influenced by the expectations of other teachers, administrators, or community members. Strong expectations can influence and shape what a teacher, administrator, parent or student feels responsible for in his or her work. In this section, we highlight three schools characterized by strong mutual expectations. The lead case in this section, St. Aloysius Elementary School, is one of the very few schools in our sample that was focused primarily on teaching and learning. The graphic representation of this school in Figure 3 highlights the prominence of collective expectations and also reflects the relationship between responsibility and expectations, due in large part to the principal's practice of hiring candidates whose teaching philosophy matched her own.

St. Aloysius Elementary is a small Catholic school with a growing enrollment that is located in an affluent section of a university city. The focus on instruction is not the result of any external formal directive or accountability system, but rather the combination of a strong school leader and high expectations for students. Of particular note in this case is the way teachers project and interpret parent expectations. The assumption at St. Aloysius Elementary is that all parents have the same high expectations as those expressed by the vocal parents of high socioeconomic status.

The second case we present, North Beach High, also has a strong leader, but the focus is on attainment, assuring that all students graduate. North Beach High is located in a blue-collar suburb of a major city, the demographics of which have recently begun to change from predominately Irish and Italian to a substantial Asian population. About 15-30 percent of the student population at North Beach is Asian, mostly Chinese.

The third case, Tatuna Point Elementary, is a K–6 school located in the heart of an affluent suburb that is almost exclusively white and Asian. The case illustrates how powerful a force parents can be in setting high expectations for teachers and providing the support that goes with those expectations. The parental presence at Tatuna Point Elementary overshadows to a large extent the labor of teachers and administrators. As we analyze the schools in this section, we show how expectations can shape teachers' work. In some cases the principal plays a central role, while in others the community is of more importance.

St. Aloysius Elementary School

St. Aloysius Elementary serves a racially and ethnically diverse population of students in kindergarten through the eighth grade. The school has experienced a recent influx of Korean students, maintains a steady population of Haitian students, and in any given year serves several transitory European and South American students whose parents come to the region to study. About 50 percent of the students are white, 40 percent African American and Haitian, six percent Asian, and four percent Latino/Latina. Fewer than one percent of students are eligible for Title I services as determined by family income. Seventy-five percent of the students are Catholic. St. Aloysius Elementary's teaching staff, consisting of one teacher per grade, is entirely white. By the principal's account, she has students whose parents work several blue-collar jobs, and others whose parents are high-status professionals and "university parents."

St. Aloysius Elementary is Mrs. Sharp's first principalship. Since she assumed the principalship five years ago, the school has undergone an almost complete turnover in teaching staff. Only three of the current seventeen staff members at St. Aloysius Elementary were there when Mrs. Sharp arrived. She attributes this turnover primarily to natural attrition through retirement, maternity leave, and continuing education, but acknowledged that in some cases teachers chose to leave, having identified themselves as misfits with the school or with her approach to education. She said that, at the end of her first year, "By virtue of things I said, people came to understand what I valued. And so, when some of those people left at the end of that year, I was able to hire people." She added that "each time that's happened, I've hired someone whose sense of education and philosophy is very much in keeping with my own." While the Catholic Schools Office publishes a list of teachers available for hire, Mrs. Sharp was wary of relying upon that list because she knew of at least one person on the list who she said would be "very inappropriate" in a setting with children. She said that she is fortunate that she is given a great deal of latitude by the church pastor to hire teachers of her choice, although he has official, final authority. All but one of the current teachers is Catholic, and the majority are young professionals with fewer than ten years' experience. Those teachers with more experience reported a good working relationship with their younger colleagues, saying that where there might have been tension, instead there was give-and-take with mutual learning. Because most teachers were hired within the past five years, several in the same year, salaries and seniority are relatively uniform across the staff. Some teachers noted that they have an unusually collegial staff and attribute this relationship partially to the fact that so many of them came to St. Aloysius Elementary at the same time and learned the ropes together. The teachers earn approximately $10,000–$14,000 less than entry-level public school teachers in the area, and many work second jobs in the evening and on weekends. Mrs. Sharp said she tries to be sensitive to their work schedules when organizing meetings or school events. She has also authorized teachers to tutor students privately after school, which she said "provides them with the additional income they need." She added, "It's also enabled us to reach out to the segment of the community that had never been a part of our school before—the ESL children." The school's immediate surroundings include upper-end real estate, a few shops and restaurants, and, within walking distance, a large university.

More than half of St. Aloysius Elementary's students live in the same zip code as the school, while the rest live in mostly suburban towns, some up to forty-five minutes away. There was no playground in the small schoolyard at the time of our visit, but a fund drive is underway to purchase equipment. The building is well maintained, with prominent displays of student work, mostly compositions and test papers.

Not all students who apply to St. Aloysius are admitted. If it appears that a child's needs cannot be met at St. Aloysius Elementary, Mrs. Sharp recommends another school within the archdiocese that she believes can better suit those needs, be they behavioral, academic, or other. When pressed on this point, Mrs. Sharp described an informal understanding between schools and in the archdiocese, that different schools have different missions and "for good reason." She described schools where the academic performance was not equal to that of St. Aloysius Elementary, but explained that those schools provide a real service to the inner-city and immigrant communities which she perceives to have different needs.

Non–English speakers are fully integrated into classrooms at St. Aloysius Elementary. The teachers have developed informal committees to gather ESL materials and to share ESL teaching techniques. Teachers report that their classes benefit from exposure to other cultures and languages, and that they are able, though with some difficulty, to devote the necessary attention to both their native English and non-English-speaking pupils. The St. Aloysius Elementary student population is racially and ethnically diverse, but it is less diverse in terms of socio-economic background. Fewer than one percent of students are eligible for Title I services as determined by family income. Not all children come from wealthy families, but few come from abject poverty, so they are less likely than students in other schools described here to suffer the range of social, physical, and emotional risks associated with living in poverty. Unlike other schools in our sample, teachers at St. Aloysius Elementary made no reference to students' home lives or living environments as an obstacle to teaching or student learning. This is largely due to the students' predominantly middle- to upper-class status, but it is also reflective of a norm at St. Aloysius Elementary that values individual responsibility for teaching and learning, and a perceived intolerance for scapegoating of any kind, even when presented with legitimate challenges to learning.

Tuition at St. Aloysius Elementary was $2,150 in 1996–1997, approximately twice that which is charged by some inner-city Catholic schools in the area. Some financial assistance is available in the second year of attendance for families meeting the school's need criteria, but the admissions process is conducted without knowledge of families' economic circumstances. When asked to describe how she believed St. Aloysius Elementary is perceived in the community, Mrs. Sharp said she and the pastor both think the school is viewed as "an inexpensive private school." She believed that many view the school as an alternative to the prestigious and expensive secular private schools in the area, and that those schools are St. Aloysius Elementary's competition.

Expectations Shape Teachers' Work

Mrs. Sharp has had relatively free rein from the church pastor to exercise discretion in hiring staff and managing the school budget. Mrs. Sharp was very happy with her current teaching staff and described them with terms such as "professional," "skilled" and "collegial." When asked what she looks for in new hires, she said that they should believe "all children can learn, [and be someone] who looks for the ways in which they learn and will have a multiplicity of activities . . . a person of good will and values."

She attributed much of the coherence within the school to having hired people whose philosophies of teaching matched her own, but was quick to say that she was not a directive principal and that the staff has developed into a cohesive group largely on its own. As an example, Mrs. Sharp said that the teachers requested that one of the four faculty meetings per month be devoted entirely to collegial discussion related to curriculum and pedagogy. She also noted that, last year, the staff agreed to seek additional accreditation beyond that awarded by the archdiocese, because they knew they could get it and because the coherence and academic quality it required "would appeal to people looking for a good school for their children."

Without exception, teachers described an atmosphere of high expectations at St. Aloysius Elementary. Some stressed a high priority on "reaching every child" and "making sure no one is left behind," while others referred to a serious and supportive environment where everyone is expected to put forth excellent work.

Teachers did describe a range of abilities within their classrooms and the particular challenge of teaching ESL students, but none referred to this as an obstacle to teaching. Rather, they described a school culture where teachers are expected to improvise and to "reach everyone." This belief in high expectations for all children applies to both academic and social learning at St. Aloysius Elementary.

Academically, children are expected to achieve at the highest level possible for them. Teachers said, with varying degrees of certainty, that they believed every student can learn the skills taught at their grade level, and in many cases students exceed those expectations. When asked if all of her students could learn the skills expected of their grade level, one veteran teacher responded, "If I see they're having trouble, I'll tutor. They're given the time for help. We just stay with it until they know it." She continued, "I never worry [about them going to the next grade] because they always know what they're doing." These comments reflect the teacher's philosophy and her expectation that students will "stay with it" too. Students praised this particular teacher for her willingness to give extra help, for her unbending belief in them, and for her equally unbending expectation that they will learn and retain what she teaches them. Teachers recognized that students have varying ability levels; they described the challenges they face in teaching ESL students and that these students face in learning. The teachers maintained "high expectations" for the ESL students by insisting on the highest degree of effort while, in some cases, adjusting performance expectations.

For example, the fifth- through eighth-grade teachers developed an ESL program that defined what teachers expect of their non-English-speaking students. One teacher told us, "We expect them to increase their English understanding and comprehension of English. We expect them to maintain math skills and improve. We listed a set of criteria that we're going to expect from ESL students." Student report cards in the upper grades at St. Aloysius Elementary have a column for performance and another column for effort. There is no effort column in the lower grades, but teachers write comments that include a description of student effort, behavior, and progress. Only one teacher described occasionally inflating letter (or number) grades based upon student effort or extenuating circumstances that might be particularly challenging for an individual child.

When asked how they were able to maintain high expectations for all children despite the range of student abilities and preparation, several teachers said that they did not expect identical work from every child, but that performance grades accurately reflected the range in student products and effort grades (or comments) focused on the expectation that every student do his or her absolute best. Although not every child can produce exemplary work, those children putting forth their best efforts can be rewarded with an "A for effort." Teachers indicated that students were not graded in comparison with one another or on a curve, but often on the basis of rubrics. One example of a rubric was a scoring sheet the teachers developed for the Science Fair. Students first received an information sheet explaining what was expected of them. Several weeks later they received a sheet stating that their topic would be due on a certain date, and their outline on another date. Finally, they received the actual scoring sheet that listed all the criteria upon which they would be graded.

Most faculty members assumed students would finish high school, some of them graduating from prestigious high schools, and that the "vast majority" would go to college. When asked what parents expected of them and the school, teachers responses seemed to place equal emphasis on instilling Christian values and on challenging the students. One teacher, comparing St. Aloysius Elementary to another school where she taught, commented, "[The previous school] was much more working class, very few of the parents had gone to college and education was not number one on everybody's list of priorities. . . . Whereas here, I think people really respect your pushing their kid to do their best and I like that. . . . The students are much more motivated [here]. The parents are much more supportive . . . and the students, quite honestly . . . my students seem to be smarter and more interested in doing well and living up to the expectations that I have set for them, they have set for themselves, that their parents have set for them as well."

Another teacher described the school as being in the business of "educating the whole child," and said that parents expected that teachers would be there before and after school "modeling that philosophy" for the students. Several parents verified this assessment of parent expectations. One parent said that she worried at first that the school might be too much pressure for her son, but that she's discovered he thrives in the "challenging environment." Other parents of younger children expressed a desire to get their children an "early start on their education," and in an environment that is disciplined and orderly.

When asked what parents expected, Mrs. Sharp remarked, "I think all the parents are setting high expectations, even though some of them may not be able to articulate them very well. I feel very strongly that they all want high academic expectations for their children. They all want their children to be good human beings. . . . There is a group that will voice that more strongly than many others will and so yes, we do respond, we hear them and we consider how we're going to respond to them. For the parents who may be less able to articulate expectations or may be less aware of the quality of education that is being provided to their children, I think they recognize there's something special. I try to deal with the parents on an individual basis, as opposed to a movement. . . . We have our parking lot brigade here, we have a few parents. . . . I've got a few teachers here that are very adept at diffusing that. The very unity of our philosophy helps that."

The parents we met in a focus group described a variety of expectations for the school. Some of the parents' expectations focused specifically on teachers, but overall they seemed not to differentiate individual people's roles. One father said, "I guess I certainly expect the school to educate. You know, academic education is certainly what they start out with, and the school seems to do that well. And the only way that can happen is if the environment in the classes allows the children to do that. . . . I think that comes from the expectations that the teachers have of the children, and I think that is a difference that seems to . . . that is a difference between this school and some of the public schools that I've heard kind of anecdotal talk of. In some of the public schools, some of the kids seem sort of lost somehow. And that doesn't seem to happen so much here at [St. Aloysius Elementary]."

Parents also described wanting frequent communication from teachers and the school, and wanting the school to be responsive to their children's individual needs. They remarked that teachers at St. Aloysius Elementary do not teach the same lessons repeatedly, but seem to vary their teaching. Parents noted that the teachers continue their own professional development, something the parents valued and expected and believed distinguished St. Aloysius Elementary from public schools. Teachers perceived that parents have high expectations of them and of the school. Speaking to the question of expectations of teachers and of the school as a whole, a parent who was highly involved in the school commented on the effects of social class and proximity to the university: "The higher the level of the parent educationally, the higher level the child will reach. . . . The parents are going on to postgraduate work and then they're expecting at least that their children will get to that level, and I do think it lifts the place. . . . I think it is a very good influence on

the school that that's there. It's like strings from above pulling you up."
This comment speaks both to the way parents at St. Aloysius Elementary were perceived by staff, and to the expectations those parents communicated in various ways to the staff.

Teachers' Sense of Responsibility Reflects Expectations

The staff at the school responded to what was expected of them by the principal, parents, and their colleagues. Those collective expectations affected teachers' personal sense of responsibility. Their sense of professional responsibility was largely informed by the schools' collective interpretation of its community's needs and expectations.

Without exception, St. Aloysius Elementary's teachers expressed feeling responsible for the learning of every individual child, and for maintaining high expectations for all children. Everyone described feeling responsible for their students' social development. In some cases this was characterized as religious teaching and in others as training in good manners and behavior. When asked for what she felt responsible, one teacher responded definitively, "Well, first, academics. To make sure that the child is learning what they should be learning. That they are on level. If they are above level, that they're being challenged. If they're below level, that they're receiving the extra help they need. As far as, like, socially, teaching them the right and wrong. . . . Even though not everyone is Christian, you're teaching them about God and loving each other and working together. So, I want to develop them. . . . My responsibility is to develop their mind, academically, develop their soul or spirit, morally, and [help them] to be able to survive in life."

A first-year teacher's comments about her personal sense of responsibility cover most of the points raised by her colleagues: "I feel that I am responsible for teaching them the tools so that they are accountable, so that they are responsible for themselves, their work. I think I'm responsible for setting a high level of expectations so that they know that's what they're expected to meet, so that I don't accept mediocre work. I definitely feel responsible for that . . . for setting a tone in here that's serious yet light-hearted enough that they feel comfortable enough to interact with me and they're not scared of the teacher. I feel responsible for sending home information so their parents are up to date as to what's going on exactly in this class every day. I feel responsible for them going home every day . . . and knowing what they've learned so that they can't say "nothing" when their parents ask, because they know [my] ears burn even if I'm millions of miles away."

Several teachers described doing whatever was necessary to help a child learn to his or her full potential—"to do the best that he or she can." Some teachers implied that they "just get to know" students' abilities and work habits, but no one offered an explicit explanation of how they gauge a student's potential or what is his or her "best." Those teachers who said they felt responsible for "individualized learning" and "educating the whole child" explained that this means making oneself available to students for extra help before and after school.

Others emphasized teaching children with varying learning styles differently. When asked to expand upon this idea, one teacher made a clear distinction between students whose grades suffer because they do not do their work and those who "don't get it" and do poorly on tests: "If you're choosing not to turn in your homework, not to do your assignments, I think the responsibility falls on you [the student]. If test grades are the big problem, I think sometimes I'd look to me. . . . If half the class is not understanding what's on the test, that's my fault I think. And then I'd look at how I was teaching or what I was neglecting to teach or what was the method I was using that wasn't reaching half the class."

We asked teachers what responsibility they felt to compensate for problems students might experience out of school, at home or in their communities. The teachers indicated that this was not a big issue at St. Aloysius Elementary, but described sensitivity to such problems as part of their jobs.

Examples offered usually related to marital problems between parents, or parents whose work schedules prevented them from being as involved with their children as other parents. They implied a willingness to address children's social, emotional, or physical well-being as part of their "whole child" orientation, but they clearly did not view themselves as solely or primarily responsible for these nonacademic areas.

North Beach High School

North Beach High School has just over 1,200 students and is located in what one teacher called an upwardly mobile blue-collar community. The majority of the student population is of Irish or Italian descent. About 25 to 30 percent of the students are Asian, mostly Chinese, who have proficient language skills; high school students who are not proficient in English attend the other high school in town. The school operates as one large family. As one respondent said, "It's like a big family, you know, and I think a lot of things get done sometimes based on relationships as opposed to a structure."

In interviews, two teachers identified the principal and assistant principal as the "mother and father" of the school. Many of the 175 adults who work in the school are graduates or parents of graduates—the principal, assistant principal, and three deans graduated from the school. North Beach High School teachers and administrators grew up together, attended the same schools and churches, and shared cultural traditions. Membership in this close-knit community includes a sense of obligation to take care of all of its members. In the case of schooling, this means that children will graduate from high school.

North Beach High School is committed to seeing that all students graduate and, essentially, does not let any student drop out. The assistant principal explained: "Basically, we hang onto kids forever. . . . We work with the one to two percent who drop out, we work with them forever and we try and try . . . because we're going to pay now or later." The principal added, "I'd like to have a dollar for every kid who dropped out of school and who came back and earned it."

North Beach High School reports a dropout rate of 1.3 percent. The assistant principal was concerned because it had "creeped up" from 1.1 to 1.3 percent. She said that she would "even violate the attendance policy on the side of kids" to keep the them in school. The student advisor system is tied into the homeroom structure and assures that one adult consistently touches base with every child each day of his or her high school years. Students have the same homeroom teacher for four years. The homeroom teacher goes to graduation and gives their homeroom students their diplomas.

The school administration is more laissez faire on instructional issues. The principal had confidence in the subject knowledge of his teachers and expected them "to perform their best, realizing they're all different—different personalities, different vocabularies sometimes."

Tatuna Point Elementary School

Tatuna Point is an elementary school located in a relatively affluent suburb, where academic expectations are high and student achievement is taken seriously. Second graders talk about going to Ivy League colleges and teachers know that is what many parents expect. As one lower grade teacher explained, "Standards are very high academically; it's expected by the parents, the community, and the staff, and we work hard to meet those expectations."

Parents are involved in almost every aspect of the school. Parents are vocal about expressing demands, and they are active in providing support for what they demand. Parents know how to articulate their demands loudly and are ready to take the steps necessary to achieve them—whether by voicing their discontent to teachers, administrators, or district officials, or by organizing and participating in formal institutions that control and regulate school activities.

As one parent said, "There's a lot of parent involvement. . . . Parents are willing to be very vocal and express their concern, or shall we say 'whine.' Most of the parents, because they're highly educated, put a real premium on education, and therefore expect a lot from the schools . . . expect high performance from the schools, and therefore make a lot of demands on the staff, on the principal, on the curriculum. But on the other hand, the majority of those parents say, 'I want this, but what can I do to help you get it?' . . . My take is that they're willing to back up their demands, if you will, with support, either financial or hands on."

The parents do in fact back up their demands. According to the principal, last year the PTA counted over 8,000 hours of volunteer time, not including those who forgot to sign in. On any given day, parents can be found assisting the school secretary, working in classrooms, shelving books, staffing the computer lab, or helping coach a sport or other activity. The PTA donates $50,000 yearly in capital goods, such as playground and computer equipment.

In 1991, a group of parents established the Tatuna Point Elementary Educational Foundation, a nonprofit foundation dedicated to raising funds to provide additional resources for the improvement of the quality of education. Each family at the school is asked to make a cash contribution of $350. Approximately 40 percent of school families give to the Foundation. The funds have supported additional teachers, consultants, and classroom aides. Students at the school also raise money through an annual walkathon sponsored by the Foundation. Parents are also very active on the school council.

The principal explained, "The Foundation buys people, the PTA buys stuff . . . and the school council keeps it all coordinated and going together." This parental effort overshadows the work of the teachers. One parent noted that, as a newcomer to the school, she heard much about the parents—the PTA, the Foundation, and the site council—but very little about teachers.

Despite the school's academic program and relatively high performance levels, parents at Tatuna Point Elementary questioned whether their children were sufficiently challenged academically. Parents were frustrated by what they claimed was a lack of individualized attention. As one parent explained, "The teacher [ought to] get to know each child and know how to deal with each child separately instead of expecting all thirty-two to do the same thing." Most parents were confident in what they believed was best for their child's education and would exert their influence in the classroom, in the principal's office, or at the district level to ensure that their child benefited from a high-quality education tailored to the child's particular needs.

The principal explained, "They know how to use the system. They know how to access the system. . . . If they didn't like what I did, they'd know who to go to. They know who is my boss. They're not shy about calling the superintendent if they have a problem."

The Tatuna Point Elementary Education Foundation has been instrumental in getting classroom aides for the lower grades. The aides are closely monitored by the Foundation's board of governors. The Foundation, the school site council, and some independent parents conducted an evaluation of resource teachers and classroom aides to assess whether students received more individualized attention as a result of the increased support. Teachers were requested to keep a log of aides' time every day for one week, and classrooms were formally observed by a team of parents. The evaluation report stated, "In the primary grades, 77 percent of aide time was spent working with small groups or individual students and 23 percent was spent in clerical duties. In the upper grades, 38 percent of aide time was spent in working with small groups or individual students and 62 percent was spent in clerical duties."

Parents found the upper-grade condition unacceptable and requested that the principal discuss the issue with the upper-grade teachers to assure that classroom aides were used more appropriately. One teacher explained that if they pay for the aides, they can dictate how teachers use the aides. The same teacher summarized the parents' sentiment, saying, "We're not going to fund it unless you're doing it our way." Parents also disagreed with the local district's opposition to tracking students according to ability. There are gifted-and-talented classes, but they are limited to the top two percent of children.

Parents were frustrated by the limited available space and felt that their children remained in a system designed for "less able" students. Parents at Tatuna Point often bypassed the school leadership to go directly to the district to ensure their children's placement in the accelerated program. Although teachers appreciated and welcomed the participation and support of parents in classes and valued the additional resources they brought to the classroom, they also resented when parents made determinations about how teachers should do their jobs.

The parent activism was certainly felt by the teachers and the principal. Teachers knew that if they were not doing what parents expected, they would hear about it, either verbally or in writing, by way of the principal or even the superintendent. One upper-grade teacher commented, "I think my greatest pressure comes from the parents and from what they're asking of me or what their expectations are of me." The same teacher said, "I am happy when I have no parent letter in my box." Teachers at Tatuna Point worked long hours and the work was certainly influenced by the demands of parents, whether expressed directly or through the principal. In spite of outside pressures from parents, district requirements, or administrative mandates, the teachers still asserted that their actions were first and foremost driven by what they viewed as the children's best interests. The teachers did appear to do what was expected of them, but the principal argued that they did so from self-motivation and personal dedication. As the principal explained, "The accountability structure here is very often self-imposed by the teachers."

Summary

The schools in this section demonstrate a different solution to the problem of accountability. The first group of schools essentially turned all accountability problems into matters of individual teacher responsibility. These schools have all developed, in somewhat different ways, a relatively powerful culture of expectations that shapes individuals' views around a common purpose. These schools operate without highly visible internal accountability structures, but they accomplish many of the same purposes through expectations.

At St. Aloysius Elementary, Mrs. Sharp has been highly influential in constructing a community of teachers, students, and parents focused on academic learning, largely through the influence of strong expectations. At North Beach High School, the culture of common expectations comes from both the school leadership's ethic of a "family" environment and from the cohesive culture of the local community, which is transmitted to the school through the staff, who are natives of the community themselves and graduates of the school. Expectations at North Beach are focused mainly on attainment—getting students to stay in school and to graduate—rather than on academic learning. The expectations at Tatuna Point Elementary seem to originate largely from aggressive and demanding middle-class parents who pressure teachers and administrators; the latter see themselves as somewhat beleaguered but heavily influenced by these parental expectations. The expectations of parents in Tatuna Point Elementary are beginning to translate into an incipient accountability structure evolving in the Foundation's strong influence over the expenditure of its funds.

In all three cases, collective expectations exercise a heavy influence on teachers' individual conceptions of their responsibilities. Mrs. Sharp deliberately selects teachers who share her views that all students can learn; the teachers at St. Aloysius Elementary share a view that de-emphasizes family background as a determining factor in student learning, instead emphasizing student and teacher effort. At North Beach High School, collective norms about the custodial role of schools and the importance of attainment heavily influence the way teachers think of their work with students. And at Tatuna Point Elementary, teachers internalize the norms of competitive academic achievement or risk the disapproval of parents.

INTERNAL ACCOUNTABILITY: THE ALIGNMENT OF RESPONSIBILITY, EXPECTATIONS, AND ACCOUNTABILITY

In the schools we have examined so far, individual conceptions of responsibility and collective expectations tend to guide the actions and motivations of teachers. These factors appear to operate in a way that is incidental to any formal arrangements or consequences that are visible within the school. Teachers may feel responsible for maintaining order in classrooms and hallways, and this sense of responsibility may be translated into shared expectations, for example, but in many schools there are no visible arrangements for enforcing this obligation and little in the way of direct consequences for failing to meet those expectations.

In this section we discuss three schools in which a strong internal accountability system has emerged, which appears to influence the actions of members of the school community. These three schools operate within quite different external accountability policy structures, yet within each school, teachers (and parents in the case of one of the schools) are held accountable for meeting a set of shared expectations. Regardless of the differences in the external policy structures, in these schools accountability is a strong internal operating principle. We consider how expectations can shape an internal accountability system within these three schools. While not a formal external policy mechanism, the internal accountability system appears to strongly influence teacher behavior and corresponds closely with teachers' understanding of their personal responsibility.

Unlike those discussed previously, the schools discussed in this section are characterized by visible accountability structures with consequences for failure to meet set expectations. These schools illustrate the idea outlined in our working theory that internal accountability systems are likely to influence individual actions if they are closely aligned with individual responsibility and collective expectations. These three schools vary in the content of their shared expectations, but they are similar in that the alignment of personal responsibility with shared expectations, combined with some consequences, has led to an internal accountability system that actually affects actions and behavior. The internal accountability systems in these three schools appear to have the greatest impact on behavior, but they still operate within an external policy structure. The degree to which the external policy structure affects behavior appears to be related to the degree of alignment between the external policy and the internal accountability system. If there is a conflict, the internal system appears to have a greater influence on behavior.

The lead case is Turtle Haven Pilot School, a locally chartered urban elementary school serving a high proportion of minority and disadvantaged students. Turtle Haven demonstrates the emergence of internal accountability in an environment of shared expectations for high-quality academic work, as represented by the high degree of alignment in Figure 4. Saint B's is an urban Catholic elementary school serving a predominantly working-class student population. St. B's demonstrates an internal accountability system extended to include parents. Pine Creek, an urban elementary school serving predominantly poor white students, demonstrates the alignment of responsibility, expectations, and internal accountability around relatively low expectations for student academic work.

Turtle Haven Pilot School

Turtle Haven Pilot School is a small elementary school located in a low-income community in a large eastern city. As a pilot school, or a locally chartered school, Turtle Haven is administratively affiliated with an urban school system of over 60,000 students, but exempted from many of the district regulations. The building itself is not owned by the school district—the school is housed in an unused wing of a parochial school. The building is old and in disrepair, but the display of student work in the hallways and classrooms livens up the atmosphere. Although located in an old building, this is a brand-new school, in only its second year of operation. The city's pilot schools were founded as part of an agreement with the local teachers' union in an effort to provide models of excellence that would spread to all of the city schools. Pilot schools are expected to be "models of innovation," and their advocates believe they will lead to improved student performance in other city schools. Because pilot schools are expected to provide models for other city schools, the models are supposed to be replicable systemwide, although the city has no formal plans for replication.

The Turtle Haven Pilot School was originally promoted for its "technology-based curriculum, active parent participation, and individualized instruction." The school opened with grades K1(a readiness class for four-year-olds), K2 (the second kindergarten year), first grade and second grade, then during its second year expanded to include third grade. The school also operates an extended-day program, providing afterschool services for children until 5:30 in the evening. There are currently 200 children enrolled, 57 percent of whom are eligible for free or reduced-price meals. Turtle Haven participates in the city's choice system, and as a result students are bused from many different parts of the city. About 65 percent of the students are African American, 25 percent Anglo, nine percent Latino/Latina, and one percent Asian and Native American. The classrooms at Turtle Haven have many similarities.

Desks are arranged in clusters of four or five. Each room has a meeting area with a big blue gym mat on which children sit. In each classroom the teacher posts a morning message—a handwritten greeting outlining the day's activities. Children appear to be actively engaged in work, frequently working on different projects at the same time. Most classrooms are not quiet, but the noise appears to be the productive sound of children working.

As a pilot school, Turtle Haven is exempt from union regulations governing the hiring of staff. Hiring is conducted directly at the school site, and as a result the staff characteristics are somewhat different from those of a typical city school. Many of the teachers are young—in their mid-twenties—with little prior teaching experience. The teaching staff is diverse, with six African Americans, six Anglos, two Latinos, and one Asian.

External Context

Turtle Haven has a unique external accountability context. Having been granted a pilot status, the school is evaluated every three years and in theory can be closed if it has not met the goals of the pilot school initiative. It is not yet clear how such evaluations will work. Staff at the school expressed confidence, however, that whatever evaluation mechanism is used they will certainly meet and exceed the district's expectations. The threat of losing pilot school status did not have a strong influence on the teachers' understanding of accountability. In this way, Turtle Haven is similar to Phoenix Charter School in that the accountability arrangement under which it operates is not a heavy influence upon conceptions of accountability, insofar as it offers greater freedom *from* accountability. Turtle Haven also operates within the context of districtwide mechanisms designed to hold all city schools accountable. Since hiring a new superintendent, the district has embarked on an ambitious systemic reform initiative—several components of which relate directly to accountability.

For example, this reform includes the implementation of "citywide learning standards" that outline specific expectations for each grade level. Children must demonstrate performance in relation to the standards by creating the "products" designated for each grade level. These products are performance-based projects directly related to the objectives of the learning standards. The district also administers the Stanford

9 achievement test each year. This test was selected because it was most closely aligned to the learning standards. Although the district has developed standards and designated products, it is still not clear to teachers how these products will be used to judge a school's success. Most of the teachers at Turtle Haven were working to help all students meet these standards, but they were unclear whether or not the district would collect the products, and if so, how the district would evaluate the products. The district has not provided schools with a detailed rubric by which to evaluate the products, so it is difficult for teachers to determine "how good is good enough?" when evaluating student products.

This confusion was not unique to Turtle Haven, but common among the public schools in this district included in our sample. Turtle Haven differed from other public schools, however, in its efforts to incorporate the standards and products, vague as they were, into the school's self-generated academic program. Nor was it clear to teachers how standardized testing would be used to hold schools accountable. Several teachers did mention that they felt accountable for student performance on these tests, but others said they felt more accountable to parents than to the district for a student's test performance. One teacher explained, "Formal assessments, like the Stanford 9, parents want their children to excel on those types of tests. We don't teach to the test, but we have to be accountable for how the children do on the test."

The district has begun to design mechanisms for holding schools accountable, but these mechanisms are not yet visible at the school-site level. There are very few rewards and sanctions that recognize a school's performance. Therefore, we characterize the external accountability context as relatively weak. Within this weak external accountability structure, however, Turtle Haven has developed its own internal accountability system with a strong set of expectations closely aligned with personal responsibility.

Expectations

> "They [expectations] taken together create sort of a school culture . . . that's very defining and distinctive and says, this is what we're about." (Turtle Haven teacher)

Turtle Haven's principal, Mary Carter, has made a very deliberate effort to make her expectations clear to teachers. It is no coincidence that classrooms look very similar. At the beginning of the year, she distributed a list of "components or things" that should be found in every Turtle Haven classroom. This list included physical objects, such as a morning message board and student work posted on the walls, and activities such as choice time and morning meeting. In this document, she outlined her expectations about parent involvement. Each teacher is expected to hold four family events during the year, and 100 percent attendance is expected. Teachers must also hold parent conferences and communicate regularly with parents by letter and phone.

Interviews with Turtle Haven teachers indicated that most of the staff have internalized these expectations and make every effort to live up to them. The responses of most teachers regarding the principal's expectations closely matched what the principal told us are her expectations. Several teachers listed expectations that repeated the written guidelines Ms. Carter had presented at the beginning of the year. Among the expectations they believed Ms. Carter had, teachers mentioned choice time, use of the Responsive Classroom model, morning meeting, and planning successful family events. One teacher, after listing many of the expectations outlined in Ms. Carter's written guidelines, explained the importance of these clear expectations. She referred to the "components or things" as "structures that support expectations we've agreed we would have. I feel that's important. It's one thing to say, theoretically, it's your job to involve families. It's another thing to say, here's a way we expect you are going to do it, which is to have a certain number of classroom events. That makes it concrete and makes it so it's clear."

The specific expectations noted by the teachers appear to be directly connected to Ms. Carter's broad and general expectations of teachers and the learning experiences they provide for their students. On this subject, Ms. Carter commented, "One thing is around curriculum development and being able to construct a learning environment that engages all children, that allows children to grow and develop and learn in . . . creative ways, in thoughtful ways, in ways where the teacher can take on a lot of different roles. Not just standing and giving information, but being a facilitator and this sort of person that guides their understanding."

In addition to this expectation of academic student-centered instruction, Ms. Carter also mentioned the importance of a social curriculum and community-building. All teachers were expected to use the Responsive Classroom model and were provided with the necessary training. Ms. Carter sees community-building as her most important responsibility as a principal. She explained, "What's most important is instructional practice and curriculum, but before that is community, is building community. A very significant learning community. But then everything else falls under that. . . . I see my work as a principal as being more of a community activist, and more of teaching children what is possible in healthy communities than what is already existing. Giving them another model, another context in which to see the world and in which to see themselves."

The teachers' understanding of these general philosophical expectations appeared to be closely aligned with what Ms. Carter told us. For example, when asked what Ms. Carter expects of her, one teacher responded, "You are expected to think about how what goes on in your room emanates from kids' interests." Other teachers responded that teachers were expected to "teach in a meaningful way, and to have high expectations of kids and to teach social behavior too." One teacher said Ms. Carter thought that "the social curriculum is on equal footing with the academic curriculum." Several teachers referred to the expectation that they use the Responsive Classroom model. One teacher explained the model's emphasis: "Teaching kids how to listen to each other, how to ask questions, how to be kind, how to be helpful, how to be responsible, and that's a huge part of the day."

Teachers at Turtle Haven work in an environment of clearly articulated administrative expectations. The expectations are communicated through writing, through informal conversations, and during staff meetings and professional development activities. Our observations in the school and interviews with teachers revealed that most teachers made every effort to align their teaching practice to these expectations. Ms. Carter has clearly articulated her expectations for pedagogical practice and technique. She also has expectations related to the expectations the teachers have of their students.

Although the school works with a large percentage of poor and minority students, a population for which other schools in our sample set relatively low standards, the teachers at Turtle Haven believe that all children are capable of learning at high levels. Teachers in other schools we studied explained low student performance by arguing that "these kids have so many needs, it is more difficult to teach them." We did not encounter this argument at Turtle Haven. Ms. Carter explained her expectations for student performance: "I have higher expectations [than the city]. . . . When I first came to [the city] and I looked at the standards the teachers were using, I was appalled. I mean I was really. . . This was before the new standards came out. So I took the standards from [a neighboring city], which I thought were more comparable to my thinking around what kids should be able to do in first grade and used those. Yes, I think my expectations for learning are higher in general for students, not just in first grade, but in general. I don't look at a child and assess what they're capable of. I feel like so much of that goes on in [the city]."

Teachers at Turtle Haven appeared to mirror Ms. Carter in her philosophy about expectations of students. All teachers strongly resisted the belief that children from disadvantaged families and communities were less likely to succeed. At a meeting with the entire school staff and the researchers working on this project, the teachers were asked the source of their expectations for children. One teacher referred directly to Ms. Carter's conviction that all children are capable of great things, and mentioned that this belief leads teachers to challenge all students. At this same meeting, two Turtle Haven teachers spoke strongly against the tendency in inner-city schools of characterizing families and communities as the source of the problem. One teacher called this characterization "vindictive and victimizing" and enabling educators to make excuses. Another teacher said, "Inner-city kids do not need to be saved, they need to be treated fairly and with respect."

Expectations Influence Responsibility

In this context of strong expectations, how do expectations influence or work in conjunction (or conflict) with individual teachers' sense of personal responsibility? Unlike schools discussed earlier in this report, Turtle Haven appears to have a close alignment between personal responsibility and the principal's expectations. In some cases it seems Ms. Carter's expectations shaped an individual's understanding of responsibility, while in other cases it appears that Ms. Carter hired teachers who already possess a sense of personal responsibility that is closely aligned with her expectations.

For example, many teachers mentioned feeling personally responsible for their students' social development. One third-grade teacher, when asked for what she felt responsible, referred to many "study skill" related areas—helping children develop the ability to work independently, and to develop their confidence and listening skills. She also mentioned a responsibility for teaching students to respect each other, cooperate, and respect adults. Although she mentioned that these were schoolwide expectations, she also felt very responsible for them personally. In this example, there was a clear alignment between the teacher's sense of personal responsibility and the expectations outlined by Ms. Carter.

Another teacher discussed the importance of such an alignment: "Not that we're trying to prove something to make Mary pleased, but we really believe and we buy into the practice that all children can and will learn if you set the stage, and you set high expectations. And if these are your ideals, not rhetorical ideals, that you believe in, you have a place here." This alignment within the Turtle Haven school was also apparent in the case of the one teacher who saw a conflict between her sense of personal responsibility and Ms. Carter's expectations. This particular teacher saw her philosophy of teaching as more traditional than that of Ms. Carter and the other teachers in the school. She believed that "before they're allowed to go, they should be given the basic steps . . . to have self-control, to be able to know that, . . . 'I have something to do. I'm going to take my time to read the directions. Do I understand?' Like if I set up centers and let them move through centers, they have to know that at the end of a certain amount of time . . . these things have to be turned in. And my class just isn't there yet to just go at centers. And I'm viewed as being very traditional because of that. In terms of behavior, I really feel that there should be control in the classroom. I can't teach if everyone is talking at one time."

Consequences: What Happens When You Don't Meet Expectations

For the teacher quoted above, there was a conflict between her personal sense of responsibility and the expectations set by Ms. Carter. For alignment between expectations and personal responsibility to function as an internal accountability system, there must be consequences if the alignment does not exist or if an individual fails to meet the expectations. For this particular teacher, a lack of alignment led her to leave the school. This decision appeared to have been made jointly by the teacher and Ms. Carter. Ms. Carter explained the decision: "That was a meeting of the minds. And it's a good leaving. It's a good leaving because it's not a good match." The teacher explained, "I'm told that I'm too traditional, that I expect the kids to sit too much. That they're used to being out of their seats and that they should have more choices, more choice time. So, that was the decision we came to since we don't have the same philosophy. That we would just let it go."

To understand how consequences transform expectations into an informal accountability system, we asked several teachers the following question: "What happens at Turtle Haven if teachers do not meet Ms. Carter's expectations or conform to the school culture created by those expectations?" Most teachers believed that a person who did not meet expectations would first receive a great deal of support from the principal and other colleagues.

Teachers seemed reluctant to say if such a teacher would eventually lose his or her job. Most agreed, however, that a teacher who did not meet the expectations would not be happy at the school and would eventually "try to weed themselves out" of the school. As one teacher explained, "The administrator would initiate a lot of support . . . structures to try to help that person meet expectations, and that's something that would go on for a long time. Eventually, if things were not able to come together and there was a sense in the community that a certain number of children were not able to get the kind of education that we say we're committed to providing, then I think at a certain point the issue would be, we have to think about whether somebody belongs here or not."

Ms. Carter was less reluctant to describe the process by which she addressed the issue of teachers not meeting her expectations. We asked her several questions about what would happen if a teacher did not meet the expectation regarding parental attendance at the four family events, and she replied, "I would say if you've tried everything, if you've truly tried and you put all those things in place. You gave them enough time, you did the calls and all that kind of stuff, you tried different times of the day. There's a lot that you would have to be doing. Then I would be very concerned about the teacher. I would be very concerned. And that's happening as we speak." We asked further if the teacher would be back the next year, and she said, "Right now, if I had to decide today . . . no. And that's what the teacher's been told. No."

Ms. Carter explained that deciding to let a teacher go is one of the most important decisions she makes as an administrator: "I don't feel there are a whole lot of decisions that I make alone in this school, but my job is to identify the best educators for children. And to hold every teacher accountable for high-quality work for kids and families. And it can be done. I don't accept a whole lot of excuses."

Internal Accountability

At Turtle Haven, the principal has established a strong set of expectations that guide teacher behavior. These expectations are both grounded in an educational philosophy and related to specific pedagogical practice. In some instances these expectations shaped personal responsibility in teachers, while in other cases it seems that individuals were hired because their sense of personal responsibility matched Ms. Carter's expectations.

The autonomy in hiring at the pilot school has been crucial in building this alignment between expectations, personal responsibility, and internal accountability, although we did not observe this alignment uniformly across the charter schools in our study. In the few instances where there was a conflict between personal responsibility and administrative expectations, or where a teacher was ineffective in meeting expectations (even though she may have felt responsible for similar goals), the functioning of the internal accountability system was clear. There were consequences for teachers who failed to meet the expectations that had been established. Consequences connect expectations and personal responsibility to shape an internal accountability system at the Turtle Haven Pilot School.

Saint B's Elementary School

Internal accountability does not necessarily affect teacher behavior alone. At Saint B's Catholic School, we saw how strong expectations, established by administrators and teachers, aligned with personal responsibility on the part of parents and created an internal accountability system designed to hold parents accountable for involvement in their children's education. St. B's Catholic School serves 600 students in kindergarten through grade eight. The school is located in M-town, an incorporated city affiliated with one of the largest metropolitan areas in the country. Residents of M-town are mostly lower middle class. Admission to St. B's is competitive. Before being admitted to kindergarten, students must take an admission test that evaluates their fine motor skills and knowledge of letters, colors, shapes, and numbers. The school is operated by the St. B's Catholic Parish, and the parish pastor, Father L, is ultimately responsible for the school. In practice, however, it is the school's principal, Sister A, who makes most of the decisions for the school.

Like Turtle Haven, the school operates within a relatively weak external accountability system. The school is a member of the archdiocese of the metropolitan area, but archdiocese officials emphasized that their influence over St. B's was only advisory, and that the archdiocese officials had no direct authority over the school. Despite the advisory nature of this relationship, however, both the school principal and many parents asserted that the archdiocese in fact does have control over the school. The most direct way in which the archdiocese influences St. B's is the "scope and sequence" curriculum. Teachers are expected to cover this curriculum in their classrooms through the course of the year. The archdiocese also receives financial reports from the thirty-four schools and publishes guidelines on a variety of issues, including safety, governance, and curriculum.

Despite these guidelines, archdiocesan officials insisted that St. B's Catholic School may not be ordered to follow these guidelines, although it is expected to do so and usually does. Within this external context, St. B's Catholic School has developed mechanisms for ensuring that external guidelines and internal expectations are met. For teachers, these expectations are generated primarily by the principal, Sister A. All of the teachers interviewed for this case study described their performance in terms of Sister A's expectations. She visits each classroom weekly to inspect lesson plans and to review the students' agenda books (pamphlets distributed to all students, which include school rules and other relevant information and have weekly calendars with space for students to note their assignments).

In addition to these weekly walk-throughs, Sister A also evaluates all teachers annually using a standardized format, including formal observation and a written report. These internal mechanisms at St. B's exist to hold teachers accountable; more striking are the structures designed to hold parents accountable. At Turtle Haven the internal accountability system worked to hold teachers accountable for parental involvement, but at St. B's, parents are held directly accountable for their involvement in school activities. As a competitive private school, St. B's has the leverage to create and enforce rules governing parental involvement in the school community.

At the beginning of each school year, St. B's Catholic School holds a mandatory parent meeting during which school rules and policies are reviewed. Failure to attend this meeting results in a $25 fine charged to the student's tuition bill. Parents are also expected to sign an annual contract indicating that they agree to follow the school rules. These policies include a dress code and other rules that parents agree to enforce, and a parental agreement to supervise homework and sign their child's agenda book. Each family must also agree to contribute twenty-five hours of volunteer work. Parents can, however, choose not to volunteer, instead making an additional financial or in-kind contribution to the school. This year St. B's instituted a new policy designed to increase communication between parents and teachers. All parents of children in the first through third grades, without exception, are required to pick up their children in the classroom at the end of the school day. Parents are fined $1 for every minute they are late.

It appeared that these expectations of parental involvement were closely aligned with the parents' understanding of their own responsibilities. For example, one parent mentioned that parent involvement in the school was one of the aspects she valued most about St. B's. She explained, "There's more accountability here. You have to participate and what I like about this participation is that you get to know the other parents. Whereas in public schools it's more of a drop-off, baby-sit kind of deal." In reference to the twenty-five hours of mandatory volunteer work, she explained, "I like that because you're not taking things for granted. . . . Whichever way you can help you can put in those hours. You know they're there. That is your obligation." At least for this parent, there appeared to be an alignment between her own sense of responsibility and the expectations of the school.

At St. B's, the edge that turns expectations into an internal accountability system is the fines imposed upon parents when they fail to meet expectations. The accountability system works most strongly here for parents, not teachers. Perhaps that is because the competition for admission to the school is greater than the competition for jobs at the school. Admission to St. B's is extremely competitive, but the school administration has had difficulty recruiting qualified teachers.

Pine Creek Elementary School

Expectations that lead to an internal accountability system do not necessarily originate from administrators. At Pine Creek Elementary School, a strong set of expectations surround the subject of the students' capabilities and needs. These expectations function within the context of external policy, shaping personal responsibility and creating an internal accountability system.

Pine Creek Elementary School serves over four hundred students from early childhood through grade five. Pine Creek is located in the city of Flagston, a suburb of a mid-sized eastern city. The school is located across the street from a large housing development where most of the students live. More than 75 percent of the students qualify for free or reduced-price lunch. In 1994, Pine Creek Elementary School was designated a Blue Ribbon School of Excellence by the U.S. Department of Education. The school was selected because it was one of four schools in the state with the largest relative gain in fourth-grade reading scores. Not only did Pine Creek demonstrate significant growth, but the school scored significantly higher than other schools in its comparison school band. Staff development at Pine Creek is designed to hold teachers accountable for meeting self-selected goals. Teachers meet in grade-level teams every Tuesday afternoon and work toward goals they have set as a team. At the end of the year, each team must present its progress to the principal, who in turn reports to the main office. One teacher said she believed this system of staff development served to hold them accountable: "I think it's accountability. It's holding us as teachers accountable to the goals that we've set, and certainly often times it's harder to show what you've done if it's not something concrete, if there is not something written to hand to somebody."

Staff development team meetings are also used to discuss strategies for improving performance on standardized tests. Pine Creek has been designated as a Title I schoolwide project. The principal asserted that, in order to maintain the additional level of funding associated with this designation, they must show 5 percent annual growth on the Stanford 9 achievement test. Within the context of these expectations for student performance defined by the Title I law exists a set of collective expectations that relates to students' abilities.

Unlike Turtle Haven, Pine Creek teachers define their work and expectations for students in relation to their understanding of the children's background. As one teacher explained, "Unfortunately, I've heard too many say around here that what we do here gets undone when they go home. The baggage that our kids carry with them when they come to school, sometimes it's unbelievable that they function as well as they do. So, a lot of them have a hard time, because there's nothing to look forward to after school gets out." Another teacher described the students' parents as follows: "They are one-parent families; they are all on welfare, they don't have any money for breakfast; they don't have any money for sub[sidized] lunch, and there is not very good parenting."

These perceptions of the students, parents, and community are often closely linked to teachers' academic expectations of students. Teachers explained that because of their backgrounds, students were not able to achieve as much academically as other students in Flagston. For example, one teacher explained that she was particularly proud of the progress the school had made in test scores because of the home environment of most students. How the teachers perceived their students and their backgrounds appeared to be the most influential factor in shaping teacher practice and attitudes. For example, the current principal has encouraged teachers to establish learning centers within classrooms. One teacher expressed frustration with this encouragement: "We found out that a lot of these types of children . . . we've learned this through workshops and we've been told. . . . that this type of child that we have here needs more structure . . . structure every inch of the way. . . . You know, less confusion and lots of structure that they thrive on."

Personal responsibility at Pine Creek is shaped by these expectations of students. Teachers perceived the children as extremely needy, both socially and academically. As a result, many teachers expressed a responsibility almost like the role of foster parent rather than the role of teacher. As one teacher said, "Kids today are coming in with a lot more issues, they are not being dealt with at home, and you need to deal with them. You wear many hats, I think. That's your job—to do it, and it's your job to make sure you are doing it." Teachers were involved in many activities with students outside of the regular school day. One teacher runs an extracurricular sports program, another volunteers as the unofficial school photographer. Another teacher mentioned that there were some things he does for which he does not believe he should be responsible. He referred to two crisis situations where he and the school got heavily involved in a student's home life. He explained, "Yeah, there's a lot of stuff we do here that we're not responsible for doing, but we do it just because we love the kids."

Some teachers, however, expressed frustration that the students' needs led the community to expect too much of teachers and the school. One teacher said, "I think we really need to gear more on the academic areas than on the other areas, whether it's the violence prevention or whatever areas are left to us, which is fine, but it's too bad because we have got enough to do with the academics. I mean, it's expected that we provide breakfast, that we provide extra programs, we provide homework centers, and it's not so much, well . . . it's expected by some, appreciated by many."

Despite these frustrations, teachers continued to feel responsible for meeting the social and academic needs of their students. They perceive these needs to be the driving force behind most teachers' decisions. Many teachers expressed a conviction that, in order to have success in their jobs, they had to assume responsibility for the many needs of their students. One teacher explained, "I think kids are coming in with so much extra baggage today, you can't get to the ABC's until you get past that point, and it would be ignorant of me to think that you could because you are not. If they don't come in ready to learn, you have to get them to that point; that's part of your job even if you have to spend all year on it."

Teachers' expectations of students also had a strong effect on the curriculum the teachers chose to introduce to students. Although there was a curriculum prescribed by the district, many teachers altered this curriculum based upon their perceptions of the children's needs and abilities. One teacher called Pine Creek a "home-based school," meaning, "We plan our curriculum for the kids down here based according to their needs because we know . . . what type of population there is down here. So we kind of gear the curriculum toward the needs of these kids because we know what the needs are and we know that sometimes the curriculum that is set for the entire city doesn't meet the needs of the kids. When they're saying that the kids should be reading such and such and we know these kids may come to us as nonreaders. . . . We do a lot of tutoring with the kids and we do a lot of changing the curriculum to meet their needs rather than to meet the needs of the city."

These expectations of students also appeared to shape the goals established by grade-level teams. For example, the third-grade team chose to focus their efforts on teaching children to write in complete sentences. They felt that the activities provided for students were too complex and therefore chose to write their own set of questions to accompany the basal reader. One teacher explained that they "tried to write the questions from a literal standpoint because we found that the book was offering questions that were very evaluative and third graders could not do it. They were not developmentally ready to do that, but we found that they were ready to answer literal type questions in a complete sentence." In this instance, the collective expectations of students worked within an internal accountability system to lower expectations of student performance.

At Pine Creek the expectations formed among the teaching staff regarding students' needs are much stronger than any expectations from the district or principal. In the one area where the principal presented clear guidelines—staff development—these collective expectations shaped how the teachers met those guidelines. In this school, these collective expectations, closely aligned with the sense of personal responsibility to act as foster parents that most teachers feel, form the internal accountability system. As one teacher said, "You have to be willing to give extra time on Saturdays to come and watch them play basketball when they ask if you'll come to their game and you know nobody else will be there."

The consequences at Pine Creek operate not so much on individual teachers, but for the entire school. The possible loss of Title I status, or loss of recognition and discretion, appeared to be a motivating factor behind much of the work of staff development teams. Teachers collaborated to create a plan that would help students achieve that minimum level of progress. Sometimes this included changing the curriculum, moving units out of the order they appear in the book, and strategically choosing which material to cover and which to skip. Pine Creek teachers and the principal felt pressure to achieve a five percent annual rise in test scores. This goal appeared to be consistent with the teachers' collective expectations of students, insofar as most teachers believed the children could improve and learn. However, if the school were expected to meet a criterion-based standard level, that might be less consistent with the school's established internal accountability systems.

Summary

The schools discussed in this section have managed to translate individual responsibility and collective expectations into some kind of internal accountability system. These internal accountability systems operate in the context of external policy, and sometimes the internal and external are mutually reinforcing. Such is the case when the external system, personal responsibility, and collective expectations are aligned within the school.

At Turtle Haven, for example, the district's performance-based standards, although accompanied by little external accountability, appear closely aligned with the school's collective expectations. There is as yet no defined mechanism to hold teachers accountable for the implementation of these standards, but this external policy has been incorporated into the internal accountability system. In schools where the external policy is *not* aligned with the collective expectations, teachers tend to follow the internal accountability system. For example, at Pine Creek, teachers collectively decided that the district's curriculum was not appropriate for their students; still, the school pays careful attention to the accountability system imposed by the federal Title I program. In effect, Pine Creek teachers wrote the district's curriculum based on their collective expectations of students with lower abilities than those represented in the district's policy. Internal accountability systems influence behavior because they reflect an alignment within the school of personal responsibility and collective expectations, regardless of the external policy. This alignment of expectations and responsibility is also accompanied by some sense that there will be consequences if expectations are not met. At Turtle Haven, teachers are aware that they could lose their jobs if they do not live up to the expectations set by the principal and reinforced by the school community. Parents at St. B's may feel some sense of responsibility to be involved in their children's education, but they know they will be fined if they do not follow the established guidelines.

It is the alignment between expectations and responsibility, connected to certain consequences, that shapes the internal accountability within these schools. All actors feel responsible for meeting expectations, *and* there are consequences for not meeting expectations. These expectations, however, are for the most part generated internally, or, if generated externally, are modified to match preexisting expectations within the school.

CONCLUSION

Our aim in this report has been to view the problem of accountability primarily from the perspective of schools, rather than from the perspective of external policies that purport to influence schools. In taking this perspective, we have aligned ourselves with those who ask what conditions within schools determine to whom, for what, and how they are accountable (Wagner, 1989; Newmann, King, & Rigdon, 1997). In this sense, we have turned the traditional formulation of educational accountability as a problem of public policy inside out. Instead of asking how schools respond to policies designed to make them accountable to external authorities, we have asked how schools come to formulate their own conceptions of accountability and what role, if any, external policies play in these conceptions.

Our working theory of accountability, and our research methods in this study, were predicated on the belief or expectation that external accountability systems operate on the margins of powerful factors inside the school, and that understanding these factors is a major precondition to understanding how and why schools respond the way they do to external pressures for accountability. In later phases of our research, in light of what we have learned from this study about how schools construct accountability, we will focus more explicitly on the design and implementation of external accountability systems. The first and most important finding of this study is that our initial expectation about the power of school-level factors in shaping schools' conceptions of accountability was correct.

All the schools in our study had distinctive solutions to the problem of to whom they were accountable and for what. The relatively weak external accountability environment in which all of the schools operated offers some explanation for this lack of uniformity, but does not explain how or why schools arrive at the various configurations of accountability that we observed during our fieldwork. In most cases, solutions to the question of accountability were tacit, unarticulated, informal, and grew more from the individual beliefs and values of teachers and administrators as enacted in their daily practice than from formal or explicit agreements. The baseline or default solution to accountability that we observed at several schools was characterized by individual teacher responsibility, where personal discretion appeared to be dominant over organizational expectations or formalized accountability mechanisms.

Phoenix Charter School typified this theme. The responsibility-driven formulation of accountability evident in these schools was, in terms of our theoretical model, rather simplistic because it reflected little or no alignment with responsibility, expectations, and accountability, and equally little coherence about teaching and learning. However, lack of complexity should not be mistaken for lack of influence on daily practice. Individual responsibility in these schools exerted a powerful influence over day-to-day operations, although the net result was a fragmented academic program.

Another group of schools, representing the midline of complexity in our sample, exhibited discernible effects of collective expectations within the school on individual teachers' conceptions of responsibility. St. Aloysius typified this formulation. In these schools where group expectations related to teaching and learning, the academic program was more coherent than in the first category of schools. Where expectations and individual responsibility were directed toward affective needs, coherence was again evident. These schools were distinguishable from our third category of schools in that alignment and coherence were the incidental result of the schools' expectations, but there was little structure or consequence associated with these expectations, and the object of these expectations—whether academic, affective, behavioral—was still largely discretionary.

The most complex formulation of accountability observed in our sample was represented by our third category of schools, led by Turtle Haven Pilot School. In these schools, collective expectations gelled into highly interactive, relatively coherent, informal and formal systems, by which teachers and administrators held each other accountable for their actions vis-à-vis students. Teachers and administrators in this category of school were able to describe and interpret the formal external accountability systems in which their schools operated (such as testing systems, curriculum guidelines, charters, and the like), but in no case did these external systems seem to exercise the determining influence over their individual conceptions of responsibility, their collective expectations of each other or their students, or their internal accountability structures, where they existed.

Our findings did not accord with our initial expectations on one dimension. We expected that different types of schools would differ, if not systematically, at least roughly, in their solutions to the accountability problem. We deliberately designed the study to include parochial schools and charter schools, in addition to types of mainstream public schools, in the belief that parochial schools and charter schools, as the empirical literature and claims of policymakers suggest, would present us with a stronger, clearer set of examples of internal accountability systems at work.

For our sample at least, this expectation proved not to be true. The development of a school's collective expectations and its internal accountability system in our sample seems to be more a function of particular school-level characteristics than it is a function of the type of school. We should not overgeneralize this finding, but it is interesting that parochial schools and charters seemed to have the same problems as ordinary public schools in constructing a coherent conception of accountability. This study confirms widely prevalent views in sociological research that schools develop their own internal normative structures that are relatively immune to external influences, and that teaching is an essentially isolated occupation in which teachers are left largely to their own devices in deciding important issues of what and how to teach (Lortie, 1975). But the framework and findings of this study advance this view in several respects. By distinguishing among individual conceptions of responsibility, collective expectations, and internal accountability structures, we have provided a finer-grained portrayal of the forces within schools that affect solutions to the accountability problem. The persistent isolation of teaching as an occupation, in our framework and findings, means that the school's conception of accountability collapses, by default, into individual teachers' conceptions of responsibility. Schools operating in this mode, such as Phoenix Charter, Gateway Elementary, and Hutchinson High, were typically characterized by an emphasis on order and control, possibly because this was the one collective expectation on which it is possible to reach agreement in an essentially isolated work environment.

Perhaps because we conducted our fieldwork in relatively weak external accountability districts, we found that big questions about the collective purposes of the enterprise were often answered by the accretion of individual teachers' decisions, based on their views of their own and their students' capacities, rather than by collective deliberation or explicit management. The dominant pattern was not so much that schools developed their own strong internal normative structures that were in conflict with external influences, but that they failed to develop strong internal normative structures and thereby defaulted to individual teachers on major issues of collective expectations and accountability. In such circumstances, a school's incidental solution to the accountability problem—to whom, for what, and how—became simply a collection of individual, often idiosyncratic, judgments by teachers, growing out of their backgrounds, capacities, and individual theories about what students can do or need. In some cases, these judgments were powerfully influenced by teachers' preconceptions about their students' characteristics. Where teachers and administrators equated low socioeconomic status with inevitably poor prospects for student learning, they frequently wrapped their low expectations in theories about the deprivation of students, their families, and their communities, uninformed by systematic knowledge of what students were capable of learning under different conditions of teaching.

In other instances, teachers deliberately gave affective needs precedence over teaching and learning, but with the belief that physical, social, and emotional deficits must be addressed before students could achieve at high levels. Hence, in several schools in our sample, teachers assigned the most powerful causality, in their own conceptions of responsibility, to factors over which they, as teachers, had little or no control, and assumed the least powerful causality to those over which they had the greatest control—the conditions of teaching and learning in the school. The exceptions to the baseline, responsibility-driven mode in our sample are instructive. They all challenge the isolation of teaching, often in halting and tentative ways, sometimes more aggressively and directly. And they do so usually by introducing the idea that collective expectations—among teachers, between teachers and students, between principals and teachers, and among families, communities, and schools—should influence individual teachers' conceptions of responsibility. Sometimes these collective expectations mirrored a culture of low expectations for students, but often they challenged these low expectations in important ways. At times collective expectations were therapeutic in nature—they cast the school in the role of substitute for deficient families and communities; sometimes they reflected the high academic expectations that school people attributed to families; and other times they explicitly aimed to correct low expectations of students in the community or the school. Usually, the development of more explicit collective expectations was associated with the presence of a principal whose model of leadership embodied an explicit attempt to overcome the isolation of teaching, by shaping the normative culture of the school through recruitment of teachers and through direct involvement in the instructional life of the school. And sometimes the development of a stronger set of collective expectations—through the active agency of a leader and the engagement of teachers—led to the creation of observable internal accountability structures, informal and formal, that carried real stakes and consequences for members of the organization.

In our sample, the relationships between the external accountability structures within which schools operated and their internal solutions to the problems of responsibility, expectations, and accountability were slippery, subtle, and often downright contradictory. In the default mode, teachers and principals often dealt with the demands of formal external accountability structures (curriculum guidance, testing, and the like) either by incorporating them in superficial ways—claiming, for example, that they were consistent with existing practice when they clearly were not—or by rejecting them as unrealistic for the type of students they served. Without a way to address collective expectations within the school, external accountability measures can only work through individual teachers' conceptions of responsibility. Some teachers seemed quite adept at deflecting external accountability measures or unable to translate the accountability measures into daily practice. In instances where schools had developed some version of collective expectations, sometimes these expectations were aligned with external accountability systems, and sometimes they were not.

In a few cases, we witnessed principals and teachers engaged in some sort of collective deliberation about how to incorporate external accountability requirements into their internal conceptions of responsibility, expectations, and accountability. But in most cases, teachers and principals viewed external accountability systems like the weather— something that might affect their daily lives in some way, something they could protect themselves against, but not something they could or should do much about. In a few cases, the responses of teachers and principals to external accountability systems seemed to contradict in some fundamental way the theory behind the external systems, such as the charter schools in our study that seemed to experience no special demands or requirements stemming from the need for their charters to be renewed. This finding about the slippery, subtle, and contradictory relationship between internal and external accountability may simply be an artifact of the design of our study. We deliberately did not, at this stage, seek schools that were operating in strong and obtrusive external accountability systems. Some schools in our sample were located in cities that are in the early stages of developing stronger external accountability systems. Some cities are located in states that are in the early stages of implementing a new accountability system.

The charter laws operating in the states where we conducted our study were in the early stages of implementation, and these states had not yet directly confronted the issue of charter renewal. The weakness of the effects of external accountability systems may simply be attributable to the state of policy. We will confront this issue more explicitly in later stages of the study, when we will observe schools in more visible and powerful external accountability environments. Taking the limitations of our design and sample into account, there are still important things to be learned from this initial study about the relationship between internal and external accountability systems.

It seems highly unlikely to us that schools operating in the default mode—where all questions of accountability related to student learning are essentially questions of individual teacher responsibility, will be capable of responding to strong, obtrusive external accountability systems in ways that lead to systematic, deliberate improvement of instruction and student learning. The idea that a school will *improve* its instructional practice and, therefore, the overall performance of its students implies a capacity for collective deliberation and action that schools in our sample did not exhibit. Where virtually all decisions about accountability are decisions made by individual teachers, based on their individual conceptions of what they and their students can do, it seems unlikely that these decisions will somehow aggregate into overall improvement for the school. For schools operating in the default mode, the question for future research on the effect of external accountability systems is whether these schools can, or will, respond by developing congruent internal expectations and accountability systems.

Perhaps more importantly, a related question is how these schools will get the capacity to develop these new internal norms and processes. Schools that are not in the default mode—schools that have developed internal expectations, internal accountability systems, or both—raise a different set of issues about the relationship between internal and external accountability.

Our study suggests that these schools answer the question of what they are accountable for in very different ways—some schools focus on students' affective needs, others on high aspirations for students' academic performance. For these schools, the issues are the degree of alignment between their internal expectations and accountability systems and the demands of external systems, and the level of conflict and accommodation that arises from the confrontation between internal and external accountability. Are schools that manifest some capacity to deal collectively with the accountability problem internally more likely to adapt and align their internal norms and systems to the requirements of external systems, or are they likely to be more resistant to changing their internal norms and systems? Do these schools have the capacity to do the work of accommodating and adapting new external requirements? The existence of internal expectations and accountability structures, in other words, does not necessarily predict how a school will respond to new external requirements regarding teaching and learning. We will pursue these questions in the next phase of our research.

In this report, we have tried to array schools in a three-fold typology showing the range of accountability formulations that we observed in our fieldwork: schools in the default mode where all questions of accountability for student learning collapse into questions of individual teacher responsibility; schools that exhibit common expectations that influence and are influenced by individual conceptions of responsibility; and schools where expectations and individual responsibility are aligned to such an extent that this combination effectively functions as an internal accountability systems with stakes and consequences for members of the organization. The edges of these three types of schools are blurry in interesting and informative ways, suggesting both the possible limits of our working theory and the diversity of ways that schools have of coping with the accountability problem.

One thing, however, seems quite clear from our study to date. Conditions *within* schools are logically and empirically prior to conditions *outside* schools when constructing a working theory of educational accountability. That is, we cannot know how an accountability system will work, nor can we know how to design such a system, unless we know how schools differ in the way they construct responsibility, expectations, and internal accountability. This finding is fundamental to the study of educational accountability in all its forms. Schools will vary in their response to external accountability systems, depending on the level and type of solutions they have in place to the problems of responsibility, expectations, and internal accountability. Studies of accountability and attempts to design new accountability systems will succeed to the degree that they consider the sources of variability and explain their impact on the way schools respond to external demands. Accountability systems are often constructed by policymakers and administrators out of normative theories of how schools *ought* to act, uncorrupted by understandings of *why* they act the way they do.

Our study suggests that such systems should take their initial point of departure not from normative theories about how schools *ought* to act, but from a finer-grained understanding of *why* they act the way they do. Our research also suggests that the attitudes, values, and beliefs of individual teachers and administrators—about what students can do, about what they can expect of each other, and about the relative influence of student, family, community, and school on student learning—are key factors in determining the solutions that schools construct to the accountability problem. Put bluntly, many educators simply do not believe that they have the capacity to influence student learning in the ways that external accountability systems suggest they should. Hence, external accountability systems will be relatively powerless in the absence of changed conceptions of individual responsibility and collective expectations within schools. In our study, we have come to call this problem, "When accountability knocks, is anyone home?" A strong normative environment inside the school, based on a belief in the capacity and efficacy of teachers and principals to influence student learning, coupled with the knowledge and skill necessary to act on those beliefs, are prior conditions necessary for the success of strong external accountability systems.

5

Unwarranted Intrusion

"May you live in interesting times"—so runs the famous Chinese curse. In federal education policy these are interesting times indeed. For reasons that have thus far defied definitive political analysis, a nominally conservative administration has, with No Child Left Behind (NCLB), presided over the single most far-reaching nationalization of education policy in the history of the United States. In doing so, it has put the goal of its own education reforms, performance-based accountability, at risk.

Prior to NCLB, ensuring accountability in schools had been primarily a state and local responsibility, with the federal government and national organizations like the National Governors' Conference and the National Conference of State Legislatures playing a supportive role in the development of state and local policy. Post-NCLB, the federal government has essentially preempted the field of education accountability, setting national parameters on the details of state and local accountability systems.

Theories of federalism usually stress the idea of comparative advantage among levels of government. Over time, the argument goes, local, state, and federal governments sort out their roles in a given policy area according to broad understandings of which levels of government best perform which functions. This piece, published shortly after the advent of NCLB, argues that NCLB is a major, perhaps fatal, strategic error because it places the federal government in a position in which it has no comparative advantage.

As with any major policy reform, performance-based accountability is a work in progress. Major issues like the use of tests to judge the performance of students, schools, and districts; the frequency and level of testing; the use of information on performance as a tool of reform; and the effect of high-stakes testing on students' learning and persistence in school are essentially under constant review and discussion as accountability policies roll out. The major advantage of the pre-NCLB division of labor was that states and localities could experiment with a wide variety of solutions to the central problems of performance-based accountability and, capitalizing on the variations among them, increase our collective knowledge.

By centralizing education reform in the hands of federal policymakers—not noted for either their patience or sophistication in this area—NCLB has effectively narrowed the range of experimentation with accountability policies, consequently narrowing the learning that can occur across states and localities and increasing the risks of failure and adverse effects.

Inside the Washington, D.C., beltway, the reauthorization of the Elementary and Secondary Education Act (ESEA) is seen as either a sea change in federal education policy or a half-measure designed to demonstrate the political leadership's willingness to "do something" on education. On one side are supporters of the legislation who point to its substantial tightening of school accountability; its granting of more flexibility to states and school districts in the use of federal funds; and its commitment to applying sanctions to and providing aid for failing schools. On the other side are those who argue that the bill doesn't go far enough. Supporters of school choice believe that opportunities for real reform were lost when conservatives and New Democrats failed to persuade their colleagues and the president's advisors to include vouchers as part of the reform package.

In other words, there is no genuine opposition in Washington to accountability rules that simply fail to understand the institutional realities of accountability in states, districts, and schools. And the law's provisions are considerably at odds with the technical realities of test-based accountability. Never, I think, in the history of federal education policy has the disconnect between policy and practice been so evident, and possibly never so dangerous. What's particularly strange and ironic is that conservative Republicans control the White House and the House of Representatives, and they sponsored the single largest—and the single most damaging—expansion of federal power over the nation's education system in history.

The federal government is mandating a single test-based accountability system for all states—a system currently operating in fewer than half the states. The federal government is requiring annual testing at every grade level, and requiring states to disaggregate their test scores by racial and socioeconomic backgrounds—a system currently operating in only a handful of states and one that is fraught with technical difficulties. The federal government is mandating a single definition of adequate yearly progress, the amount by which schools must increase their test scores in order to avoid some sort of sanction—an issue that in the past has been decided jointly by states and the federal government. And the federal government has set a single target date by which all students must exceed a state-defined proficiency level—an issue that in the past has been left almost entirely to states and localities.

Thus the federal government is now accelerating the worst trend of the current accountability movement: that performance-based accountability has come to mean testing, and testing alone. It doesn't have to. In fact, in the early stages of the current accountability movement, reformers had an expansive view of performance that included, in addition to tests, portfolios of students' work, teachers' evaluations of their students, student-initiated projects, and formal exhibitions of students' work. The comparative appeal of standardized tests is easy to see: they are relatively inexpensive to administer; can be mandated relatively easily; can be rapidly implemented; and deliver clear, visible results. However, relying only on standardized tests simply dodges the complicated questions of what tests actually measure and of how schools and students react when tests are the sole yardstick of performance.

If this shift in federal policy were based on the accumulated wisdom gained from experiences with accountability in states, districts, and schools, or if it were based on clear design principles that had some basis in practice, it might be worth the risk. In fact, however, this shift is based on little more than policy talk among people who know hardly anything about the institutional realities of accountability and even less about the problems of improving instruction in schools.

THE IMPLEMENTATION PROBLEM

The idea of performance-based accountability was introduced in the mid-1980s by the National Governors Association, led by Bill Clinton, then the governor of Arkansas. It took the form of what was then called the "horse trade"—states would grant schools and districts more flexibility in making decisions about what and how to teach in return for more accountability for academic performance. This idea became the central theory of today's accountability reforms. It was an appealing idea in principle: Governors and state legislators could take credit for improving schools without having to commit themselves to serious increases in funding.

The movement got a major boost in 1994, when Title I—the flagship federal compensatory education program—was amended to require states to create performance-based accountability systems for schools. The vision behind the 1994 amendments was that Title I would complement and accelerate the trend that began at the state level; they required states to develop academic standards, assessments based on the standards, and progress goals for schools and school districts, all within ambitious timetables. The merger of state and federal accountability policies—or alignment, as it was called—was supposed to occur by the year 2000. By the end of the decade, it was difficult to find more than one or two states lacking some form of statewide testing program and public release of the results. However, in all but a few states the basic architecture of performance-based accountability systems remained relatively crude and underdeveloped. In those few states where the idea had been developed most extensively—Texas and Kentucky, for example—the systems worked well enough, according to the testimonials of their sponsors, to legitimate the idea that they were successful in general. Even in these states, however, there were legitimate criticisms of the accountability system's actual effect on academic performance and dropout rates.

Nevertheless, by the late 1990s it was abundantly clear that the states had fallen well short of what the crafters of the 1994 Title I amendments had envisioned. It was also clear that the federal government possessed very little leverage with which to force them along. States varied vastly in their administrative capacities to implement performance-based accountability systems. Many did not have testing systems in place that met the federal requirements. Most did not have the capacity to administer and monitor testing programs of the scale required to meet the federal goals. More important, creating accountability systems at the state level is essentially a political act, not an administrative one, and the federal government's harmless knuckle-rapping was hardly going to overcome the intransigence of a state legislature or governor. Indeed, the ability of the U.S. Department of Education to monitor and enforce compliance with the 1994 law was limited; budget cuts whittled away at the department's Title I staff just as their responsibilities were increasing. As is always the case, the department's senior political appointees were reluctant to make life too difficult for governors and chief state school officers, who are among their key political constituencies. The rub: By 2000, the target date for full compliance, fewer than half the states had met the requirements. In this environment, it came as no surprise to learn that by the year 2000 many schools with Title I–eligible students were simply unaware of the program's major policy shift in 1994.

This situation should have signaled to the Bush administration and Congress that there were complex issues of institutional capacity at the state and local level that could not be brushed aside by simply tightening the existing law's requirements. If more than half the states were unable or unwilling to comply with the requirements of the previous, less stringent, more forgiving law, why would one expect all the states to comply with a much more stringent and exacting law? Part of the problem is political. Even though virtually all the states have joined the accountability bandwagon, for many states it is largely a symbolic act. The basic designs of the systems are still primitive; the authority of state education officials to oversee school districts is still limited in many cases; and the political consequences of imposing large-scale, statewide testing in states with strong traditions of local control are risky. Consequently, support for accountability among state legislators and governors is often highly volatile.

Another part of the problem is administrative. Mounting a statewide testing system is a task beyond the capacity of most state departments of education. Those that have embarked on large-scale testing are stretched to their limits just managing test-development work or monitoring testing contractors. Many states are not doing this work particularly well; others still don't know what the work entails. Still another part of the problem is technical. Standardized tests inevitably become highly politicized and, in the course of the debate, the limits of testing are subjected to public scrutiny. Many policymakers enter the accountability debate not knowing much about testing, and they often discover, much to their chagrin, that what they don't know can hurt them. Many legislators, for example, are surprised to hear that off-the-shelf standardized tests may not validly measure the content specified in state-mandated standards and that norm-referenced tests (tests that deliberately create a normal distribution around a mean) may not be effective in measuring changes in performance.

THE CAPACITY GAP

The working theory behind test-based accountability is seemingly—perhaps fatally—simple. Students take tests that measure their academic performance in various subject areas. The results trigger certain consequences for students and schools—rewards, in the case of high performance, and sanctions for poor performance. Having stakes attached to test scores is supposed to create incentives for students and teachers to work harder and for school and district administrators to do a better job of monitoring their performance. If students, teachers, or schools are chronically low performing, presumably something more must be done—students must be denied diplomas or held back a grade; teachers or principals must be sanctioned or dismissed; and failing schools must be fixed or simply closed. The threat of such measures is supposed to be enough to motivate students and schools to ever-higher levels of performance.

This may have the ring of truth, but it is in fact a naïve, highly schematic, and oversimplified view of what it takes to improve student learning. The work that my colleagues and I have done on accountability suggests that internal accountability precedes external accountability. That is, school personnel must share a coherent, explicit set of norms and expectations about what a good school looks like before they can use signals from the outside to improve student learning. Giving test results to an incoherent, atomized, badly run school doesn't automatically make it a better school. The ability of a school to make improvements has to do with the beliefs, norms, expectations, and practices that people in the organization share, not with the kind of information they receive about their performance. Low-performing schools aren't coherent enough to respond to external demands for accountability.

The work of turning a school around entails improving the knowledge and skills of teachers—changing their knowledge of content and how to teach it—and helping them to understand where their students are in their academic development. Low-performing schools, and the people who work in them, don't know what to do. If they did, they would be doing it already. You can't improve a school's performance, or the performance of any teacher or student in it, without increasing the investment in teachers' knowledge, pedagogical skills, and understanding of students. This work can be influenced by an external accountability system, but it cannot be done by that system. Test scores don't tell us much of anything about these important domains; they provide a composite, undifferentiated signal about students' responses to a problem.

Test-based accountability without substantial investments in capacity—internal accountability and instructional improvement in schools—is unlikely to elicit better performance from low-performing students and schools. Furthermore, the increased pressure of test-based accountability, without substantial investments in capacity, is likely to aggravate the existing inequalities between low-performing and high-performing schools and students. Most high-performing schools simply reflect the social capital of their students; they are primarily schools with students of high socioeconomic status. Most low-performing schools also reflect the composition of their student populations. Performance-based accountability systems reward schools that work against the association between performance and socioeconomic status. However, most high-performing schools elicit higher performance by relying on the social capital of their students and families rather than on the internal capacity of the schools themselves. Most low-performing schools cannot rely on the social capital of students and families and instead must rely on their organizational capacity. Hence, with little or no investment in capacity, low-performing schools get worse relative to high-performing schools.

Some changes in the new law provide relatively unrestricted money that states can use to enhance capacity in schools if they choose to. However, neither state nor federal policy is currently addressing the capacity issue with anything like the intensity applied to the test-based accountability issue. So an enormous distortion is occurring in the relationship between accountability and capacity, a distortion that is being amplified rather than dampened by federal policy.

ABUSING TESTS

During the cold war, just about anyone who raised questions about the distribution of wealth in America was branded a Communist, thus chilling debates over social justice. Debate in the realm of education reform is being similarly chilled. Critics who suggest that there might be problems with the ways in which tests are being used for accountability purposes have been essentially marginalized. They're smeared with accusations of being against accountability of any kind and of being apologists for a broken system. The idea that the performance of students and schools can be accurately and reliably measured by test scores is an article of faith in test-based accountability systems. Consequently, tests are being misused and abused in ways that will eventually undermine the credibility of performance-based accountability systems.

Probably the most serious problem lies in the use of test scores to make decisions about students' academic progress—decisions about whether they can advance to the next grade or graduate from high school. The American Psychological Association's guidelines for test use, as well as the consensus of professional judgment in the field of educational testing and measurement, specifically prohibit basing any consequential judgment about an individual student on a single test score. The primary reason for this principle is technical, not ethical. Test scores have a significant margin of error associated with them. That margin of error increases as the number of cases decreases; individual scores are typically much less reliable than aggregates of many individual scores. The best that can be said about an individual test score is that it falls within a range that is described by its coefficient of reliability. Unless the range is extremely small, which it isn't for any standardized test, the likelihood of error is high.

The solution to this problem is to use multiple measures of a student's performance when making consequential decisions. But this solution is more expensive because it introduces a new level of technical complexity into the system. For instance, say that high school graduation was based on a composite of grades, test scores, and portfolios of students' work. Developing such a composite would not only be a challenging technical feat; it would also introduce a certain amount of human judgment into the system. Policymakers tend to distrust the professionals who make such judgments.

A similar problem arises at the school level. Under Title I, schools are expected to meet their annual yearly progress goals. This involves calculating a school's annual gain in test scores from one year to the next. Title I also requires disaggregating these scores by students' ethnic and economic backgrounds. But research has shown (see Thomas Kane, Douglas Staiger, and Jeffrey Geppert, "Randomly Accountable," in *Education Next,* Spring 2002) that these measures are highly unreliable for schools the size of a typical elementary school, and they are particularly unreliable for even smaller groups of students. Schools are often misclassified as low or high performing purely because of random variation in their test scores, unrelated to any educational factor.

The standards and accountability movement is in danger of being transformed into the testing and accountability movement. States without the human and financial resources to select, administer, and monitor tests are now being forced to begin testing at all grade levels. This is the surest way to guarantee that the test will become the content. Instead of creating academic standards that drive the design of a standards-based assessment, low-capacity states will simply select a test based on its expense and ease of administration. Thus the criticism that many state assessments are invalid because they fail to test the curriculum that is being taught. The more the issue of validity is submerged in the political debate on accountability, the more likely that charges of "teaching to the test" will be essentially accurate. A test with no external anchor in standards or expectations about student learning becomes a curriculum in itself, which trivializes the whole idea of performance-based accountability.

PROGNOSIS

The idea of performance-based accountability plays to the greatest weaknesses of the American education system. After World War II, most industrialized countries nationalized their education systems, but not America. Just the idea that students in Louisiana should be held to the same academic and performance standards as those in New York was enough to inspire heated political debate for decades. One consequence of leaving decisions about content and performance to states and localities for so long is that they never developed the institutional capacity to monitor the improvement of teaching and learning in schools, to support the development of new knowledge and skill in teachers and administrators, and to develop measures of performance that are useful to educators and the public.

The difficult, uneven, and protracted slog toward clearer expectations and supports for learning has barely begun in most states and localities. The history of federal involvement in that long endeavor is at best mixed and at worst a failure. The current law repeats all of the strategic errors of the previous ESEA reauthorization, only this time at a higher level of federal intervention. The prognosis is not good. The best we can hope for is that the capacity problems of states and localities will become more visible as a political issue at the state and federal levels, triggering responses that will help schools overcome the obstacles they face in improving the quality and intensity of teaching and learning. Likewise, it is to be hoped that the technical failures of testing will gain higher visibility and trigger a response that focuses more on the assessment of student learning and less on the administration of tests. The worst that can happen is that test-based accountability will widen the gap between schools serving the well-off and the poor, thereby confirming, at least in the public's mind, that expecting high levels of learning from all children is unrealistic.

As with many policy innovations, performance-based accountability in education is mutating into a caricature of itself. Never has this been clearer than in the reauthorization of Title I. The idea of giving schools and school districts greater flexibility in return for greater accountability for student performance—the original principle behind the "horse trade" of the 1980s—makes a great deal of sense. What we have discovered, however, is that accountability for performance requires substantial investments in organizational capacity: State departments of education need the capacity to select, implement, and monitor sound measures of performance; schools need support in developing internal coherence and instructional capacity; schools and districts need help in creating reasonable, diverse ways of assessing student learning; and teachers need support in acquiring the knowledge and skill required to reach larger numbers of students with more demanding content. As performance-based accountability becomes test-based accountability these critical issues recede, and a sensible policy becomes a nightmare.

6

Change and Improvement in Educational Reform

The disconnect between policy and practice has been, as this essay argues, endemic in American education. Sometimes this disconnect has been relatively benign, as, for example, when A Nation at Risk used a largely fictional portrayal of the problems of American education to galvanize a generation of education reform.[1] Sometimes it is actually quite destructive, as in the case of vast underinvestment in capacity-building in the federal government's No Child Left Behind Act. The basic lesson of nearly fifty years of policymaking in education at both the federal and state levels is that there is not necessarily a relationship between what policymakers say will happen and what actually does happen as a consequence of policy.

A more subtle but far more important lesson is that institutional change—including changes in the rhetoric of policy and in the accompanying regulatory superstructure—does not necessarily result in educational improvement. Shifts in policy improve teaching and learning only if they are accompanied by systematic investments in the knowledge and skills of educators.

This essay diagnoses the political and institutional incentives that lie at the origin of the confusion between change and improvement. It also assesses the consequences of this confusion for the current phase of educational reform. It brings to this collection an appropriately skeptical note: We should not always trust the rhetoric of policymakers. We should hold them accountable for creating the conditions that will make it possible for educators to be accountable.

Education policy in the United States has arguably not been much about education, at least the sort of education that occurs among teachers and students in classrooms. It has, however, been a great deal about policy, the kind of high-level political discourse that generates controversy and electoral credit for public officials. The great political and social struggles around education in the twentieth century have been about issues like the expansion of access to schooling (e.g., mandatory attendance), the institutional forms of schooling (the comprehensive high school, vocational education, what to do about the middle grades), and inequalities of opportunity among different types of children (financing inequities, compensatory education, desegregation, special education). While these struggles have been significant in their own right and have changed much about the institutional structure, rules of access, and social conditions of schooling in the United States, they have done little directly or intentionally about what teachers and students experience on a daily basis in classrooms. Indeed, the major theme of education policy seems, until recently, to have been the disconnect between policy and practice (see, e.g., Cuban, 1993; Sarason, 1993; Tyack, 1974; Tyack & Cuban, 1995).

Throughout the twentieth century, a rich and powerful series of debates about educational practice ran in parallel with policymaking—the struggle for the soul of progressive education, the emergence of child development theory and practice, the emergence of cognitive and behavioral approaches to instruction in reading and writing, and the like. But the two discourses of policy and practice have rarely intersected, and when they have, they have done little to inspire confidence in either policy or practice, as in the longstanding debate over evolution and creationism, or the more recent struggle between phonics and whole-language instruction in reading (see Ravitch, 2000a, 2000b).

To say that policy and practice have been engaged in parallel play is not to say that the two discourses have not influenced each other, usually in unintentional and perverse ways. The emergence of the American comprehensive high school is a case in point. The comprehensive high school was a largely structural reform designed to accommodate huge increases in enrollment in the first half of the twentieth century, with only the thinnest of pedagogical theories behind it. This structure has been enduring and persistent, and has profoundly influenced access to learning for generations of high school students and the conditions of teaching for generations of teachers, often in manifestly destructive ways. But the reform itself was never much about how teachers taught and students learned. In fact, that may have been its major advantage as a policy idea. It was a largely empty structural vessel into which educators and communities could pour whatever content and pedagogy they wished. Those reformers who focused on issues of teaching and learning have typically moved outside the existing structure of the comprehensive high school to demonstrate that alternative conceptions of learning could coexist in other settings. And still, the comprehensive high school survives. Still, the parallel discourse about what good teaching and learning looks like for adolescents survives. The two have had not much to do with each other (Boyer, 1983; see Powell, Farrar, & Cohen, 1985).

Now, two decades after *A Nation at Risk*, this parallel relationship between policy and practice seems to be changing in ways that are unprecedented in American educational policy. The course of educational reform has led, probably inadvertently, over the past twenty years toward the classroom—toward a more explicit connection between what policy says and what teachers and students are expected to do. The question now is whether this connection will occur and, if it does, what influence it will have.

A Nation at Risk has relatively little to say about this issue. In fact, the report itself is a good example of old-style policy-as-usual—broad language carrying no specific proposals, designed to mobilize *others* to act, locating responsibility for its proposals in a broad array of actors distant from its point of origin in Washington, D.C. It could hardly have done otherwise, originating in a presidential administration that had three years earlier run on a promise to dismantle the U.S. Department of Education and dramatically reduce the federal presence in education, declaring education to be wholly a state and local responsibility. Politically, the report was masterfully engineered by then-secretary of education Ted Bell as a way of positioning himself and an initially reluctant administration in a proactive role in education and salvaging the department without committing the administration or the federal government to actually doing anything (Harvard Graduate School of Education, 1995).

Not surprisingly, then, the report is clearer on diagnosis than on prescription. It defines the central problem as low expectations for academic work in schools, weak preparation for teachers in academic content, and insufficient time on academic work in schools. It suggests that the remedies to these problems are the joint responsibility of teachers, local school administrators, school boards, and states—with a modest and vaguely defined role for the federal government in supporting others' work. More importantly, while the report is quite critical of the performance of schools in general, it is quite vague in its diagnosis of what has produced this problem. Presumably, the same institutional structure that produced the problem is the one that the report calls upon to exercise responsibility in solving it. It is as though the problems described in the report were a sort of unintentional side effect of teaching, administration, and governance of schools. Bringing these problems to the attention of teachers, school administrators, school board members, state legislators, and governors was sufficient to engage their full energy—suddenly—in a new, more powerful way. Not surprisingly, many educational practitioners saw in the report another example of policy-as-usual: a broad critique with vague prescriptions, ungrounded in anything that looked or smelled like a real school.

But *A Nation at Risk* did legitimize an already growing political movement that had begun in southern and border states, like Florida, South Carolina, and Kentucky, and, in time, gradually spread to virtually every other state. The so-called reform movement in the early 1980s was protean and incoherent, covering everything from increases in teachers' salaries to school finance reform to merit pay for teachers to school-site management and internal restructuring. It was a political cause in search of a theme, fueled largely by self-defined progressive southern politicians, like Richard Riley of South Carolina, Bob Graham of Florida, and Bill Clinton of Arkansas, looking for ways to bring their states into the mainstream economic and political life of the country. It wasn't until the Education Summit of 1989 in Charlottesville, Virginia, between then-president George Bush and the governors, chaired by Bill Clinton, that what we currently regard as education reform began to emerge. The significance of this meeting was unprecedented in the history of U.S. educational policy: the chief elected executives from the states, sitting with the president of the United States to discuss a common strategy for educational reform.

The vision of reform that emerged from this meeting probably would have surprised the authors of *A Nation at Risk* in its specificity and strategic focus. The deal—or the "horse trade" as then-secretary of education Lamar Alexander called it—was increased discretion for results. The federal government and states would focus their policy on results, defined as student learning, and schools and localities were expected to exercise their judgment and expertise to achieve those results. Only in cases of outright failure would the federal government or the states intervene in the affairs of local schools—and then only to remedy immediate causes and leave. This idea was the kernel of what we now call education reform: that the government's job is to regulate and reward *results*, and it is the job of school people to produce them. This idea began to work its way through state reforms and through successive reauthorizations of the federal Elementary and Secondary Education Act (ESEA) over the next decade-plus. At the heart of this theory is the belief—shared by New Democrats and Republicans—that bureaucracy, government regulation, and institutional complexity sap human creativity and energy. Removing the dead hand of bureaucracy and overregulation by focusing government on results frees people to do what they know is right and effective. Education reform henceforth would come to mean accountability for results. And it is this theory that has been developed and modified in the laboratory of federalism for the last decade or so.

While accountability for results has proven to be a powerful and durable political idea, it has had no more basis in the reality of practice for most educators than previous policy ideas. Throughout the entire post–Nation at Risk period, education reform was largely done to, rather than done with, educational professionals. To a large degree, the dominant interests in state reform were general government officials and business interests. Educational interest groups—including the nominally powerful teachers unions—have been put in the role of responding to proposals initiated elsewhere, usually influencing policy only on the margins. Educators were largely considered to be part of the problem rather than part of the solution. The irony, of course, is that these same professionals were those who were charged with implementing performance-based accountability. The same people whose judgment and initiative is required to make accountability for results work are the people who produced the failures that created the occasion for reform. State reformers, obviously, do not have much sense of irony (see Fuhrman, 2001).

Another deep irony of this reform period is that it is premised on the belief that focusing government regulation on performance frees people in schools to do what they know is right and effective, but, of course, most of what people in schools know how to do they have learned by working in the same schools that policymakers think are failing. What educators knew how to do was what they were already doing, not what policymakers were asking them to do (see Chapter 2).

Fast-forward to the present: forty-eight or so of the fifty states now have some version of performance-based accountability systems, broadly defined as standards for content and student performance, assessments of student learning, public release of data on student and school performance, and some degree of consequences or "stakes" for poor performance. These systems vary widely in the specifics of their architecture—whether they involve specific stakes or consequences for schools and students, how frequently they test, how explicit the content and performance standards are, how difficult the tests are, etc.—but performance-based accountability has become the main theme of state education policy (see Goertz & Duffy, 2001).

With the adoption of the No Child Left Behind Act in 2002—the centerpiece of federal education policy—the federal government is now in the position of being the chief enforcer of performance-based accountability at the state and local level. The new law is unprecedented in the specificity of its requirements on state and local agencies: annual testing in grades three through eight, specific targets for annual yearly progress in student performance, mandates for quality control in hiring of teachers, state and local remedial measures for failing schools, and exit options for parents of children in failing schools. No Child Left Behind goes far beyond any federal role envisioned by the 1989 educational summit, much less the calculatedly vague *A Nation at Risk*, and far beyond any previous definition of the federal role in education. Performance-based accountability is now federal *and* state policy.

The reform movement is far enough along at the state and local level to have revealed that the central idea behind the "horse trade" of performance for discretion and control is highly suspect. The premise that educators know what to do and all they need are the correct incentives to do it is essentially wrong. *Some* educators know what to do; *most* don't. *Some* are able to learn what to do on their own; *most* are not. About the same proportion of educators are capable of responding successfully to performance-based accountability as were successful under the previous regime. Educators, like most practitioners, learn most of what they know from what they do. It should not surprise us that the best predictor of what they will do at Time 2, other things being equal, is what they were doing at Time 1. The main lesson of the reform movement thus far is that increasing performance in schools is complex and difficult work—much more difficult than simply changing policy.

A large part of this difficulty has to do with the fact that performance-based accountability challenges the chronic and powerful disconnect historically between policy and practice in education. This disconnect is deeply rooted in the institutional structure of education in the United States. It is the consequence of a governance structure that promotes superficiality and instability in local leadership, that chronically under-invests in the knowledge and skills of teachers and school-level administrators, and that sends conflicting and multiple messages to people in schools about the nature and purpose of their work (Hess, 1999).

There is simply no way to solve the problem of large-scale improvement in educational performance without connecting policy and practice more directly and powerfully. It is this connection that we have been avoiding in variety of ways, through a variety of pretexts, throughout the twentieth century, but especially since *A Nation at Risk*. Schools simply cannot do what they are being asked to do without more explicit and powerful guidance and support for instructional practice and without major changes in investments in knowledge and skill for educational practitioners.

Put simply, educational reformers are gradually, unavoidably, and reluctantly approaching the inevitable conclusion that schools cannot simultaneously be the cause of failure and the source of success. Asking teachers and administrators to increase academic performance for students without fundamentally altering the conditions under which they failed to produce student learning in the first place is a dead end. Teachers and administrators generally do what they know how to do—they do not deliberately engage in actions they know will produce substandard performance, nor do they intentionally withhold knowledge that they know might be useful to student learning. If schools are not meeting expectations for student learning, it is largely because *they do not know what to do*. And, given the longstanding disconnect between policy and practice, neither do policymakers. In its least desirable face, educational reform can become a kind of conspiracy of ignorance: policymakers mandating results they do not themselves know how to achieve, and educators pretending they do know what to do but revealing through their actions that they don't.

Under these conditions, "change" can become an attractive nuisance. Policymakers "change" policy in order to keep faith with their constituents—raising standards, increasing the difficulty and frequency of testing, raising the stakes for students, threatening failing schools with adverse consequences. Practitioners reciprocate by engaging in their own brand of "change": teaching test items; expanding the amount of instructional time but not the actual content or quality of instruction for students who fail to meet standards; holding students out of testing grades who are at risk of failure; providing public recognition for students and teachers who meet performance expectations but not explaining how they did; and so forth. What's interesting about these conditions of "change" is that they are almost perfectly symbiotic—both sides are benefiting from the "changes" each is undertaking—and also almost perfectly pointless in educational terms. Both sides are operating in a mutually and tacitly acknowledged zone of ignorance.

This view of policymaking as "change making" also dovetails nicely with the pathologies of the governance structure for education in the United States. Administrators are selected and promoted largely on the basis of their ability to inspire confidence in communities and locally elected school boards, not usually on the basis of their knowledge of instructional practice. They seek approval and recognition by proposing agendas of "change" that maximize public visibility but minimize actual impact on instructional practice. Local board members collude in the dance of change by identifying themselves with the agenda of leaders. Since the effects of changes proposed by leaders are ephemeral, leaders often survive by moving on to other communities with other boards looking for "change." This phenomenon—called *policy churn*—is a powerful pattern in American education policy (Hess, 1999).

And it runs exactly counter to the requirements of performance-based accountability. Over the long term, it is impossible to improve student performance without eventually improving the quality of teaching and learning that occurs in classrooms and schools. This work is hard, precisely because it is counter-cultural in virtually every respect: it requires the mobilization and use of knowledge that is not presently in schools and classrooms, it requires the active engagement of people whose knowledge is primarily about teaching and learning rather than about the tailoring of ideas to an unstable political environment, and it requires the design and operation of institutional structures that alter the way people learn to do their work.

In the default mode, the governance and organizational structure of American education is all about change and not much about improvement. Performance-based accountability forces the issue of whether schools and school systems can be about the improvement of learning for adults and children. There are two possible scenarios from here forward. The first is that the parallel play of policy and practice will continue, driven by deeply institutionalized forms and incentives, and, ultimately, it will become clear that performance-based accountability has failed to materially improve conditions of teaching and learning in schools, except for those schools that manage to succeed under any set of external conditions. The second scenario is that performance-based accountability will force the forms and incentives of American education into a new relationship to learning, which will actually improve conditions for learning in schools.

As should be clear, part of the problem here is semantic, and in this instance semantics matter a great deal. The term *change* has become so corrupted in its application to education, at least in the United States, that it is practically useless as descriptor of anything related to the core functions of schooling. The problem of American education is not, as many proponents of change argue, that schools and the people in them "resist change." Quite the contrary, school boards, superintendents, and principals are all rewarded and reinforced for "changing" routinely and promiscuously. The problem is that schools are poorly equipped to *improve* the conditions of teaching and learning for teachers and students. To be sure, improvement requires change, in some sense. But the key semantic distinction is between *change* that has little or no measurable, cumulative effect on learning and that is driven by forces disconnected from teaching and learning, and *improvements* that are designed to direct attention and resources toward deliberate enhancements in the knowledge and skill of teachers and students designed to improve their performance. Another way of saying this is that change has a clear meaning only in an instrumental sense—change that *leads to* improvements in human capacity.

Thoughtful students of educational change acknowledge that few reforms ever reach teaching and learning, much less alter it in any fundamental way, and they agree in principle that useful change is, in some sense, about making the conditions of teaching and learning better (see Fullan, 2001).

But research on educational change, and its consulting spin-offs, are fundamentally concerned with advising people how to "manage change," rather than with questioning the value and role of change. The literature and practice of educational change is deeply concerned with how to convince people that they should change, how to make the need for change more compelling and palatable to a range of actors, how to hone and develop the skills of leaders to lead change, how to design organizations to be more or less perpetual change machines (because, after all, the world is constantly changing), and so forth. "Change in the service of what?" is a less compelling question in this literature. Even less compelling is the question of whether successful schools don't actually engage in less change of a visible sort, less fancy change-mastering and -leading, and more concentrated work on fewer big ideas directly connected to their core processes of teaching and learning than less successful schools. Even the most confirmed students of educational change would agree that the level of visible change activity in schools, or school systems, is no predictor of how successful they are likely to be.

The semantics of educational reform have traditionally been quite slippery around this issue, and the period since *A Nation at Risk* is no exception. The political rhetoric of reform, as we have seen, has been rather carefully designed (a) to mobilize commitment to change, but (b) to diffuse responsibility for the actions and consequences that follow from change, and (c) to avoid acknowledging that the problems that require change are produced by the very people and institutions that are being asked to engage in the changes required to fix these problems. The circularity here is obvious, and it can only be broken by teleology— that is, by assigning a purpose and direction to change and by assessing the value of change by the degree to which it makes progress toward that purpose.

Another semantic problem of educational reform is its tendency to substitute rhetoric for what might be called a "theory of action." The "horse trade" underlying performance-based accountability is a classic example of this. "Discretion for results" sounds attractive as an organizing idea for a policy, but, in fact, there is no well-worked-out theory of how you get from performance-based accountability to improvements in teaching and learning. Performance-based accountability may have a powerful political logic behind it, but it has no causal theory that would explain how applying increased scrutiny to performance will in fact lead people in schools to do their work more effectively. Worse, as we begin to sketch out the details of what such a theory might look like, it is apparent that it doesn't much look like "discretion for results." In fact, it begins to look like *less* discretion of a particular kind for *greater consistency* and *higher levels* of results (see Chapter 4).

With this congenital slipperiness of policy rhetoric in mind, let me stipulate a simple, some would say simplistic, definition of improvement: *Improvement equals increased quality and performance over time.* Put quality and performance on the vertical axis and time on the horizontal; improvement consists of moving in a roughly northeasterly direction. It is important to talk about both quality and performance as objectives of improvement for two reasons. First, agreement on what constitutes quality practice precedes and informs improvement in performance in education. In order to know what kind of performance we are trying to produce, we must first know what we are trying to do to produce that performance. Second, it is impossible to say whether performance has value unless one is prepared to defend the quality of the performance expected and the quality of the measures that act as proxies for that performance. So, for example, it makes no sense to talk about "improving reading performance" unless one has in mind some set of high-quality practices that would lead to increased proficiency in reading among students. Nor does it make sense to define reading performance in a way that is easily achievable but trivial in its value to students. Time, in the definition, speaks for itself. It takes time to improve, and we expect more or less steady progress in quality and performance over time.

Underneath this model of improvement lie two key ideas. The first is that there is such a thing as an *instructional core* that can be improved. In the United States, this is a controversial idea, since the culture of teaching has grown up around the idea that teaching practice is somehow irreducibly idiosyncratic and that "good" teaching is more an individual trait than a function of knowledge and skill. These beliefs about teaching are, of course, a dead end, because if there is no objective way to discriminate among more and less effective teaching practices and all practices are matters of personal taste and determined by individual traits, then there is no way to engage in any kind of discourse about teaching, much less improve it. In fact, all professional practices involve a core of knowledge that is relatively specifiable and teachable, surrounded by a zone of discretion in which practitioners are expected to use their judgment in adapting practice to specific circumstances. Trait theories of teaching are more a symptom of the intellectual underdevelopment of teaching practice than a valid characterization of the nature of the work.

The instructional core is defined by the relationship of the student and the teacher in the presence of content. In this model, it is possible to talk about the knowledge and skill of the teacher in relation to the content, the knowledge and skill of the teacher in relation to the student's mastery of the content, the knowledge and skill of the student in relation to the content and the student's knowledge of the teacher's expectations around the content, and the ways in which the content is refracted through the understanding of the teacher and student. There are, of course, many more things that education is about than instructional practice, and these things have value, but if education is not, in some fundamental sense, about the interaction of the teacher and student in the presence of the content, then it is, more likely than not, not about much.

The second key idea underneath the improvement model is that of *capacity* or *capability*, defined as the resources, knowledge, and skill that the teacher and student bring to the instructional core and the ability of the organizational surroundings—the school and the larger institutional environment—to enhance and support the resources, knowledge, and skill of the teacher and student. Capacity both *inheres in* teachers and students and it *comes to* them from external sources.

Improvement occurs, then, by raising the capacity of key relationships in the instructional core: by increasing teachers' knowledge of content and their knowledge of how to connect the content to specific students, by increasing the prerequisite knowledge that students bring to their interactions with teachers and by deepening their own knowledge of themselves as learners, by increasing the complexity and demand of content, etc. (Cohen & Hill, 2001; see also Chapter 3).

There is no other way to enhance capacity, as it is defined above, than by deliberately investing in the knowledge and skill of teachers and students to do the work of learning. This means literally using the school and the institutional structure that surrounds it as a mechanism to deliver resources and supports to teachers and students to enhance their learning. A controversial idea: that schools should become places dedicated to adult and student learning.

It is difficult to imagine schools succeeding on a large scale in responding to performance-based accountability without some deliberate theory of improvement. Some schools—those least in need of improvement—will no doubt manage their relationship to performance-based accountability systems by making more intensive use of the social capital that surrounds them in their affluent communities without actually doing much about teaching and learning. Some schools—those in need of improvement but out of range of the resources and opportunities necessary to improve the instructional core—will try to respond to performance-based accountability by doing what they have done in the past with greater focus and intensity. And many schools will try, at least initially, to meet the demands of performance-based accountability by gaming the system—teaching test items, moving content around in the calendar, holding students out of the testing stream, etc.—until they run out of such options. Sooner or later, if performance-based accountability is going to work as a policy, it will need a theory of improvement that is actually on the ground, in action, instantiated in an institutional structure, affecting the work of people in schools.

Notice I said "if performance-based accountability is going to work as a policy." In the world of policymaking, one always has to entertain the possibility that policies are more or less purely symbolic acts, and that the major point of policymaking may not be to influence the world but to display concern, generate short-term electoral credit, and move on to the next issue. It is quite possible that governors, state legislators, business interest groups, and now, after No Child Left Behind, bipartisan national political leaders, including the president and congressional leaders, are not primarily interested in the stated purposes of performance-based accountability but are using the issue of accountability to frame the issue of education for their electoral constituencies. If performance-based accountability is a largely symbolic policy, then it is a peculiarly ill-suited one. The key distinction between performance-based accountability and earlier reforms, dating back to the beginning of the twentieth century, is that it actually carries the evidence of its own success. We will know whether the policy is working or not by the evidence that the policy itself produces. Symbolic policymaking requires a certain discreet distance between the rhetoric of policymaking and data on its effects, so that policymakers can always assert that they did not intend what the data show. In essence, policymakers are playing with fire by requiring the measurement of school performance: They are betting on a policy that essentially has no theory of action behind it, and they have bet the credibility of policymaking institutions (if not their own credibility) since elected. What is at stake then in this experiment with performance-based accountability is the logic of confidence around public education. As long as the relationship between policy and practice was characterized as parallel play, everyone could be a winner. Policymakers and school leaders could engage in policy churn, reaping the benefits of new initiatives without ever having to deal with their consequences. Schools could manifest their commitment to "change" by engaging in activities that had little effect on their core functions, and by marginalizing those examples that did. The public could orient itself toward whichever aspects of schools they chose, since policymakers sent a welter of messages to multiple constituencies about how their interests were served by specific changes. Parallel play served everyone's interests well, except possibly the interest of students in learning. But then, students have never been a well-represented constituency in education.

The problem with performance-based accountability is that it stipulates the measures by which schools will be determined to be successful or not, those measures are in turn verdicts on the success of the policies themselves, and the policy disrupts the traditional logic of confidence around schools by asserting that schools are primarily responsible for student learning. As if this weren't enough, it is probably impossible to succeed at performance-based accountability without violating the principle of parallel play between policy and practice.

If the path to performance is primarily through deliberate practices of improvement, designed to enhance the resources, knowledge, and skill in the instructional core, then policy must necessarily be *about* practice, not about symbolic change and policy churn. This possibility is all the more problematical because the United States has little experience with policies that are designed to connect policy and practice in useful ways. A few examples will suffice.

It seems clear from both research and practice that professional development—highly focused on specific content and the pedagogy that goes with it and delivered as close as possible to the classrooms and schools in which it will be used—is a promising way to improve instructional practice. In most states and school districts and schools, no infrastructure exists for delivering professional development in this way. The obvious remedy for this would be for policymakers at the state and local level to invest in building up an infrastructure of intermediary institutions that would work with schools and districts on the delivery of heavily content-focused professional development. The political incentives to support this kind of investment are extremely weak and the level of sophistication required to do it well is way beyond that of most political leaders.

It is dawning on a number of actors involved in serious work on instructional improvement that the "discretion for performance" model of accountability in the horse trade is deeply flawed. Teachers and their organizations are, in fact, asking for more explicit curriculum guidance in order to meet performance standards. And their analysis is compelling. Under the system of parallel play, the curriculum grew in response to essentially political imperatives—subjects were added to the curriculum in response to constituency pressures, textbooks ballooned in size and topic coverage in response to politically driven state adoption processes, activities in classrooms multiplied in response to teacher initiatives, and special programs constructed their own version of the curriculum for "their" students. Teachers who are actually trying to figure out how to respond to pressure for student performance very quickly understand that improvement of performance requires focus, and focus requires discipline, both in practice and in the external demands that administrators put on teachers. Under these circumstances, having a simpler, more explicit, more focused curriculum begins to seem to teachers to be more advantageous. And, of course, the policy structure around schools is designed to produce complexity, controversy, and flux, rather than stability, simplicity, and focus. Where are the political incentives that will draw policymakers and educational leaders into a different view of curriculum guidance?

One of the first things that dawns on schools and districts when they begin to receive performance data is the *range* of variability in student performance at any given grade level. This is certainly true in urban schools, but it is also true in nominally "high-performing" schools in more privileged communities. The trend in performance-based accountability systems, exemplified in No Child Left Behind, is toward *more* disaggregation of results by level of performance and type of student, directing attention away from average school performance levels and toward the way schools serve specific populations of students. As a matter of practice, we know very little about how to accelerate learning in specific domains from students whose performance is well below those of their peers. Most so-called remediation consists of putting students in the same kind of instructional settings in which they failed in the first place for longer periods of time, on the theory that it was the students who failed rather than the teachers who taught them. As the variability in student performance becomes clearer, the paucity of effective remediation and acceleration practices will become clearer, as will the relative lack of a knowledge base in this area and an institutional infrastructure to bring it into schools and classrooms. Who will own this problem politically, and who will generate the kind of sustained focus of resources and knowledge to address it?

These are a few examples of what happens when policy and practice move from parallel play to a necessary connection. The problems are daunting and the signs that policymakers are prepared for them are weak and erratic. It is unclear at the moment whether policymakers have any idea what they have done by unleashing performance-based accountability.

A Nation at Risk was a largely symbolic event in the early history of the current generation of education reform. It represented policy-as-usual in many respects, not the least of which was its tendency to define problems and push the responsibility for solving them onto other players in other settings, and to reinforce the idea of parallel play between policy and practice. It added legitimacy to a growing reform movement that did not begin to take on its present focus until 1989. And as the idea of performance-based accountability has developed, it has become progressively clearer that it is both highly subversive and vastly underspecified. If performance-based accountability is about anything other than symbolic action, then we are facing some major challenges in the way we think about schools and their improvement. The work of improvement is very different from the work of change as it has been traditionally defined in education. It requires more focus, more sustained effort, greater attention to the core processes of instruction, and more discipline in holding the policy agenda steady while providing the resources and support for teachers and students to respond. It is unclear whether either the policy system or the administrative structure of education is built for this work.

7

Doing the Right Thing, Knowing the Right Thing to Do

The Problem of Failing Schools and Performance-Based Accountability

This essay examines the problems of performance-based accountability and school improvement from the perspective of low-performing schools. It represents a preliminary statement of some of my findings from a year and a half of visiting low-performing schools, trying to understand the work of school improvement in the most difficult cases, and trying to be of some assistance to the people charged with running and teaching in such schools. It is a fitting concluding chapter for this book, since it supports and extends the main argument presented throughout: that policies work only when they take into account the exigencies and uncertainties of teaching and learning inside schools and classrooms. The two schools featured in this article—Thornton and Clemente (both pseudonyms)—are real schools. Nonetheless, they reflect an array of patterns and problems I found in low-performing, improving schools.

At the heart of this piece is the idea that improvement is a developmental process, not an act of compliance with policy. Schools "get better" by engaging collectively in the acquisition of new knowledge and skills, not by figuring out what policymakers want and doing it. The development of human knowledge and skills—both individually and collectively—is not a simple, linear trajectory, as models of external accountability would seem to suggest. Development is often a ragged, uneven process characterized by significant gains in knowledge, skill, and performance, followed by fallow periods in which people confront the limits of their existing knowledge and try to discover the next set of problems that will lead to the next level of increase in performance. Accountability measures that penalize schools for failing to improve at a constant, and arbitrary, rate simply wind up making it harder for them to sustain and build on their accomplishments.

While the thoughts and arguments of this piece are decidedly preliminary, they raise significant questions about the design of existing accountability systems, not least those of No Child Left Behind. I hope these arguments will lead to a round of deeper research focused on the actual problems that improving schools face and their implications for the design of policy.

> All happy families resemble one another, but each unhappy family is unhappy in its own way.
> —Leo Tolstoy, *Anna Karenina*

In the next two or three years, a very large number of schools, most of them in urban areas, most of them with largely poor, minority student populations, will be classified as failing under the newly authorized accountability provisions of No Child Left Behind. The process by which this will happen is straightforward. The state sets a performance target for reading and math (science later) defined as the "proficient" level on its (federally approved) test. A school's starting point is its initial position on that test. All schools must meet the "proficient" standard, for all students, by the school year 2013–2014. Each school's annual performance target is the difference between its starting position and the state's "proficient" standard. That is, each school is expected to score annual gains across its entire population of students in a linear fashion. Lower-performing schools are expected to make larger incremental gains because the target is further away. Likewise, higher-performing schools are expected to make smaller incremental gains. Failure to meet these improvement targets for two consecutive years carries consequences. In the first year, students attending failing schools must be offered the option of moving to another, higher-performing public school.

In the second year, parents of children in failing schools must be offered the option of using their share of the federal Title I allotment to schools to purchase supplemental educational services from an approved provider on the open market. In the third year, the school becomes the subject of "corrective action," which requires the district to formulate a plan for the school that might include replacing staff, decreasing management authority at the school level, appointing outside experts to advise the school, lengthening the school day or year, or restructuring the school. The corrective action plan must also set targets for improvement by academic subject, it must provide that 10 percent of Title I funds in the school be spent on professional development, and incorporate a teacher mentoring program. Up to this point, the measures required by the law are cumulative—that is, schools in corrective action are also required to provide public school choice and purchase of services. If the school fails to meet its target under corrective action in one year, the district must take one of the following actions: the school can be closed and reopened as a charter school, it can be contracted to a private management company, it can be put in state receivership, or it can be subjected to any other federally approved governance arrangement. If at any point in this process the school has two successive years of meeting its target, it ceases to be failing school, but it continues to be subject to the target performance requirements. Performance failures, however, are cumulative. That is, the further behind its performance target the school falls, the greater the gains it is required to make in order to meet performance expectations.[1]

These are the basic ground rules for accountability under which most schools with high proportions of poor and minority students will operate for the foreseeable future. Under the most generous interpretation of No Child Left Behind, the law is designed to galvanize and focus the attention of educators around the problem of failing schools. Under a less generous interpretation, it is designed to remove large numbers of children and schools from direct public management and to move public education funds from public schools to privately managed schools and supplementary service providers operated with public funds. Whatever the intent, large numbers of schools and school systems are facing the problem of how to respond to the requirements and incentives of No Child Left Behind.

THORNTON AND CLEMENTE: THE FIRST CUT

Consider the following portraits of two schools I have visited in the last year that are currently classified as "failing:"

Thornton Elementary School

I am observing a second-grade classroom at Thornton Elementary.[2] The teacher is working with a third of the students in one corner of the classroom doing guided reading, a form of literacy instruction in which teacher and students jointly read aloud and discuss a book with an explicit focus on the author's meaning as well as the readers' responses to the text. Guided reading is new to the teacher, a veteran of twenty years. She is concentrating very hard. The students are also working very hard, and seem to be successfully reading and responding to the book. Each student in the class will rotate through guided reading in the course of the literacy block—the 90-minute period every morning devoted to reading and writing at Thornton—in one of three groups. While the teacher is focusing on the eight students in the guided reading group, the remaining two-thirds of students in the classroom—about sixteen—are doing a variety of things. Two reading specialists are working individually with two students, obviously struggling readers, on specific problems of phonics and word identification. A classroom aide is supervising a group of students who seem to be filling out worksheets. Some students are reading on their own and writing in journals. There are books in considerable quantity available to students. Student writing is prominently displayed on the walls. In general, the classroom appears to be orderly, quiet, and efficiently run. Behavior problems are few. Students seem compliant and relatively happy. Above all, the adults seem to be very focused, working hard, and highly motivated.

The principal and superintendent have worked out a professional development strategy for the school that focuses time during the school day and during designated professional development days on priority instructional areas. The teachers uniformly say that this is the best work they have done. The teaching force at Thornton is a veteran group; the least experienced teacher has been there twelve years.

Over the course of the morning I visit several classrooms at Thornton. Each looks roughly the same in structure and texture. To the casual observer, it would be difficult to see why Thornton is a failing school.

Teachers are working hard. Students are highly engaged. There are extra adults to work with failing students. The classrooms and hallways are orderly and clean. Thornton certainly looks nothing like the stereotype that laypeople might carry in their heads about failing schools—chaotic, disorderly classrooms, teachers obviously out of their depth with both content and student discipline, low-level student work, etc. In fact, most observers would probably say that, overall, Thornton represents a strong and positive environment for students. Most observers would be hard-pressed to say what Thornton should be doing differently, or why it's failing.

I have been invited to the school by the superintendent and the principal because, after some initial modest success on the state reading and writing test, Thornton's test scores have gone flat. The student population at Thornton is more than 80 percent poor, with equal numbers of African American and Latino students. The school is in an economically depressed city, and the patterns of student performance at Thornton reflect similar patterns in other elementary schools in the district. The state reading and writing test is a challenging test for even the highest-performing schools in the state. For Thornton, it is daunting. The superintendent and principal report that teachers in the school are heavily demoralized by their designation as a failing school. They feel that they have given the school's new literacy program their best shot. They feel they have dramatically changed their practice. The changes they have made are clearly visible in all the classrooms in the school, they feel, and they are still not making progress against the standards of performance they are expected to meet.

Clemente Middle School

Shift now to Clemente Middle School, a school of about one thousand students, grades six through nine, in a large northeastern city. Essentially all the students at Clemente meet the income requirement for free or reduced-price lunch—the prevailing measure of poverty. They are predominantly Afro-Caribbean, Spanish-speaking recent immigrants, with a significant number of African American students. A large proportion of the students are from families that might be classified as the working poor—they perform the basic services of the economy with very low compensation. It is mid-morning, and I am observing a seventh-grade language arts class, taught by a novice teacher—a Teach for America corps member, one of several in this school. The teacher is a new graduate of a prestigious northeastern liberal arts college. She is young, energetic, highly engaged in her work. She is African American and obviously has strong rapport with her students. The students in the class—about fifteen today—are a mix of African Americans and Afro-Caribbean Spanish-speaking immigrants. One student sits off by herself in a corner, focusing on something on her desk—probably a "time-out" discipline problem. The rest of the students sit comfortably at moveable desks, focused on the teacher. The lesson has to do with topic sentences and lead paragraphs, a key element of the state's middle-grades writing test, which these students will be taking next year. The teacher is carrying on a lively discussion of a topic that students are asked to use as the basis for their writing. As students volunteer ideas and write them down in their notebooks, the teacher actively engages them in a discussion of what they will say and how they will say it.

This classroom is one of a number I have observed this morning and the patterns are similar: active teachers, highly engaged students, instruction targeted at skills that are, at the same time, useful on their face and included in the state reading and writing test. I do not see a discernible difference between the novice and experienced teachers on these dimensions. The principal takes me to visit a couple of classrooms where he knows he has problems with the teachers. These classrooms are noticeably less engaging places for students; the teachers are clearly struggling with the fundamentals of teaching; they are also seemingly aware that they are not doing great work. One of the students asks me, in the course of the visit, if I am from the state. A review team recently visited as part of the state process for classifying schools as failing. Faculty and students know they are in a failing school, they are used to being visited, and it does not make them happy.

Clemente has four assistant principals, each of whom has instructional and professional development responsibility for a grade level in the school. The assistant principals are clearly present in classrooms. The principal and assistant principals have a strategy for professional development in key subjects with teachers. While time is limited, teachers participate and say the work is valuable to them in the classroom.

Clemente Middle School is a vibrant and exciting place visually. It is a relatively new building, with a large atrium as a central feature. It has a privately funded arts program in which students produce stunning examples of visual arts and writers from the neighboring city visit, while teachers and students conduct author studies of their work. The building exudes energy. Student work is visible everywhere, especially in the atrium.

Again, I am in the school because performance, after a brief gain, has gone flat, well below the target level required to keep the school from being classified as failing. The superintendent and the principal want me to see, hear, and feel what the school is like, not just examine the test scores. The superintendent thinks the principal of the school is one of the best in the district, and is worried about losing him to a neighboring district with much higher-performing schools. The principal says, in passing, that he has had to learn to ignore much of the feedback he gets from the state in order to focus on the things that need to be done to improve the school. Teacher turnover in the school and district is about 15 percent per year. About 40 percent of the teachers in the district have four or fewer years experience. Virtually none of the Teach for America members stays after their two-year term is over. The district invests heavily in professional development in literacy and math, but the superintendent says that once the new teachers have received the basic staff development program, they are attractive recruits for neighboring suburban districts that offer them significantly higher salaries.

Again, to the lay observer, Clemente would not be thought of as failing school. It has at least its share of marginal teachers, which in a school of one thousand is probably a significant number. But what you see as you walk the halls and visit classrooms are powerful examples of students doing interesting and creative work, teachers working hard to engage students in learning that is clearly connected to what the state tests measure, and students largely responding in the ways teachers want them to. Take away the discouraging test scores, and you have a school that most lay observers would say is a decent place for kids to learn.

I want to stress that these schools are *not* atypical of the legions of schools that are about to be classified as failing under No Child Left Behind. I have been in several failing schools in several localities over the last few years, and I would say that Thornton and Clemente are more representative of what I have seen than not. Failing schools are, for the most part, schools that have received repeated messages about their failure over long periods of time. They are not just coming to consciousness of their low performance. In every instance I have observed, these schools have been the object of intensive efforts to make them work better. People in these schools—teachers, administrators, students—are aware that they are in organizations labeled as failing, and, with certain exceptions, they are not happy or complacent about it. Failing schools, liberal critiques to the contrary, are usually not resource-poor environments. They are heavily staffed, they have large numbers of specialists who work directly with students, and they have considerable access to outside guidance and expertise in most settings. They also frequently have access to community resources that bring considerable assets to the schools. Failing schools do not have uniformly weak leaders. Some do. Some don't. The point is that "strong" leaders—as in the case of Thornton and Clemente—are often just as baffled about what to do about their situations as "weak" leaders. Strong, competent leaders may have more motivation to find out what to do; they usually don't actually know what to do, though they may be more inclined to seek help. In fact, I have come to the conclusion that most school leaders who claim to know what to do about seriously failing schools are bluffing. The leaders, in my experience, who are making the most progress—including those at Thornton and Clemente—are the ones who confess honestly that they don't know what to do and try to get help.

To be sure, I have also been in failing schools over the past several years that more closely resemble the common stereotype of such schools: schools that show little or no evidence of consistent expectations around the quality of instruction or student performance; schools in which the adults assign responsibility for low student performance to families and communities rather than to themselves; schools in which the resources available to support student learning are managed, if at all, in a chaotic and scattered way; schools in which teachers and students cannot answer the most basic questions about the purpose and direction of their work.

In general, what we have found in our research on accountability is that failing schools fundamentally lack what we have come to call "internal accountability."[3] That is, they lack agreement and coherence around expectations for student learning and they lack the means to influence instructional practice in classrooms in ways that result in student learning. In our research, high internal accountability, or coherence and agreement around expectations for teaching practice and student learning, leads directly to observable gains in student learning. Some failing schools lack internal accountability on anything but the most basic expectations—order in the hallways, for example. But, as the Thornton and Clemente examples illustrate, some failing schools are actually engaged in developing internal accountability, have had some success in generating increased student learning, but are still at risk of failure, and under the terms of No Child Left Behind are likely to lose their franchise before they have an opportunity to meet the performance requirements of the law. In the final section of the paper, I will return to the question of what to do about failing schools that manifest no apparent capacity to generate sufficient internal accountability to influence student learning, but I would like to stay with Thornton and Clemente because I think they teach us something valuable about the process of improving failing schools and about the design of accountability systems.

I wanted to begin this paper with these two examples because my thesis is that existing policies toward failing schools, including No Child Left Behind, are based on either faulty knowledge about school failure, or no knowledge at all. And, therefore, policies that are nominally designed with the intent of improving failing schools are actually likely to have the opposite effect—to prevent improving schools from succeeding. Our policies are based on extremely thin cultural stereotypes about failing schools, stereotypes that reflect commonly held beliefs and values deeply embedded in American culture and political discourse. Among these core beliefs are that schools fail because the people in them—administrators, teachers, students—don't work hard enough; they are lazy, unmotivated, and self-serving. The purpose of policy is to make people use their existing capacities to the maximum—to wake people up, to make them work harder. Schools also fail, we believe, because they are not led by strong, energetic people with vision and charisma. The people who lead schools, the argument goes, are products of a bureaucratic culture that rewards compliance over creativity. So policies should encourage new kinds of people to lead schools and new forms of school organization to break the lock of traditional bureaucratic culture. Schools also fail, in the conventional view, because the people in them lack the appropriate sense of urgency and focus on the essential tasks of learning. Given the opportunity, the argument goes, adults and students in schools will do whatever they want to do, rather than what they are supposed to do. So policies should give schools clear guidance coupled with clear rewards and sanctions that send a clear message about what the work is supposed to be. Finally, the conventional view is that schools fail because they lack the proper incentives to succeed. If schools and the people in them were threatened with closure or loss of enrollment, the argument goes, they would somehow be motivated to discover what they needed to do in order to succeed. These beliefs, I think, are embedded in accountability policies that focus on external rewards and sanctions as motivators for teachers, administrators, and students. These policies also focus on changes in governance and incentives on the theory that the "right" external incentive structure will "drive" schools and school systems to recruit and hire the "right" kind of people who will, in turn, lead schools toward the "right" kind of goals.

I have spent the better part of my professional career studying the impact of incentives and policies on schools, so I am not going to argue that incentives don't matter. They do. Nor would I argue that schools can't improve, to a degree, by getting people more focused, encouraging them to make better use of their existing capacities, and making them work harder. One of the main insights I take away from my recent visits to failing schools is how clearly most of these schools have gotten the message that the policies are sending them. The problem is not that they haven't gotten the message. The problem is that the message doesn't tell them what to do about the problem, other than to "get better." The answer that current policy gives failing schools to the question "What do I do next?" is "Get better." Thomas Schelling, surely one of the most astute economic theorists on the subject of incentives, once said to me when I was a graduate student, "The problem with most incentive structures is *not* getting people to do the right thing. It's getting people to figure out what the right thing is to do."

This is the problem I would like to focus on. This is the problem that is exemplified by Thornton and Clemente. Given that failing schools confront widely varying conditions and are being forced to operate under relatively uniform expectations, how do we think about dealing with school failure in policy and practice? How to we think about the right thing to do?

Another misconception influencing American policy is the notion that some schools are "successful" at meeting the government's and society's expectations, and that these schools can act as beacons or examples for failing schools. If failing schools would just do what successful schools are doing, they would get better.

At the same time I have been visiting failing schools, I have, as a normal part of my work with teachers, principals, and superintendents, also been visiting successful schools in very successful districts. Two things strike me about these visits. First, many so-called successful schools are afflicted with the same problems as so-called failing schools. Second, for the most part, critics and policymakers don't pay attention to the problems of successful schools because, as a category, like Tolstoy's happy families, they are all judged to be the same. A very large proportion of so-called successful schools are producing performance, as nearly as I can tell, almost entirely on the social capital of parents and communities. That is, they face many of the same problems of quality in teaching and learning as less successful schools, but these problems are not socially or politically visible because the income and cultural capital of parents and communities overrides the defects of the schools. These schools remind me of that joke about a certain successful politician from a wealthy family who was "born on third base and thought he hit a triple." They have little or no understanding of why they are successful, they only know that they are. Among the so-called successful schools I have visited there are some that acknowledge that they have serious problems with the quality of academic instruction. I find these schools to be just as interesting as so-called failing schools, and the problems they are working on look very much like the problems that failing schools are working on. These successful schools are, of course, under much less pressure, and they have much higher opinions of themselves. They are careful to protect themselves from any possibility of being judged as substandard, so they do not advertise their problems to their constituencies or the world at large. They work hard at preserving their credibility with their communities while they are working on fundamental problems of instructional quality. And they are largely ignored by existing accountability systems.

I am, as a result of my work with schools, highly skeptical that so-called successful schools have anything systematically to teach so-called failing schools. In fact, I would argue that schools like Thornton and Clemente have a great deal more to teach some nominally successful schools than vice versa. Later, I will propose two different classes of schools—"improving" and "not improving"—and I think these two classes of schools do have much to teach each other. But I'm getting ahead of myself. Let's return to Thornton and Clemente.

THORNTON AND CLEMENTE: THE SECOND CUT

As we debriefed our observations of classrooms at Thornton with the superintendent, the principal, and the lead teachers, a number of patterns became clear. First, while teachers were clearly working hard to apply their new knowledge on literacy instruction, no one was paying attention to the overall instructional quality and intensity of what was happening to students while the teachers were doing guided reading. All one needed to do was to walk around the classroom and observe what students who weren't involved in guided reading were actually doing— that is, what was on the desk in front of them, what was the purpose of whatever it was, and what did the student actually know about the purpose of the work. What became clear when we did this was that, while instructional intensity and cognitive demand were high among those students involved in guided reading, not much was going on with the other students when they were not in the group, with the exception of the two students who were working one-on-one with the reading specialists. But second, those students presented another problem. The work they were doing with the reading specialists, while it was quite skillfully designed and done, was not explicitly connected to the work that these students were expected to do when they were not in remediation. That is, the intervention was successful, but it wasn't successful as a cumulative goal that would bring these students into the mainstream of the class. And third, when we asked students to describe to us, in real time, what they were doing, what its purpose was, and how they would know whether they had been successful at doing it, most of the students were unable to answer.

So it's not surprising that Thornton had some initial gains with its literacy program and then its performance went flat. What happened was that students were exposed to a potentially powerful reading intervention—the introduction of guided reading—that substantially increased the amount of time and intensity of instruction for them relative to what they had been doing. This new activity got the teachers and students focused on coherent work around reading in a way that could be observed and improved. What was *not* happening was that no one was monitoring the overall intensity of instruction for students when they were not participating in guided reading, and the coherence of the tasks that various people were doing in the classroom. Clearly, the next increment in performance will come from increasing the level of intensity, cognitive demand, and coherence for all students, whether they're in guided reading or not. This will require the teacher to pay much more attention to the orchestration of activities in the classroom and to have much more clarity and agreement with students and support staff around the purpose of the work.

What often happens when you present this problem to teachers is they reply that they are already working at full capacity and simply can't do anything more around classroom management. Then, with the support of someone who is knowledgeable about instructional practice, teachers come to understand that they can actually do the work and that it is not as demanding as they thought it was. And so they move to the next level of practice. At that level, they often confront some other constraint that causes performance to, again, level off. Typically, at this next level, they come to terms with the fact that certain of their practices are simply not working for certain students, and the performance of those students is lowering the overall performance of the class. Often, teachers go through the same period of wondering whether they have the skill and knowledge to do the work, initially thinking it is impossible to do, and with support they discover they do have the capacity to do the work, and, again, performance rises.

Several things are happening here. First, it often takes another set of eyes to see what principals, students, teachers, and support staff don't see, because they are working on solving the current problem, not on identifying the next one. At Thornton, the teachers were working so hard at mastering guided reading, they didn't have time to focus on what else was happening in the classroom. Second, teachers and students get more powerful in their practice, often against their own expectations, when they are brought to acknowledge a barrier and then put in the way of knowledge about how to get over it. Notice, it is important to understand that teachers and students don't get better by applying knowledge and skill they already have—they are stuck because their existing knowledge isn't enough. They get better by having access to new knowledge, and discovering that they can use it in ways that they did not fully appreciate before. Third, it is increasing the level of intensity, cognitive demand, and coherence around instructional practice that produces gains in student performance, and that process requires that everyone, including students, teachers, and support staff, develop increasing agreement about what the work is. As noted above, this is what we have called internal accountability. If you walk into a classroom and sit down next to a student, ask them what they are doing and why, and you don't get a clear answer, it is highly unlikely that any powerful learning is taking place.

At Clemente, as we debriefed, a different set of problems emerged. This will sound odd, but bear with me. The teachers at Clemente were working *too* hard. Yes, that's what I said. Novice teachers and veteran teachers of students in the middle and upper grades often equate "good" teaching with teaching that keeps students amused, interested, and seemingly engaged—which usually means eyes forward, paying attention, not causing any discipline problems, and responding in a timely way to the teacher's questions.[4] So what had happened at Clemente was that the "good" teachers in the building—including some novices and some experienced veterans—had adopted a style of practice in which the teachers were doing virtually all the work in classrooms and the students were doing very little. The teachers felt they were giving it their best shot, and to a layperson's eyes they were doing even more than that. The students were engaged and amused, and they certainly weren't complaining. But when you looked at the classroom as a setting for *student work* it was clear that not much was happening. A straight transcript of classroom discourse, for example, would reveal that, in order to keep students' attention focused on the front of the room, teachers were asking predominantly factual questions—questions that could be answered literally by the student pulling the information straight out of the text on the desk in front of them. When teachers did ask questions that required higher levels of cognitive demand—interpretation, argument, analysis—the overall pace of previous questions meant that waiting even a short period of time for a student response seemed like ages, so the teacher quickly moved on to the next question before the students could fully engage the previous one. The actual written work that students were being asked to produce—remember, this is a class aimed at preparing students to pass the state writing exam, which includes open-ended writing prompts—was likewise short and truncated, apparently because the teachers had made the judgment that the students needed, again, a faster pace, with more concrete tasks, in order to stay engaged.

What was happening at Clemente is what often happens in the early stages of instructional improvement—teachers are developing rudimentary norms of practice designed to signal their collective commitment to students' success. They are, in effect, developing internal accountability around student learning and performance, albeit at a very rudimentary level. In the absence of careful and thoughtful analysis of the kind of practice that would lead teachers and students to be successful on a demanding writing exam, teachers were doing what they thought they should do—working hard, being enthusiastic, demonstrating that they can hold the attention of the students—without much thought for the actual work that students were doing. Students, of course, responded. The dirty little secret of schools is that students generally do what adults tell them to do, especially if the adults seem interested in them. An outside observer would see what most people would regard as "good teaching" going on in a significant number of classrooms and wonder why the results weren't more impressive.

More importantly, teachers were generally *doing what they knew how to do*, rather than doing what was necessary to produce the result they were trying to produce. In the absence of specific guidance that what they were doing wasn't going to get them where they were trying to get, they would, other things being equal, continue to do what they regarded as "good teaching," and what many people would tell them was good teaching, without recognizing that it was precisely that kind of teaching that was producing the performance they were disappointed with. In order to get different results, they would have to learn to do something they didn't know how to do, and in order to do that they would have to have access to skills and knowledge that would help them understand and enact those practices in their classroom. Doing what they regarded as the "right thing" was not enough. They would have to figure out what the right thing was to do and then figure out how to do it.

The question at Clemente, however, significantly different from at Thornton, is how much to invest in helping teachers improve their literacy practice when the probability is that they won't be there to use the skills they have developed. The Teach for America teacher I described earlier is on a straight course toward burn-out. She is doing what she regards, and what her peers tell her is, "good" teaching. She is doing most of the work of teaching herself, which means that she has no way of creating strong norms for how the work will be distributed in the classroom. Her students are getting a free pass. Her practice is driving her students exactly in the direction of the performance the school has produced in the past—some initial gains in basic reading and writing, but not much evidence of improvement beyond that. In order to get the students to the next level, this teacher and her peers have to redesign the work in the classroom, which requires a substantial infusion of new knowledge and a significant amount of work to apply it. And if we work with her in the way we would work with Thornton teachers, we will, in the short run, be making her work even more difficult and challenging than it already is, against a probable result that she will either leave teaching altogether or move to a nominally easier setting, where the demands are lower and where she feels her skills are more useful. You can't begin to solve the problem of Clemente's performance without making the work more demanding, but making the work more demanding means increasing the likelihood that you will lose your investment in that teacher.

Another problem special to Clemente is its sheer scale: one thousand-plus students, sixty-some teachers, four assistant principals, and assorted other support personnel. One can argue about whether middle schools should be the size of Clemente, but in the short term that is not a negotiable item in the district where Clemente is located. The school has already made significant progress at creating a strong and supportive culture around student learning; it is an inviting place for students to be, a place where a critical mass of adults clearly cares about the students. Also, there is clearly a nucleus of teachers who are developing strong norms about what good teaching looks like, even though those norms aren't very well aligned with the performance the school is being asked to produce. But the problems of bringing these nascent norms into the classrooms of Clemente are considerably more complex than those of Thornton. All four assistant principals have to be on the same page and knowledgeable about which teachers need which kinds of development. Each assistant principal has to work with a group of fifteen to twenty grade-level teachers, most of them at the low end of experience. Each teacher has an entry point for developing her practice and her own set of dispositions about the collective expectations of the school. Teacher by teacher, the work looks difficult. At this scale it looks formidable.

Within weeks of visiting Clemente, I visited a middle school in a neighboring state that was at the far opposite end of the socioeconomic spectrum from Clemente. Let's call it Buckingham. Buckingham is, by any standard, an impressive and exceptional public school—a high-performing school that can explain how it got that way. Even though it is in an affluent community, it consistently out-performs its peer schools, as does the district in which it resides. The district superintendent is a leading practitioner in his field, an active learner himself, and a skillful developer of talent in other people. The principal of Buckingham is young and energetic and clearly a competent instructional leader, although very inexperienced. The district and the school provide substantial support to teachers, and they exert substantial pressure for teachers to improve their practice and student learning. The school and the district have no problems with the accountability system. The problem the superintendent posed was interesting: Students leaving the school and moving into the high school were having difficulty meeting the high school's expectations for reading, understanding, and interpreting high-level content. This problem did not show up in the state assessment, but it did show up in the assessments of high school teachers. To meet this challenge, Buckingham had undertaken an ambitious program of reading instruction across the middle school curriculum. Teachers in science, mathematics, history, and social studies, as well as those in English/language arts, were spending some portion of each day working on problems of reading in their content areas. The results of this strategy were disappointing, and the question the superintendent and principal were posing was why. What was interesting to me is that I saw almost exactly the same thing happening at Buckingham that I had seen at Clemente. The teachers were doing most, if not all, the work.

The teachers had clearly internalized a model of teaching in which they were expected to be focused, well-organized, energetic, engaging, fast-paced, and, above all, in control. But if you took the objective of the school's focus on reading across the curriculum, it didn't align with what the teachers were actually doing in the classroom. If you took a literal transcript of the classroom discourse, it was mostly teacher talk and mostly composed of questions that could be answered by retrieving facts from texts. If you sat next to a student and watched what they were doing, what you saw was students looking at the teacher waiting to be called on, and then going to the appropriate place in the text to retrieve the fact. What the high school teachers wanted was students who could read high-level text, analyze it, have ideas about it, and articulate those ideas. What middle school instruction was doing—and doing with ruthless efficiency—was teaching students how to answer factual questions in class.

I give this example to make the point that Clemente and Buckingham are both *improving schools*. They are essentially working on the same problem, albeit under vastly different conditions with vastly different stakes. Buckingham flies under the radar, because its socioeconomic community provides it with a high base of student performance on which to engage in its improvement. The state test won't even measure Buckingham's improvement—they will have to develop their own measures because the school has already topped out on it. Clemente is squarely in the center of the radar screen of the accountability system, with conditions that make its engagement in improvement a very high-stakes enterprise. I would propose that Clemente teachers visit Buckingham, and vice versa, if I didn't suspect that the principal of Buckingham would pick off the best Clemente teachers and offer them substantial raises to switch schools. But clearly, because Buckingham and Clemente are both improving schools, they have something to learn from each other. They have, in fact, more to learn from each other as improving schools than either of them has to learn from a "successful" school that is not improving.

In the world of performance-based accountability, high-performing schools are made to appear to be the same, even when they are not, while low-performing schools present a wide variety of conditions that make it hard to prescribe uniform solutions to their problems. All high-performing schools look the same, whether they are improving or not; low-performing schools look very different from one another. Tolstoy lives.

ACCOUNTABILITY AND CAPACITY: THE PRINCIPLE OF RECIPROCITY

As noted earlier, I have been working over the past several years with colleagues studying how schools respond to performance-based accountability systems. One major principle of accountability that I have drawn from that work is the principle of reciprocity, which can be stated as follows: For each unit of performance I demand of you, I have an equal and reciprocal responsibility to provide you with a unit of capacity to produce that performance, if you do not already have that capacity. The principle of reciprocity should work with equal force at all levels of the system. The state, for example, should not withhold diplomas from students who fail high school exit examinations without first having demonstrated that the students have actually been taught the content on which they are being tested, and that they have had an opportunity for remediation if the teaching initially failed. This idea sounds simple, but how many states and localities can actually demonstrate that they have taught the content on which students are being tested? Likewise, schools being required to perform at ever-increasing levels of performance for all students should not be expected to meet performance standards unless local jurisdictions and states have demonstrated that they have made the investments in teachers' and administrators' knowledge and skill that are required to meet the standards. The principle of reciprocity captures the relationship between performance and capacity. I should be expected to perform at the limits of my capacity, but I should not be expected to do those things for which I do not have the capacity unless you accept joint responsibility with me to create that capacity. I do not directly have to produce the capacity that you require, but I have to assure that you have access to that capacity and I have to accept my responsibility as co-producer of that capacity.

The reason the principle of reciprocity is so central to the operation of accountability systems is that it completes the essential political logic of performance-based incentives. *My* authority to command or induce you to do something you are not currently doing depends, in large part, on *your* capacity to actually do it. You may be motivated to do it. You may agree with me that it should be done. Or you may be willing to do it just because I have a legitimate grant of authority to require you to do it. But if you can't do it because you do not have the capacity to do it, then my authority is diminished because I have induced or required you to do something you cannot do. I can flog you harder, I can penalize you, I can threaten you, but I cannot make you do something you do not know how to do.

When accountability systems require schools to perform at levels that exceed their current capacity, the authority of those systems and the people who run them is thereby diminished. Asking people to do the impossible without helping them to master the skills necessary to do it is a formula for political resistance and ultimate failure. One is reminded of the Russian saying, coined during the decline of the Soviet system, "We pretend to work. They pretend to pay us." I have noticed this attitude developing in urban school systems as they begin to assess their positions under No Child Left Behind.

Thornton and Clemente are both improving schools, and they are both failing schools under the terms of the current accountability systems in which they operate. They will almost certainly both be classified as failing schools under No Child Left Behind, and there is a high probability that they will, in the near term, continue to fail to meet their performance targets, although they will probably continue to improve. They are not failing because the people in them don't, for the most part, recognize their limitations or fundamentally believe in the principles on which the accountability system is based. In fact, people who work in both schools *accept* that they are not doing as well as they should. This is why they have asked for help. Thornton and Clemente are failing, I think, because of a fundamental design flaw in current accountability systems, and that flaw has to do with the failure of policymakers to bring capacity-building measures into alignment with performance measures in the design of accountability systems. Ultimately, performance-based accountability systems, and the people who sponsor them, will fail politically if Thornton and Clemente fail. Another way of saying this is that if performance-based accountability systems can't improve Thornton and Clemente, which are already improving schools, they certainly won't improve schools that are in more serious trouble.

One point of view, growing out of the bravado of current political rhetoric around accountability, is that schools like Thornton and Clemente should be *allowed* to fail, and that other (unspecified) schools, staffed by other (unspecified) people should take over responsibility for educating the students currently enrolled at Thornton and Clemente, because these other schools couldn't possibly be worse than Thornton and Clemente. Thornton and Clemente demonstrate, I think, how suspect this view is. The successors to Thornton and Clemente will confront the identical problems that their predecessors confronted. Maybe the successors will have done a better job of solving them; possibly— probably—they will not. In the meantime, taking students out of Thornton and Clemente and moving them somewhere else means that we lose whatever capacity for improvement we have already invested in and we create, or increase, the problem of capacity somewhere else. The skill and knowledge of how to begin the process of improvement—however rudimentary—are part of the longer-term capacity we need to solve the problem of failing schools.

How is it that Thornton and Clemente can be improving and failing at the same time? Aren't the accountability systems designed to reward and sustain improving schools, not penalize them? The reason Thornton and Clemente can be improving and failing at the same time has to do with a fundamental design flaw of current accountability policies, including No Child Left Behind. The basic design of these accountability systems—adopted primarily from Texas and Kentucky—requires states to set proficiency levels in content areas (a test-based standard of performance) and to set a fixed date (a specified number of years) by which schools must meet these performance targets. There is nothing inherently wrong with the idea of performance targets, nor is there anything inherently wrong with holding schools accountable for some kind of progress toward a target.[5] A major design flaw of current design of accountability systems, however, is that the performance targets they set are *completely arbitrary;* they have no basis in theory or evidence related to what schools actually do when they are improving their performance. The targets have no basis in any defensible knowledge about school improvement, therefore they are, for all practical purposes, useless as guides for improvement.

An analogy with environmental policy helps to illustrate this point. When the Environmental Protection Agency (EPA) sets emission standards for pollution sources, like power plants or automobiles, it goes through a process of assessing the level of pollutants in emissions and the feasible technology for removing them. The EPA sets an emission target based on its assessment of what is desirable and feasible, and bases its enforcement action on that target. These targets are always the subject of political wrangling, but the important fact is that the political debate revolves, to a large degree, around empirical evidence on what it's feasible to achieve, given existing knowledge and technical capacity around pollution abatement. Educational accountability systems are designed by setting an arbitrary target, based on no knowledge or evidence whatsoever about either the value of the target or the actual process of improvement; that target becomes binding for all schools. This is the sort of policy that could only be made by people who haven't actually looked at what schools do when they are trying to improve.

What we see when we look at Thornton and Clemente—as well as other schools I have visited—is that the process of improvement is anything but constant and linear, as the accountability policies require. Both Thornton and Clemente had initial gains, but their performance has gone flat and sits below target. This is actually a predictable pattern through the entire improvement process if you understand what it takes to move instructional practice at scale in schools and school systems. Significant gains in performance, as we noted above, are usually followed by periods of flat performance. These periods of flat performance are actually very important parts of the improvement process—they are the periods in which individual teachers consolidate and deepen the knowledge and practices they acquired in earlier stages, in which schools diagnose and identify the barriers to the next stage of improvement, and in which they diagnose the next set of problems and look for the capacity to work on them. In existing accountability systems, these flat periods are seen as failures to improve. They carry heavy penalties. From the inside, these flat periods are actually important phases of improvement; improvement continues, even though performance is flat.

The analogy that occurs to me is to extreme mountain climbing. A group of people are strategizing about an assault on a difficult 20,000-foot mountain. The goal is achievable only if each member of the group works at full physical and mental capacity, and only if the group fully develops it capacity to work *together* on the assault. Would any reasonable mountaineer argue that the best way to solve this problem would be for all members of the team to head straight up the mountain, as a group, in one continuous assault? This would be a formula for disaster; in fact, it is out this kind of bravado that most mountain climbing disasters occur. No, what actually happens is that the assault is carefully staged in order to provide time for the group to pause, reconnoiter, pool its knowledge of the mountain, regain its physical capacity, regroup, and agree on a plan for the next phase. The more effective the group, the more skillful they are at finding and using these periods of consolidation. Groups that work this way are also called survivors.

Another useful analogy is aerobic conditioning. People in modest physical shape do not work themselves into great shape in one continuous path of improvement. Substantial periods of increased cardiovascular capacity are followed by (usually demoralizing) flat periods in which it seems that no improvement is occurring at all. In fact, what we know is that during these periods the cardiovascular system is literally opening up and enlarging new capillaries to carry oxygen-enriched blood to muscle tissue—building capacity. Then, as if by a miracle, you suddenly notice that you are able to operate at a much higher level of conditioning.

In effect, the performance targets by current accountability policies are, for failing schools, completely unattainable using their existing capacities. You literally cannot get there from here. Most schools, even nominally high-performing schools, couldn't do this work using their existing capacities. In order to meet these performance targets schools have to develop successively higher capacities. Each new set of capacities speaks to the next level of problem. Each level of increased performance carries its own new set of problems. Each new level of capacity requires a period of consolidation. Acknowledging the gap between capacity and performance in accountability systems isn't, I repeat *isn't*, an argument for abandoning performance targets altogether. It is, however, an argument for a more knowledgeable approach to setting performance targets.

Improvements in school performance, as we currently understand them, probably take something like the following form:

- Schools recognize and internalize problems of performance by paying attention to evidence on student performance.
- They choose a proximate performance target—increasing reading performance, for example—and focus their work on improving their individual and organizational capacity to meet this target.
- If they succeed in choosing the right target and developing the initial knowledge and skill in teachers and students around that target, they typically see a modest bounce in student performance. Often, these initial moves, in very low-capacity schools, consist of very low-level changes: devoting a set number of minutes per day to teaching reading; realigning the curriculum so that the content that is tested is actually taught before the test is given; identifying students whose performance could easily be improved, thereby making the whole school look better, etc. I have come to call this

stage the "low-hanging-fruit" stage, or, less complimentary, the "some teaching versus no teaching" phase.

- These initial simple moves always turn out to have very short-term, very disappointing effects. But the critical moment here is that the school has decided to make some collective commitment to a goal that has to do with performance. This is the first stage of developing what I earlier called internal accountability—that is, the capacity for individuals in the school to subscribe to common expectations about what it is important to work on and what students should be able to do.

- If the organization reads its performance well, it is at this stage that schools often try to tackle a more ambitious kind of instructional improvement. This improvement is often focused on the adoption of specific curricula and instructional practice. This stage almost always requires that the school receive some kind of external help, support, and professional development. Why? Because, by definition, people in the school don't know what to do, or they would have done it already. New practices take time to acquire and implement with any consistency. They also require people to organize and manage themselves around increasingly clear collective goals—another increment in internal accountability. But schools that go through this phase almost always see gains in student performance, in part because they are learning to work together more powerfully, and in part because they are actually teaching different content in different ways. Just as predictably, performance tends to go flat again almost immediately. This is where Thornton and Clemente were in the improvement cycle. As noted above, performance goes flat because the problems of improving student performance are more complex than the strategies adopted at this stage can cope with.

- If the organization diagnoses this problem—and schools usually require some kind of external help to do this—it typically chooses the next problem to work on, based on a diagnosis of the barriers to continued improvement. Typically, the kind of problems that schools work on at this stage are either problems of increasing the consistency and cognitive demand of instruction or figuring out why the instructional strategies they adopted earlier work for some students and not for others. Simply diagnosing these problems and working on their solutions creates new capacity for collective action, bringing the next stage of internal accountability.

- The problems of improvement become more complex and demanding as performance increases; the challenges to existing instructional practices and existing organizational norms, more direct and difficult. Often schools go through some kind of crisis at around this time, where teachers and principals argue that the work has become impossible to do under existing resource constraints and that expectations set by external accountability systems are simply impossible to meet. This is a very tricky stage, because it is hard to argue that the demands of the external accountability system are reasonable—they often are not. But what teachers and administrators are also saying is that they simply don't have the capacity to make the next set of improvements, and they usually don't. They are, consciously or not, invoking the principle of reciprocity; they are demanding the skills and knowledge necessary to do the next level of work. I have come to call this the "impossible work" stage. The conditions for future improvement are present in the school, but the capacities to make that improvement are not. It is critical for schools to receive high levels of support at this stage—to get help in diagnosing the next set of problems, to get help from people with expertise about problems of student learning and instructional practice, to broaden and deepen common expectations around high-quality instructional practice, and usually to see schools in similar circumstances that have managed to move through this stage. It is at this stage that credibility of accountability systems, as systems of political authority, is tested. If people don't see the principle of reciprocity at work, they revoke the authority of the system to govern their actions. We pretend to work. They pretend to pay us.

- Schools that make it through these crises typically emerge as much different organizations—stronger, more coherent, with responsibilities more widely distributed and with much higher morale around student learning and much high cognitive demand in the classroom. But they often have difficulty demonstrating that these changes are consequential because going through a crisis saps the energy and commitment of people while it is going on, and often performance goes flat during these periods. So just as the school is feeling that it has a much better handle on student performance, its results often look less impressive than they should. This occurs because the school has built the capacity for higher-level instruction but hasn't yet seen its full effects. This is where more concentrated work on instructional practice—not less—is important, because it is important that teachers and administrators understand that not only have they changed the way instruction occurs in the schools, they have changed their own capacity to take responsibility for and manage their school's response to pressure for performance. Again, external support and assistance around targeted problems of student learning help to reinforce the idea that everyone has gotten here by developing new knowledge and skills.

- The next stage of improvement—one that very few schools achieve, even nominally "high-performing" schools—is where the school collectively takes over the management of its own improvement process, teachers and students internalize the values of managing and monitoring their own learning, administrators model their own learning for teachers and students, and individuals are empowered to invoke the principle of reciprocity in relations around accountability for performance. No one gets to tell anyone else what to do unless they themselves are prepared to become part of the solution.

This is a highly stylized map of the improvement process, in part because we need much more research to get a deeper picture of what actually happens as failing schools improve, and in part because Tolstoy was right—each unhappy family is unhappy in its own way. Each failing school faces, in addition to the general problems of improvement, a specific set of problems rooted in its own context. For example, Thornton faces a relatively stable labor force of relatively experienced teachers who, with care and attention, can be encouraged to extend and deepen their practice over time. Thornton also has the luxury of thinking about what kind of new teachers it might want to hire and forming alliances with teacher-training institutions to get those teachers when the time comes. Clemente, on the other hand, faces a labor force in which between 15 and 25 percent of its teachers turn over in the course of a single year and in which, while it's trying to capitalize on the idealism of new (unskilled) teachers, it is simultaneously hemorrhaging its investment in teacher knowledge and skill at an alarming rate. What Clemente and its school system are doing is, in effect, subsidizing surrounding, higher-performing schools and districts through its investments in its own work force. As good as Clemente's strategy is, it won't deliver higher levels of performance consistently until it gets help from policymakers in the form of stronger incentives for well-educated and - trained teachers to stay in the school and the district. Increases in performance require increases in the knowledge and skill of people working in schools; if the people with the knowledge and skill aren't there, no matter how serious and committed the school, the performance won't increase beyond a certain initial level. The problems Clemente faces are the most demanding problems of American education, far more demanding than the problems in the higher-performing schools it's subsidizing. Yet the combination of labor market conditions and incentives in the accountability system, in effect, drain capacity away from Clemente toward higher-performing schools.

THE PROBLEM: IMPROVING ACCOUNTABILITY SYSTEMS WHILE WE'RE IMPROVING SCHOOLS

Current accountability systems aren't built to do what they are supposed to do—to push and support schools in getting better. The basic design flaws are not hard to identify: The performance targets are arbitrary, not based on any systematic understanding of feasible performance targets, given our current understanding of school improvement. The annual expected targets of improvement are based on assumptions of linear improvement, when the evidence suggests that the actual process of improvement is a series of gains followed by flat periods of consolidation. The systems exhort schools and localities to provide support and professional development for schools in need of help, but don't actually invest in the infrastructure required to make sure that that help gets to the right schools at the right time with the right technical expertise. The systems heavily invest in testing and monitoring school performance and in the administration of sanctions that attach to poor performance, and heavily underinvest in the development of the knowledge and skill required to rectify the problems that failing schools face. The systems are generally unresponsive to systemic problems in getting the resources to schools that are necessary to do high-quality work, and tend to view the problems of all low-performing schools as essentially the same. In general, the systems focus excessively on getting people to do the right

thing, rather than on the much more difficult, challenging, and ultimately more important problem of figuring out what the right thing is to
do. The most discouraging aspect of current systems is that they ignore
and undervalue the struggles of people like those who work in schools
like Thornton and Clemente, creating the expectation that students
would be better off in other settings, without understanding that moving
students around is essentially moving the problems of capacity from
one set of institutions to another, without remedying the underlying
problem of how raise the capacity of the institutions where the children
are to begin with.

Currently, the problem of failing schools is defined as how to deal
with schools that come to be classified as failing by existing accountability systems. I would like to suggest that the problem of failing schools is
a problem of fixing *both* the accountability systems *and* the schools they
classify as failing. You can't fix the schools unless you fix the policy, and
vice versa.

First, the principle of reciprocity requires major investments in infrastructure at the state and local level to meet the requirements of expertise and support for failing schools. Improvement is a *process*, not an
event. Schools don't suddenly "get better" and meet their performance
targets. Schools build capacity by generating internal accountability—
greater agreement and coherence on expectations for teachers and students—and then by working their way through problems of instructional practice at ever-increasing levels of complexity and demand. At
each successive stage, the work at the next stage can look impossible.
This process has to be managed by people with expertise, and informed
by people who have worked with schools confronting similar problems
in other settings. Right now no infrastructure exists outside of a few op-
portunistic state and local examples to provide continuous support to
failing schools. This infrastructure doesn't exist partly by deliberate
choice. Policymakers have chosen to focus on the testing, monitoring,
and sanctions part of the accountability systems rather than on the reciprocal capacity-building part. It is extremely important that policymakers understand that there is a fundamental problem of political authority here. Accountability systems can fail just as surely as the schools
they classify as failing. Accountability systems fail when they fail to
command authority and consent on the part of the people they are
designed to influence. When you ask people to do unreasonable or im-

possible things and you don't respond to this fact, they revoke their consent.

Building capacity in failing schools is going to require a lot of feet on the ground—people who know something about school improvement and who know what they don't know. As my analysis suggests, I would look for these people in what I have called "improving" schools, not in nominally "successful" schools, because a large number of "successful" schools are not improving schools. Finding and organizing this expertise is going to require a kind of work that most educators aren't yet very good at and that most policymakers don't know anything about. It will require measures of instructional improvement and performance that are much closer to the ground than the state assessments that are the basis of accountability systems. It will require the creation of systems to find people with expertise in subject matter, instructional practice, and improvement, and getting them into the schools where they are needed. And it will require a new generation of people who are knowledgeable enough about instructional practice to be useful but also interested in broader questions of designing and running support systems.

Second, the basic design of the accountability systems themselves needs to be revisited, and it needs to be addressed as a problem of continuous improvement. The irony here, of course, is that before the advent of No Child Left Behind we had a vast national experiment going on around continuous improvement of accountability systems—it was called the federal system. States chose a variety of different designs, based on a variety of expectations and theories about school improvement. All the major elements of accountability systems varied—the level and type of stakes, expectations for rates of improvement, the level of difficulty and coverage of tests, the type of test, etc. The level of variability in the design of accountability systems was an accurate reflection both of variation in state and local circumstances and of the relatively weak knowledge base that underlies accountability policies. States routinely revised their accountability systems in light of experience and feedback from the field. The standardizing effect of No Child Left Behind will be to substantially reduce this variability and to limit the possibilities for state and local responsiveness to learning and changed conditions.

I have tried to point out at least two fundamental design problems with current accountability systems that are present in No Child Left Behind, and that were present in the earlier state systems on which No Child Left Behind was based. These problems are the arbitrariness of the proficiency targets against which schools' performance is measured, and the lack of correspondence between the straight-line linear expectation for annual improvement and what we know about how schools actually improve. There are other fundamental design problems that have been incorporated into No Child Left Behind, but the ones that I have identified are the ones that will have the greatest impact on schools at risk of being classified as failing.

The important thing to recognize about these design flaws is that they actually make it *more difficult* for schools like Thornton and Clemente to improve. Whether or not the proficiency target is valid, whether or not the annual performance increments required to meet that target are reasonable, Thornton's and Clemente's success is judged by that standard. The reality is that this condition makes it extremely risky and difficult for Thornton and Clemente to engage in any improvement effort that doesn't guarantee immediate gains, which eliminates many of the capacity-building measures that would ultimately turn these schools around. We actually have no idea what rate of improvement it is reasonable to expect failing schools to meet. Policymakers have chosen to solve this problem by choosing a target date and a proficiency level and dividing the required increments in performance into equal annual units. This model corresponds neither to any empirically based understanding of how schools actually improve nor to any understanding of what the feasible rate of improvement might be with a given level of support under the principle of reciprocity. This problem is compounded by the fact that the schools with the lowest capacity are required to make the largest gains—in uniform annual increments—so there is little or no slack in the system to adjust performance expectations to an understanding of the actual process of improvement or the limits of capacity in schools at the low end. This is a system that could only have been designed by people who haven't actually watched schools try to solve the problems of performance.

The solution to this problem lies in experimenting with a variety of different ways of setting performance targets, measuring performance, and scaling performance expectations to the realities of school improvement. This would have been possible under the earlier state of affairs where there was wide variation among states and localities in the design of accountability systems. It is going to be extremely difficult to do under the requirements of No Child Left Behind without some significant changes in the law itself. It is unlikely, however, that the problem of failing schools will be adequately addressed without some significant changes in the basic design of accountability systems.

Finally, accountability systems should reflect in their basic design and implementation an appreciation that all "failing" schools are not alike, and each failing school is problematical in its own way. I said earlier that the most remarkable recognition for me in my work with failing schools is that there are many such schools that look like Thornton and Clemente—schools that are seriously engaged in very important work around instructional improvement, that are, in fact, making gains, and that will probably be classified as failing under No Child Left Behind, because the process of improvement they are pursuing doesn't match the architecture of the law. I am also impressed, as I said earlier, with how similar the instructional problems of Thornton and Clemente are to the problems of nominally high-performing schools that are also working on problems of improvement. The problems that Thornton and Clemente face, while similar to each other, are quite different from the problems faced by other failing schools, and more similar than we would expect to those faced by nominally successful schools. They are, at least, improving. There are other failing schools that have yet to get on any kind of improvement path. At a very basic minimum, the accountability system should not penalize schools that are making significant improvements in instructional practice and demonstrable gains in student performance, because those schools are the repositories of the knowledge that the rest of us will have to use to understand how to deal with the schools that are not yet on an improvement path. A system that classifies Thornton and Clemente as failing schools is a failing system.

The advent of performance-based accountability systems is an important and powerful shift in the governance of American public education. It is also a highly problematical shift. It represents limited knowledge of how schools work, how they improve, and what it is reasonable to expect schools to do. The advantage of the federal system is that it allows us to be ambitious and cautious at the same time: to make major changes in the way we govern schools, and to hedge the risks in those changes with the variation of states and localities; to engage in national reforms that are not creatures of a single national jurisdiction. The problem of failing schools is a central problem of educational accountability. In some sense, it is *the* central problem of educational accountability. Solving the problem requires systems of accountability and capacity-building that are responsive to the contours of the problem itself, not to the problem as it has been constructed by policymakers. Schools can fail. But so too can accountability systems.

Notes and References

INTRODUCTION

References

Elmore, R. F. (1975a). Lessons from follow through. *Policy Analysis, 1*, 459–484.

Elmore, R. F. (1975b). Design of the follow through experiment. In A. Rivlin & P. M. Timpane (Eds.), *Planned variation in education.* Washington, DC: Brookings Institution.

Elmore, R. F. (1978). Organizational models of social program implementation. *Public Policy, 26*, 185–228.

Elmore, R. F. (1979–1980). Backward mapping: Implementation research and policy decisions. *Political Science Quarterly, 94*, 601–616.

Elmore, R. F. (with Peterson, P. L., & McCarthey, S. J.). (1996). *Restructuring in the classroom: Teaching, learning and school organization.* San Francisco: Jossey-Bass.

Elmore, R. F. (with Burney, D.). (1997). *Investing in teacher learning: Staff development and instructional improvement in Community School District #2, New York City.* New York: National Commission on Teaching & America's Future, Consortium for Policy in Education.

Hess, F. (1999). *Spinning wheels: The politics of urban school reform.* Washington, DC: Brookings Institution.

1 GETTING TO SCALE WITH GOOD EDUCATIONAL PRACTICE

Notes

1. See, for example, Lawrence Cremin's (1961, p. 157) reference to Randolf Bourne's critique of the "artificiality and dullness" of U.S. classrooms, published in *The New Republic* in 1915.

2. Dewey's own ambivalence about the connection between the exemplary practices developed in laboratory schools and the broader world of practice can be seen in his reflections on the University of Chicago Lab School: "As it

is not the primary function of a laboratory to devise ways and means that can at once be put to practical use, so it is not the primary purpose of this school to devise methods with reference to their direct application in the graded school system. It is the function of some schools to provide better teachers according to present standards; it is the function of others to create new standards and ideals and thus to lead to a gradual change in conditions." (quoted in Cremin, 1961, p. 290n)

3. Remarks at Project Atlas Forum on Getting to Scale, April 3, 1995.
4. This is, in fact, the model used by the Central Park East Elementary School in New York City to create two other elementary schools to serve parents and children who could not be accommodated in the original school.

References

Cohen, D. (1988). Teaching practice: Plus que ça change . . . In P. Jackson (Ed.), *Contribution to educational change: Perspectives on research and practice* (pp. 27–84). Berkeley, CA: McCutcheon.

Cohen, D. (1995). Rewarding teachers for student performance. In S. Fuhrman & J. O'Day (Eds.), *Rewards and reforms: Creating educational incentives that work.* San Francisco: Jossey-Bass.

Cremin, L. (1961). *The transformation of the American school.* New York: Knopf.

Cuban, L. (1984). *How teachers taught: Constancy and change in American classrooms, 1890–1980.* New York: Longman.

Cuban, L. (1990). Reforming again, again, and again. *Educational Researcher, 19*(1), 3–13.

Darling-Hammond, L. (1996). Restructuring schools for high performance. In S. H. Fuhrman & J. A. O'Day (Eds.), *Rewards and reform: Creating educational incentives that work.* San Francisco: Jossey-Bass.

Dewey, J. (1899). *The school and society.* Chicago: University of Chicago Press.

Dewey, J., & Dewey, E. (1915). *Schools of to-morrow.* New York: E. P. Dutton.

Dow, P. (1991). *Schoolhouse politics: Lessons from the Sputnik era.* Cambridge, MA: Harvard University Press.

Elmore, R. (1993). *The development and implementation of large-scale curriculum reforms* (Paper prepared for the American Association for the Advancement of Science). Cambridge, MA: Harvard Graduate School of Education, Center for Policy Research in Education.

Elmore, R. (1995). Teaching, learning, and school organization: Principles of practice and the regularities of schooling. *Educational Administration Quarterly, 31,* 355–374.

Flexner, A. (1917). A modern school. In *Publications of the General Education Board* (Occasional papers No. 3). New York: General Education Board.

Fullan, M. (1982). *The meaning of education change.* New York: Teachers College Press.

Fullan, M., & Miles, M. (1992). Getting reform right: What works and what doesn't. *Phi Delta Kappan, 73,* 744–752.

Goodlad, J. (1984). *A place called school.* New York: McGraw-Hill.

Grobman, A. (1969). *The changing classroom: The role of the biological sciences curriculum study.* New York: Doubleday.

Kilpatrick, W. H. (1925). *Foundations of method: Informal talks on teaching by William Heard Kilpatrick.* New York: Macmillan.

Kilpatrick, W. H. (1933). *The educational frontier.* New York: Century Company.

March, J., & Olsen, J. (1989). *Rediscovering institutions: The organizational basis of politics.* New York: Free Press.

Marsh, P. (1964). *The physical sciences study committee: A case history of nationwide curriculum development, 1956-1961.* Unpublished doctoral dissertation, Harvard Graduate School of Education, Cambridge, MA.

Meyer, J., & Rowan, B. (1978). The structure of educational organizations. In M. Meyer (Ed.), *Environments and organizations* (pp. 78–109). San Francisco: Jossey-Bass.

National Center for Education Statistics. (1993). *NAEP 1992 Mathematics Report Card for the nation and the states: Data from the national and trial state assessments.* Washington, DC: U.S. Department of Education.

National Commission on Excellence in Education. (1983). *A nation at risk: The imperative for educational reform.* Washington, DC: U.S. Department of Education.

Powell, A., Farrar, E., & Cohen, D. (1985). *The shopping mall high school.* Boston: Houghton Mifflin.

Rugg, H. A., & Shumaker, A. (1928). *The child-centered school.* Chicago: World Book.

Stake, R., & Easely, J. (1978). Case studies in science education. In *The case reports* (vol. 1, 2). Washington, DC: U.S. Government Printing Office.

Tyack, D., & Cuban, L. (1995). *Tinkering toward Utopia: A century of public school reform.* Cambridge, MA: Harvard University Press.

Tyack, D., & Hansot, E. (1982). *Managers of virtue: Public school leadership in America, 1820-1980.* New York: Basic Books.

Tyack, D., & Tobin, W. (1994). The "grammar" of schooling: Why has it been so hard to change? *American Educational Research Journal, 31,* 453–479.

2 BUILDING A NEW STRUCTURE FOR SCHOOL LEADERSHIP

Notes

1. Notice also that vouchers, capitation grants, and charters are quintessential structural changes, in that they imply absolutely nothing about either the content or the quality of instruction, except insofar as quality can be defined as the satisfaction of consumer preferences (a tautology). So a major

part of the political appeal of these policies, to both educators and policy-makers, is that they don't require any commitment as to what will actually happen inside the structure, hence reproducing, in another form, the buffering of the technical core.

2. For a more extensive treatment of the theoretical underpinnings of the idea of distributed leadership, see Spillane, Halverson et al. (2002).

3. The study includes ten districts in which at least 50 percent of the students are low income and at least one-third of the schools in each district received either of the highest two ratings in the state's accountability system, putting these schools in the top 40 percent of schools in the state (Ragland, Asera et al., 1999).

4. This study also found suggestive, but not conclusive, evidence that stability of leadership and good relations between superintendents and boards around core issues of instruction were a key factor (Ragland, Asera et al., 1999).

5. In my own attempts to explain my work in District #2 to practitioners from other districts, I have heard what I think must be every possible explanation of why the District #2 experience could not be useful in other settings: *District #2 is a small district, therefore its lessons don't transfer to large districts.* Actually, at 23,000 students, the district is larger than the average school district and about the same size as many districts with high proportions of low-income children. *District #2 has exceptional teachers (one of my favorites), therefore one can't expect "ordinary teachers" to do what teachers in District #2 do.* Actually, District #2 has attracted exceptional teachers by being good at what it does. *District #2 must have a different union contract than the one in my district in order to get teachers to participate in so many professional development activities.* Actually, District #2 operates under the same union contract as all other community districts in New York City, it has developed exceptionally strong working relations with the union, and it has its share of union/management issues. *District #2 must spend an inordinate amount of time "teaching to the test" to get such high scores.* In fact, teachers spend very little time preparing students to take standardized tests; the performance gains are mostly produced by high-quality instruction. After a while, one begins to think that the source of questions is not curiosity but its opposite.

References

Bidwell, C. (1965). The school as a formal organization. In J. G. March (Ed.), *Handbook of organizations.* Chicago: Rand McNally.

Cohen, D. K., & Barnes, C. A. (1993). Pedagogy and policy. In D. K. Cohen, M. W. McLaughlin, & J. E. Talbert (Eds.), *Teaching for understanding: Challenges for policy and practice* (pp. 207–239). San Francisco: Jossey-Bass.

Cuban, L. (1984). *How teachers taught: Constancy and change in American classrooms.* New York: Longman.

Cuban, L. (1988). *The managerial imperative and the practice of leadership in schools.* Albany: State University of New York Press.

Cuban, L. (1990). Reforming again, again, and again. *Educational Researcher, 19,* 3–13.

Drury, D. W. (1999). *Reinventing school-based management: School-based improvement through data-driven decision-making.* Alexandria, VA: National School Boards Association.

Elmore, R. (1993). School decentralization: Who gains? Who loses? In J. Hannaway & M. Carnoy (Eds.), *Decentralization and school improvement.* San Francisco: Jossey-Bass.

Elmore, R., & Burney, D. (1998). *Continuous improvement in Community School District #2.* New York: University of Pittsburgh, Learning Research and Development Center, High Performance Learning Communities Project.

Elmore, R. F. (1996). Getting to scale with good educational practice. *Harvard Educational Review, 66,* 1–26.

Elmore, R. F. (1997). Accountability in local school districts: Learning to do the right things. In P. W. Thurston & J. G. Ward (Eds.), *Improving educational performance: Local and systemic reforms* (pp. 59–82). Greenwich, CT: JAI Press.

Elmore, R. F., & Burney, D. (1997a). *Investing in teacher learning: Staff development and instructional improvement in Community District #2.* New York: National Commission on Teaching and America's Future, Consortium for Policy Research in Education.

Elmore, R. F., & Burney, D. (1997b). *School variation and systemic instructional improvement in Community School District #2.* New York: University of Pittsburgh, Learning Research and Development Center, High Performance Learning Communities Project.

Elmore, R. F., Peterson, P. L., et al. (1996). *Restructuring in the classroom: Teaching, learning, and school organization.* San Francisco: Jossey-Bass.

Floden, R., Porter, A., et al. (1988). Instructional leadership at the district level: A closer look at autonomy and control. *Educational Administration Quarterly, 24,* 96–124.

Fuhrman, S. H. (1993). The politics of coherence. In S. H. Fuhrman (Ed.), *Designing coherent education policy: Improving the system* (pp. 1–34). San Francisco: Jossey-Bass.

Fuhrman, S. H. (1994). *Legislatures and education policy.* In R. F. Elmore & S. H. Fuhrman (Eds.), *The governance of curriculum* (pp. 30–55). Alexandria, VA: Association for Supervision and Curriculum Development.

Fuhrman, S. H., & Elmore, R. F. (1994). Governors and education policy in the 1990s. In R. F. Elmore & S. H. Fuhrman (Eds.), *The governance of curriculum* (pp. 56–74). Alexandria, VA: Association for Supervision and Curriculum Development.

Grissmer, D., & Flanagan, A. (1998). *Exploring rapid achievement gains in North Carolina and Texas.* Washington, DC: National Education Goals Panel.

Hess, F. M. (1999). *Spinning wheels: The politics of urban school reform.* Washington, DC: Brookings Institution.

Knapp, M. S., Shields, P. M., et al. (1995). The school and district environment for meaning-oriented instruction. In M. Knapp (Ed.), *Teaching for meaning in high poverty classrooms.* New York: Teachers College Press.

Lortie, D. (1975). *Schoolteacher: A sociological study.* Chicago: University of Chicago Press.

Lortie, D. (1987). Built-in tendencies toward stabilizing the principal's role. *Journal of Research and Development in Education, 22,* 80–90.

Malen, B., Ogawa, R., et al. (1990). What do we know about school-based management? In W. H. Clune & J. F. Witte (Eds.), *Choice and control in American education* (pp. 289–432). New York: Falmer Press.

Meyer, J., & Rowan, B. (Eds.). (1992). *The structure of educational organizations, organizational environments: Ritual and rationality.* Newbury Park, CA: Sage.

Murphy, J. (1990). Principal instructional leadership. *Advances in Educational Administration, I,* 163–200.

Murphy, J., & Hallinger, P. (1988). Characteristics of instructionally effective school districts. *Journal of Educational Research, 81,* 175–181.

Murphy, J., Hallinger, P., et al. (1987). The administrative control of principals in effective school districts. *Journal of Educational Administration, 25,* 161–192.

Newmann, F. M., Rutter, R., et al. (1989). Organizational factors that affect schools' sense of efficacy, community, and expectations. *Sociology of Education, 62,* 221–238.

O'Day, J., Goertz, M., & Floden, R. (1995). *Building capacity for education reform* (Policy Brief #RB-18). Philadelphia: University of Pennsylvania, Consortium for Policy Research in Education.

Powell, A. G., Farrar, E., et al. (1985). *The shopping mall high school: Winners and losers in the educational marketplace.* Boston: Houghton-Mifflin.

Ragland, M. A., Asera, R., et al. (1999). *Urgency, responsibility, efficacy: Preliminary findings of a study of high performing Texas school districts.* Austin: University of Texas, Austin, Charles A. Dana Center.

Rosenholtz, S. (1989). *Teachers' workplace.* New York: Longman.

Rosenholtz, S. J. (1985). Effective schools: Interpreting the evidence. *American Journal of Education, 93,* 352–388.

Rosenholtz, S. J. (1986). Organizational conditions of teacher learning. *Teaching and Teacher Education, 2,* 91–104.

Rowan, B. (1990). Commitment and control: Alternative strategies for the organizational design of schools. *Review of Educational Research, 16,* 353–389.

Schmidt, W., McKnight, C., & Raizen, S. (1997). *The splintered vision: An investigation of U.S. science and mathematics education.* Boston: Kluwer Academic.

Spillane, J. P. (2004). *Standards deviation: How schools misunderstand education policy.* Cambridge, MA: Harvard University Press.

Spillane, J. P., Halverson, R., & Diamond, J. (2002). Towards a theory of leadership practice: A distributed perspective. *Journal of Curriculum Studies, 35,* 1–32.

Stigler, J., & Hiebert, J. (1999). *The teaching gap.* New York: Free Press.

Tyack, D. (1974). *The one best system.* Cambridge, MA: Harvard University Press.

Tyack, D., & Cuban, L. (1995). *Tinkering toward Utopia: A century of public school reform.* Cambridge, MA: Harvard University Press.

Tyack, D., & Hansot, E. (1982). *Managers of virtue: Public school leadership in America, 1820–1980.* New York: Basic Books.

Weick, K. E. (1976). Educational organizations as loosely-coupled systems. *Administrative Science Quarterly, 21,* 1–19.

3 BRIDGING THE GAP BETWEEN STANDARDS AND ACHIEVEMENT

Notes

1. But not so very different from mainstream definitions in the literature on professional development. For example, "Staff development is defined as the provision of activities designed to advance the knowledge, skills, and understanding of teachers in ways that lead to changes in their thinking and classroom behavior. This definition limits the range of staff development to those specific activities that enhance knowledge, skills, and understanding in ways that lead to changes in thought and action" (Fenstermacher & Berliner, 1985, p. 283). All that's missing here is the explicit connection to student learning.

2. My first tutorial on this principle was delivered by Anthony Alvarado, then-superintendent of Community School District #2, New York City, and now Chancellor for Instruction in the San Diego Public Schools.

References

Bird, T., & Little, J. W. (1986). How schools organize the teaching occupation. *Elementary School Journal, 86,* 493–511.

Borko, H., & Putnam, R. T. (1995). *Expanding a teacher's knowledge base: A cognitive psychological perspective on professional development.* New York: Teachers College Press.

Brown, J. S., Collins, A., & Duguid, S. (1989). Situated cognition and the culture of learning. *Educational Researcher, 18,* 32–42.

Clark C. M., & Peterson, P. L. (1986). *Teachers' thought processes.* New York: Macmillan.

Cohen, D. K., Raudenbush, S., & Ball, D. L. (2002). Resources, instruction, and research. In F. Mosteller & R. Boruch (Eds.), *Evidence matters: Randomized trials in education research* (pp. 80–119). Washington, DC: Brookings Institution Press.

Elmore, R. F. (2000). *Building a new structure for school leadership.* Washington, DC: Albert Shanker Institute.

Elmore, R. F. (2001). Psychiatrists and lightbulbs. In Carnoy, M., Elmore, R, & Siskin, L. (Eds.), *The new accountability: High schools and high-stakes testing.* New York: Routledge.

Feiman-Nemser, S. (1983). Learning to teach. In L. S. Shulman & G. Sykes (Eds.), *Handbook of teaching and policy.* New York: Longman.

Fenstermacher, G., & Berliner, D. (1985). Determining the value of staff development. *Elementary School Journal, 85,* 281–314.

Fullan, M. (1991). *The new meaning of educational change.* New York: Teachers College Press.

Guskey, T. R. (1989). Attitude and perceptual change in teachers. *International Journal of Educational Research, 13,* 439–453.

Hargreaves, A. (1991). *Contrived collegiality: The micropolitics of teacher collaboration.* London: Sage.

Huberman, M. (1995). Networks that alter teaching: Conceptualizations, exchanges and experiments. *Teachers and Teaching: Theory and Practice, 1*(2).

Kelley, C., Odden, A., Milanowski, A., & Heneman, H. (2000). *The motivational effects of school-based performance awards* (CPRE Policy Briefs). Philadelphia: University of Pennsylvania.

Kelley, C., & Odden, A. (1995). Reinventing teacher compensation systems (CPRE Policy Briefs). Philadelphia: University of Pennsylvania.

Lave, J., & Wenger, E. (1991). *Situated learning: Legitimate peripheral participation.* New York: Cambridge University Press.

Little, J. W. (1990). The persistence of privacy: autonomy and initiative in teachers' professional relations. *Teachers College Record, 91,* 481–508.

Little, J. W. (1993). Teachers' professional development in a climate of educational reform. *Educational Evaluation and Policy Analysis, 15,* 129–151.

McLaughlin, M.W., & Yee, S. M. (1988). *School as a place to have a career.* New York: Teachers College Press.

Miles, K. H. (1995). Freeing resources for improving schools: A case study of teacher allocation in Boston public schools. *Educational Evaluation and Policy Analysis, 17,* 476–493.

Miles, K. H., & Darling-Hammond, L. (1998). Rethinking the allocation of teaching resources: Some lessons from high-performing schools. *Developments in School Finance, 1997.* Washington, DC: National Center for Education Statistics.

Newmann, F. M., King, M. B., et al. (2000). Professional development that addresses school capacity: Lessons from urban elementary schools. *American Journal of Education, 108,* 259–299.

Sparks, D. (1995). A paradigm shift in staff development. *ERIC Review, 3*(3), 5–11.

Sparks, D., & Hirsh, S. (1997). *A new vision for staff development.* Washington, DC: National Staff Development Council and the Association for Supervision and Curriculum Development.

Stein, M., Smith, M., & Silver, E. (1999). The development of professional developers: Learning to assist teachers in new settings in new ways. *Harvard Educational Review, 69,* 237–269.

Wenger, E. (1998). *Communities of practice: Learning, meaning, and identity.* New York: Cambridge University Press.

4 WHEN ACCOUNTABILITY KNOCKS, WILL ANYONE ANSWER?

Notes

1. Newmann et al. (1997) identify a "complete school accountability system" as including: 1) Information about the organization's performance (e.g., test scores); 2) Standards for judging the quality or degree of success of organizational performance (e.g., a mean achievement score higher than other schools with comparable demographic characteristics); 3) Significant consequences to the organization (i.e., rewards and sanctions such as bonuses to teachers in the school) for its success or failure in meeting specified standards; and 4) An agent or constituency that receives information on organizational performance, judges the extent to which standards have been met, and distributes rewards and sanctions (e.g., the state department of instruction.)

2. See Elmore (1997).

3. The research reported in this paper was part of the CPRE research project, "Accountability for Results, Capacity for Reform," jointly undertaken by Stanford and Harvard Universities.

4. Our working theory is informed by Robert Wagner's conception of accountability and responsibility, as described in *Accountability in Education* (1989).

5. See Metz, in Mitchell and Goertz (1990) for more on "real schools," and standard constructions of schooling.

6. In some cases, the categorization of schools is a better fit than in others. Full case studies of each school are available upon request by contacting CPRE-Harvard.

References

Ladd, H. (1996). *Holding schools accountable: Performance based reform in education.* Washington, DC: Brookings Institution.

Lortie, D. C. (1975). *Schoolteacher: A sociological study.* Chicago: University of Chicago Press.

Newmann, F., King, B., & Rigdon, M. (1997). Accountability and school performance: Implications from restructuring schools. *Harvard Educational Review, 67,* 41–74.

Schein, E. H. (1992). *Organizational culture and leadership.* San Francisco: Jossey-Bass.

Wagner, R. B. (1989). *Accountability in education: A philosophical inquiry.* New York: Routledge.

6 CHANGE AND IMPROVEMENT IN EDUCATIONAL REFORM

Notes

1. See David Gordon, *A Nation Reformed? American Education 20 Years after A Nation at Risk* (Cambridge, MA: Harvard Education Press, 2003).

References

Boyer, E. (1983). *High school: A Report on secondary education in America.* New York: Harper and Row.

Cohen, D. K., & Hill, H. C. (2001). *Learning policy: When state education policy works.* New Haven, CT: Yale University Press.

Cuban, L. (1993). *How teachers taught: Constancy and change in American classrooms, 1890–1990* (2nd ed.). New York: Teachers College Press, 1993.

Fuhrman S. (Ed.). (2001). *From the Capitol to the classroom: Standards-based reform in the states.* Chicago: University of Chicago Press.

Fullan, M. (2001). *The new meaning of educational change* (3rd ed.). New York: Teachers College Press.

Goertz, M., & Duffy, M. (2001). *Assessment and accountability across the 50 states.* Philadelphia: Consortium for Policy Research in Education.

Harvard Graduate School of Education. (1995). *The thirteenth man: Ted Bell and the U.S. Department of Education* [Teaching case]. Cambridge, MA: Author.

Hess, F. (1999). *Spinning wheels: The politics of urban school reform.* Washington, DC: Brookings Institution Press.

Powell, A., Farrar, E., & Cohen, D. (1985). *The shopping mall high school.* Boston: Houghton Mifflin.

Ravitch, D. (2000a). *The great school wars: A history of the New York City public schools.* Baltimore: Johns Hopkins University Press.

Ravitch, D. (2000b). *Left back: A century of failed school reforms.* New York: Simon and Schuster.

Sarason, S. B. (1993). *The predictable failure of educational reform.* San Francisco: Jossey-Bass.

Tyack, D. B. (1974). *The one best system: A history of American urban education.* Cambridge, MA: Harvard University Press.

Tyack, D. B., & Cuban, L. (1995). *Tinkering toward Utopia: A century of public school reform.* Cambridge, MA: Harvard University Press.

7 DOING THE RIGHT THING, KNOWING THE RIGHT THING TO DO

Notes

1. http://www.nclb.gov
2. All schools are identified with pseudonyms under assurances of confidentiality.
3. Martin Carnoy, Richard Elmore et al. (edited volume on accountability, forthcoming, 2003; see also Chapter 4).
4. Elementary teachers, I have found, are usually much more knowledgeable and discriminating on this issue. I recently showed a videotape of a high school writing lesson to a mixed group of teachers and administrators from elementary, middle, and high schools. The tape showed a white teacher who had strong skills for engaging his largely minority students in playful and pleasant interactions in class. The work the students produced was, however, obviously very low level, and the teacher's expectations, revealed in his teaching and in a post-lesson interview, were very low. The middle and high school educators gave the lesson largely positive reviews. The elementary educators had strongly negative reactions to what they regarded as the insultingly low level of expectations for students and what they perceived as the teacher's condescending attitude toward his students.
5. There are, however, legions of technical problems with the validity and reliability of individual and school-level measures of performance over time, which policymakers often overlook when they design such systems, but that is not our subject here. See, e.g.: Board on Testing Assessment Reports.

Further Reading

Selected Readings on the Problem of Scale in Educational Reform

Cynthia Coburn has done a comprehensive review of research on the New American Schools Project, and her article makes a good companion piece to mine. She argues that future efforts should focus on four dimensions of scale: the *depth* of changes in instructional practice; the *sustainability* of those changes over time; the *spread* of the ideas and practices beyond the initial adopters; and the assumption of *ownership* by adopters of the ideas and practices embedded in reform models.

Bodilly, S. (1998). *Lessons from New American Schools' scale-up phase: Prospects for bringing designs to multiple sites.* Santa Monica, CA: RAND.

Coburn, C. (2003). Rethinking scale: Moving beyond numbers to deep and lasting change. *Educational Researcher, 32*(6), 3–12.

Cook, T. D., Habib, F., Phillips, M., Settersten, R. A., Shagle, S. C., & Degirmenciouglu, S. M. (1999). Comer's school development program in Prince George's County, Maryland: A theory-based evaluation. *American Educational Research Journal, 36,* 543–597.

Datnow, A., Borman, G., & Stringfield, S. (2000). School reform through a highly specified curriculum: Implementation and effects of the Core Knowledge Sequence. *Elementary School Journal, 101,* 167–191.

Slavin, R. E., & Madden, N. A. (1996). Scaling up: Lessons learned in the dissemination of Success for All (Report No. 6). Baltimore: Johns Hopkins University, Center for Research on the Education of Students Placed at Risk.

Stringfield, S., Datnow, A., Ross, A., & Snively, F. (1998). Scaling up school restructuring in multicultural, multilingual contexts: Early observations from Sunland County. *Education and Urban Society, 30,* 326–357.

Supovitz, J. A., Poglinco, S. M., & Snyder, B. A. (2001). *Moving mountains: Successes and challenges of the America's Choice comprehensive school reform design.* Philadelphia: CPRE.

Selected Readings on Distributed Leadership

The idea of distributed leadership has been developed and elaborated by my former student and current colleague James Spillane. His work focuses on the specific ways in which knowledge and expertise are distributed in schools and school systems, and how leadership follows the contours of this knowledge. In recent years, Spillane has published a substantial amount of research on the subject of distributed leadership that should be part of the context of discussions of leadership and instructional improvement in education.

Spillane, J. (2002). Local theories of teacher change: The pedagogy of district policies and programs. *Teachers College Record, 104,* 377–420.

Spillane, J., Reiser, B., & Reimer, T. (2002). *Policy implementation and cognition: Reframing and refocusing implementation research.* Evanston, IL: Northwestern University.

Spillane, J., Hallett T., & Diamond, J. (2003). Forms of capital and the construction of leadership: Instructional leadership in urban elementary schools. *Sociology of Education, 76*(1), 1–17.

Selected Reading on the Improvement of Teaching Practice

Since the publication of my paper "Bridging the Gap Between Standards and Achievement," Hiebert, Gallimore, and Stigler have written a widely read article that addresses a fundamental issue that my analysis does not treat: Is there a knowledge base that can be used to engage in the systematic improvement of teaching practice in the United States, and if not, can one be created? Their article makes a good companion piece to this one.

Hiebert, J., Gallimore, R., & Stigler, J. (2002). A knowledge base for the teaching profession: what would it look like and how can we get one? *Educational Researcher, 31*(5), 3–15.

Selected Readings on Accountability

Carnoy, M., Elmore, R., & Siskin, L. (Eds.). (2003). *The new accountability: High schools and high-stakes testing.* New York: Routledge.

Finnigan, K., & O'Day, J. (2003). *External support to schools on probation: Getting a leg up?* Chicago: Consortium on Chicago School Research/Consortium for Policy Research in Education.

Fuhrman, S., & Elmore, R. (Eds.). (2004). *Redesigning accountability systems for education.* New York: Teachers College Press.

Mintrop, H. (2003). *Schools on probation: How accountability works (and doesn't work).* New York: Teachers College Press.

Newmann, F., King, B., & Rigdon, M. (1997). Accountability and school performance: Implications from restructuring schools. *Harvard Educational Review, 67,* 41–74.

Selected Readings on Federal Policy and the No Child Left Behind Act

Fuhrman, S., & Elmore, R. (Eds.). (2004). *Redesigning accountability systems for education.* New York: Teachers College Press.

Kaestle, C. F., & Smith, M. S. (1982). The federal role in elementary and secondary education. *Harvard Educational Review, 52,* 384–408.

Kim, J., & Sunderman, G. (2004). *Does NCLB provide good choices for students in low-performing schools?* Cambridge, MA: The Civil Rights Project at Harvard University.

Kim, J., & Sunderman, G. (2004) *Large mandates and limited resources: State response to the No Child Left Behind Act and implications for accountability.* Cambridge, MA: The Civil Rights Project at Harvard University.

Peterson, P. E., Rabe, B. G., & Wong, K. K. (1986). *When federalism works.* Washington, DC: Brookings Institution.

Vinovskis, M. A. (1999). Do federal compensatory education programs really work? A brief historical analysis of Title I and Head Start. *American Journal of Education, 107,* 187–209.

Selected Readings on School Capacity and Improvement

Cohen, D., & Ball, D. (1999). *Instruction, capacity, and improvement* (CPRE Research Report RR-43). Philadelphia: Consortium for Policy Research in Education.

Massell, D. (2000). *The district role in building capacity: Four strategies* (CPRE Policy Brief RB-32). Philadelphia: Consortium for Policy Research in Education.

National Governors' Association. (2003). *Reaching new heights: Turning around failing schools.* Washington, DC: NGA Center for Best Practices.

Acknowledgments

Parts of the work presented here were funded by a grant from the U.S. Department of Education to the Consortium for Policy Research in Education.

"Knowing the Right Thing to Do: School Improvement and Performance-Based Accountability," a shorter version of Chapter 7, "Doing the Right Thing, Knowing the Right Thing to Do: The Problem of Failing Schools and Performance-Based Accountability," was written in collaboration with and published by the National Governors Association Center for Best Practices in 2003. The original, unabridged paper produced here does not necessarily reflect the views of the National Governors Association or its members. For a copy of the national Governors Association publication, please go to www.nga.org.

"When Accountability Knocks, Will Anyone Answer?" is reprinted with permission from the Consortium for Policy Research in Education.

"Unwarranted Intrusion" is reprinted with permission from *Education Next,* Spring 2002.

"Building a New Structure for School Leadership" and "Bridging the Gap between Standards and Achievement: The Imperative for Professional Development in Education" are reprinted with permission of the Albert Shanker Institute.

About the Author

Richard F. Elmore is the Gregory Anrig Professor of Educational Leadership at the Harvard Graduate School of Education and a senior research fellow at the Consortium for Policy Research in Education (CPRE), a group of universities engaged in research on state and local education policy, funded by the U.S. Department of Education. He has previously held positions with the U.S. Department of Health, Education, and Welfare and the U.S. Office of Education.

Elmore's research focuses on the impact federal, state, and local education policies have on schools and classrooms. His primary areas of interest include accountability, school choice, school restructuring, and how changes in teaching and learning affect school organization. His most recent books include *The New Accountability: High Schools and High-Stakes Testing* (edited with M. Carnoy and L. Santee Siskin, 2003); *Restructuring the Classroom: Teaching, Learning, and School Organization* (with P. Peterson and S. McCarthey, 1996); *Who Chooses, Who Loses? Culture, Institutions, and the Unequal Effects of School Choice* (edited with B. Fuller and G. Orfield, 1996); and *Restructuring Schools: The Next Generation of Educational Reform* (1990).